Duane H. Larson

Times of the Trinity

A Proposal for Theistic Cosmology

PETER LANG
New York • Washington, D.C./Baltimore • San Francisco
Bern • Frankfurt am Main • Berlin • Vienna • Paris

BT
111.2
.L37
1995

Library of Congress Cataloging-in-Publication Data

Larson, Duane H. (Duane Howard).
    Times of the trinity: a proposal for theistic cosmology/Duane H.
Larson.
        p.   cm. — (Worcester Polytechnic Institute studies in science,
technology and culture; vol. 17)
    Includes bibliographical references and index.
    1. Trinity. 2. Trinity—History of doctrines. 3. Time—Religious
aspects—Christianity. 4. Religion and science. I. Title. II. Series.
BT111.2.L37   231'.044—dc20   94-37760
ISBN 0-8204-2706-3
ISSN 0897-926X

Die Deutsche Bibliothek-CIP-Einheitsaufnahme

Larson, Duane H.:
Times of the trinity: a proposal for theistic cosmology/Duane H. Larson.
–New York; Washington, D.C./Baltimore; San Francisco; Bern; Frankfurt
am Main; Berlin; Vienna; Paris: Lang.
    (Worcester Polytechnic Institute studies in science, technology and
    culture; Vol. 17)
    ISBN 0-8204-2706-3
NE: Worcester Polytechnic Institute: Worcester Polytechnic Institute ...

The paper in this book meets the guidelines for permanence and durability
of the Committee on Production Guidelines for Book Longevity of the
Council of Library Resources.

Printed in the United States of America.

Times of the Trinity

Worcester Polytechnic Institute
Studies in Science, Technology and Culture

Lance Schachterle and Francis C. Lutz
Co-Editors

Vol. 17

PETER LANG
New York • Washington, D.C./Baltimore • San Francisco
Bern • Frankfurt am Main • Berlin • Vienna • Paris

Acknowledgements

A continual theme of this project is the affirmation that a person is only so within a field of relationships. Just as no one is an island; no one is simultaneously self-sufficient and authentically human. Certainly this applies also to authors. I could not have completed this project without the help of many people in an ever expanding and influential field of relationships. I thank them, and do disrespect to the many whom I cannot name here; may they infer who they are and my gratitude nevertheless. Among those I can name are those charged with particular guidance of my thinking, especially John Polkinghorne, Robert John Russell, and Ted Peters. Where I am correct in my exposition and insights, the credit should be theirs; where I err, I err alone. I am further privileged to have been part of two wonderful communities who have given me deeply of their love and support: the congregation of St. Andrew's Lutheran Church, San Mateo, California, and colleagues of the Lutheran Theological Seminary at Gettysburg, where I am happy currently to serve. I am also grateful to Heidi Burns for her editorial help and to Richard Burgess for technical support. Without the support of these people, in many ways, this project would not have come to fruition. Finally, my deepest thanks goes to Kathy, who, when taxed so often and so deeply by my investment in this project, nevertheless plumbed deeper her wealth of patience, understanding, and encouragement. She sets an example at which I can only marvel.

Contents

I

Introduction

...the doctrine of the Trinity has a wholly actual and not just a historical significance for us and for the dogmatics of our age, even though this is a very different age from that of Arius and Athanasius. In other words, it means that the criticism and correction of Church proclamation must be done to-day, as it was then, in the form of developing the doctrine of the Trinity.

Karl Barth, *Church Dogmatics*, I.1

This is a book about theology engaged with science. It takes a distinct problem in theology, assesses its correlate in the natural sciences, and then seeks to resolve the problem with some resources from deep within theology's own tradition. This, in turn, could suggest that theology, on this point at least, is coherent with natural science. In the broadest terms, then, this book is a post-modern exercise. By that, I do not mean the trivial acknowledgement that this book could not have been written earlier. I suggest, rather, that the very notion of theology engaged with science, wherein both enterprises *theoretically* might inform each other, is not a typically "modern" project insofar as it does not strictly abide by the categories of the Enlightenment. Thus, it is fair to say that this book intends more toward acceptance of a post-modern vision.

It is said today that our's is a post-modern age. By the predicate of "post-modern," different writers mean different things. Those philosophers and theologians who identify the beginnings of modernism with the so-called "turn to the self" take Descartes as the period's chief origin, Kant as the definer of its critical limits, and Schleiermacher as its theological genesis. Such modern critical limitations and definitions have meant specializations within the body of knowledge. The "renaissance person" is exceptional in the modern world precisely because expertise in one area is commonly thought to constitute one's identity. Kant's separation of faith from reason, so to make room for faith, also led to the perception of theology as a non-science, and of science as the only truly rational enterprise. The argument that theology *per se* should be regarded as a legitimate science in the academy—as opposed to the scientific study of religion—is still a minority argument.[1] This wholesale divorce, of course, was not Kant's intent, though many argue it is at least part of his legacy. Nevertheless, the pluralization of knowledge, as well as the pluralization of authorities, are two children of modernism.[2] Critical reasonable pursuits have their established grounds and protocols; theology its own. And even theology's own protocols became all the more diversified under the scapels of critical, historical and practical reason. Schleiermacher's famous rearrangement of the theological curriculum into its tripartite structure is the still vital example. It is an irony. The modern and democratic mind maintains a pluralism of authorities, which by their own authoritative definitions cannot and will not engage each other in the pursuit of consensus. It is the modern mind that seeks, however limited, a hegemonous authority, and yet fails because its authority is a "specialty." Only the modern mind could engage in a warfare between science and religion.[3]

The popular contemporary revolt against authority *sui generis* may be the uncritical response to the authoritarianism of specialization. In western culture, at least, we have begun to grow weary of the many claims to authority all about us, just as we have begun to grow weary of the fractiousness of experts. Of course, we affirm genuine know-how. But we more desire expertise that is on equal ground with other expertises in contributing to the public good. We desire neither a melting pot nor a panoply of discrete options. We desire the unity of knowledge; personal integrity in community; a whole inclusive of, but more than, its parts. Wholism is said to be a primary element of whatever it is that is emerging as post-modernism. Opposed to the specializations and the consequent reductionisms of modernism, post-modernism is characterized by an emerging consciousness of the mysterious and intimately related ecology of the universe.

This sentiment, of course, involves intellectual efforts other than theology. Perhaps they indeed set theology's agenda. Literary theorists speak of post-modernism in terms of the deconstruction of once-assumed authorities; this extends even to the claim that the printed signifier is automatically suspect. A presumed permanence of a sign itself, as well as its "meaning," implies conceptuality, and concepts are idols. Even "Being" as a concept is an idol. So says the Heideggerian. But that is not the all of it. Even the concept of deconstructing Being implies a "primacy of the question of Being," which, too, has been denounced as idolatry.[4]

Much of the recent rise in antipathy to science and technology in western culture, too, is said to be symptomatic of emerging post-modernism. Many in the popular culture rightly question the hubris of technocracy, as if applied science will solve every vicissitude of creaturely life, regardless of "Being's" profoundly, if not essentially, tragic character. Human ingenuity is brought here before the prophet, and told rightly that we are not so self-sufficient and ascendant as we had conceived in the imaginations of our hearts. The natural and human sciences have come to the same conclusion, though public policy in its use of the applied sciences lags yet far behind. Of course, there is no unanimity of opinion, or even monolithicity of philosophical perspective, among the members of the scientific community. But, while necessarily focussed on their own endeavors, most scientists would affirm indeed that no one science is more "basic" than another. Fortunately, the distinction even between "hard" and "soft" science is coming to be recognized as the unwarranted and pejorative distinction it is. Indeed, there is likely no community of selves more accountable to one another than the community of science. This intra-community accountability itself demonstrates that science is achieving a "wholism" in its own practice and identity that quite transcends the earlier, modern, paradigm of the one scientist creatively at work in his—the pronoun itself indicates part of the authority problem—lonely laboratory.

What might these meandering reflections summarize, but that, if it is has not yet been completed, culture must turn away from the "self"? The modern period is giving way to a new way of understanding the world. Self, sign and science are the reconfiguring subjects in the current project of modernism's transcendence. Theology must negotiate this sea-change with respect to its own methods and with respect to how it engages other disciplines, particularly the sciences.

Background

Numerous writers in the fields of Christian theology and the natural sciences have only within the past decade or so vigorously begun to reassess their relationship in ways that are mutually beneficial, as well as critical.[5] This new emerging relationship has often meant that the sciences have provided many data for the practice of theology. This phenomenon, of course, is not new. Except for early neo-orthodox theology of this century, theological systems have drawn many of their resources from the sciences, even after theology's dethronement from the status of "queen of the sciences." As popularized history puts it, however, rarely has theology performed the same function for natural sciences in return, excepting perhaps the dogmatic prescription of a cosmology or an anthropology that can only constrain science from the free inquiry necessary to it. Geocentrists and anti-evolutionists are unfortunate examples of such overprescription, even if the extinction of the former reemphasizes the errancy of the latter.

In spite of these celebrated prototypes of theological anti-science, theology and natural science have indeed provided for positive advances in each other's fields. One could hardly deny that scientific discovery provides much fodder for thoughtful theologians today. While little in the way of systematic or dogmatic theological claims finds its way into good science and properly so, Christian theology's deep concern with and affirmation of the natural world as God's good intention is a long cherished principle that frees and affirms science in its endeavors. From Basil of Caesarea through Luther and Calvin, the Christian claim has been that good science in its own right is to be celebrated; in fact, the Christian unconcerned with science is no faithful Christian! The liberation of science from theology after the Reformation indeed was an initial and revolutionizing advance for the sciences, as now they could seek and recognize order and pattern in the natural world apart from any preconception that this was necessarily so. Reason discrete from revelation was an advance for science endorsed by revelation.[6]

Of course, if one wishes to maintain some sort of mutuality in the practices of natural science and theology, one must admit that "advances" thereby made in each field always pose new problems. It would be easier for practitioners of one discipline not to attend to the problems of others, and therefore there is always some catching up to do. As a Christian theologian, my guess is that the responsibility of "catching up" is most daunting for theology. Relatively little attention has been paid to crucial scientific insights since the birth of relativity theory in 1907. Perhaps this lack is in part a deficiency of our public education system. Almost a century later, many Americans respond with surprise, if not disbelief, to a description of Einstein's theories and their consequences. The ante is all the higher for theologians. How might relativity theory and cosmology, for example, impinge upon and reform classical articulations of Christian eschatology? How might the epistemological reformation of a once presumed objective scientific consciousness now logically allow, if not imply, a theistic metaphysic as its context? And how, practically speaking, are these specialized-yet-related concerns to be marshalled into a renewed Christian orthopraxy that is attentive to its environment?

These are, admittedly, grotesquely large questions. Yet, my main argument in this book derives from them. The primary Christian view of time and eternity has remained fairly consistent through the ages until the modern day.[7] One might trace the ingredients of a consistent Christian point of view with respect to the relationship of time and eternity from Augustine and Boethius through the Newtonian synthesis of the Enlightenment. It was rather commonly accepted, for example, that time was considered as created by deity along with the rest of the created order. Also, time was viewed as a "singular" phenomenon; all matter in the created and dynamic order shared the same "time." For its part, the Boethian notion of eternity as the "whole, perfect and simultaneous possession of endless life" was commonly accepted, too. Until Newton, at least, the natural sciences (such as they were) held these and other ideas pertaining to time and eternity in common with Christian thought.

While this *Weltanschauung* was common with the natural sciences even after the Newtonian synthesis, the Christian tradition showed itself to be incongruent when it encountered the proclamation of relativity and the new theories about atomic and subatomic nature offered by the quantum physicists. With Einstein and Planck, one was faced with the revolutionary divergence in physical theory from the Newtonian conception, leading into such complex areas as current speculative proposals in quantum cosmology. Relativity theory, the theory of the quantum and the generally rehearsed Big Bang cosmology at least appear now to give us a different understanding of time. Of course, the voyage of Darwin's Beagle and an enlightened, rationalist, philosophical compass had already prepared for the parting. But, influenced in part by the works of Michael Polanyi and Thomas Kuhn,[8] theologians and scientists have effectively forged a re-engagement. Among the discussion points, we have found that the conception of time and eternity, particularly, needs reassessment. The critical theological question is thereby hard pressed once again. How, if at all, might an "eternal" God relate to the temporal world, especially as this "world" may now be characterized by most western, physical cosmologies as having a plurality of times?[9]

Project Intention

This writer will not suggest a complete answer here. My intentions are a bit more modest. My interest as a theologian is to explore a central claim of the Christian faith and to reflect upon its possibilities in providing at least a foundation for describing an eternal God's relationship to a temporal cosmos. More specifically, my aim is to show that a reappropriation of the classic Christian doctrine of the Trinity is a theologically coherent and intellectually fruitful way to describe God's action in the world.

At first sight, one may wonder what in the secular world such an esoteric and paradoxical, indeed mystical, notion as the Trinity has to do with the sciences, time, and eternity. Indeed, the doctrine of the Trinity has not enjoyed a good reputation since Schleiermacher relegated it to an afterthought in his dogmatic treatise, *The Christian Faith*. Until the mid-twentieth century (and beyond for the theologically slothful), the doctrine of the Trinity seemed to be one of those unappealing-but-necessary components of an orthodox menu; like asparagus on Tuesday evening, it had to be consumed, though the reasons why remained unclear to the young and untutored at the table. Even the tutors would have some difficulty providing a satisfactory explanation. The doctrine of the Trinity, it was said, was an essential "mystery" of the faith that had to be accepted on faith. Or, the justification might be an *argumentum ad accordiam*; "The Bible says it, so believe it!" Or the tutor might go a bit further with an attempt at first-grade metaphysics. The doctrine of the Trinity was interpreted as an attempt to explain the "paradoxical" nature of reality, as in how one substance (like water) could take three different forms. Of course, this was a misuse of the term "paradoxical," as well as a basic misunderstanding of the doctrine of the Trinity. Most often this misuse and misunderstanding has revealed itself in theological obfuscation or, ultimately, in unabashed dismissal of a notion so irrational and embarrassing as that of the Trinity. This has been a consequence with those who number themselves among Christian faithful people, while it has long been, of course, irrelevant to those numbered without.

But the doctrine of the Trinity was never intended as paradox, obfuscation, or even—at best—"simply" mystery. Since Karl Barth's recognition in this century that the doctrine was the cornerstone on which to base all his systematic reflection,[10] and this recognized keenly by Claude Welch,[11] the doctrine of the Trinity has enjoyed a vital and surprising resurgence of interest, especially so within the past decade. The doctrine is recognized more now as the fundamental background by which to understand God's salvific action in and through Jesus Christ, as well as all God's action of creativity, providence and sustenance toward a new and just future. Equally, it is the prism by which Christian faith is to understand how such transcendence over the state of cosmic affairs is simultaneously so involved in the personal and corporate history of mundane affairs. Somehow, the early church fathers and mothers recognized, the cosmic bears upon the mundane, and vice-versa. The God of Abraham and Sarah who deigned to guide God's people in the forms of smoke, fire, and flesh, the early writers were convinced, included in deity's character the attributes argued as necessary in the Greek lycea, as Paul himself would argue in Athens. Time and space were involved here in a collaboration with that which is beyond space and time. Consequently, these same trinitarian constructionists maintained, salvation was not to be construed only individually or personally or existentially (to put it anachronistically); it had to embrace all of reality, time, and space in real fashion if it were to be any authentic "salvation" at all, especially salvation from the onslaughts of temporality's decay and death. All this was set forth, of course in terms appropriate to their day, by the scriptural writers and theologizers who would follow them for the next four centuries. It is this intention of describing "God's wholism" that is being recaptured in the fertile work of so many writers today. It is this intention of wholism, primordial in the Christian scriptural witness, which makes the doctrine of the Trinity pertinent to such issues as physical description and the relation of time to eternity.

The recognition of this intent is implicit in the work of Jürgen Moltmann.[12]

Moltmann's recent work in developing a trinitarian theology of creation, for example, focuses precisely on the problem of conceiving the action of God in creation without loss to God's transcendence, rather than supposing that God acts dispassionately apart from the creation. Moltmann's work suffers, however, from inattention to scientific research, particularly with regard to the subject of time, which could so positively inform new configurations in the doctrine of the Trinity today. Neither his theological method nor his doctrine of the Trinity are informed by scientific method or its discoveries. Even so, were Moltmann's claim that the Trinity is essentially temporal argued from the approach of a scientific research program, as such programs are understood by Imre Lakatos[13] and then theologically adapted in the work of Nancey Murphy,[14] then the doctrine of the Trinity might be understood as both theologically coherent and cosmologically relevant. Thus, one subtheme of this book is to address some of the lacunae in Moltmann's work.

The general structure of the argument is as follows. In chapters two through six I will have in mind continually a proposal of a theological research program along the lines propounded by Murphy following the Lakatosian method. Such a program begins with the proposal of a core thesis, which is followed by a series of auxiliary theses in support of the primary one. Lakatos argues that criticism directed at the theses of the "protective belt" is, in fact, beneficial to the research program, as long as there is no direct attack on the core thesis itself. When there is such an attack, the viability of that particular research program is rather destroyed. A fruitful research program, on the other hand, will sustain the auxiliary theses with data and prediction of novel facts, which themselves may sustain further the core theorem. The perihelion effect of Mercury, for example, when discovered was a novel fact that was predicted in principle by and further supported Einstein's theory of General Relativity. Only with chapter seven, however, will I propose an example of a theological research program that could extend from my "hard core" thesis: that the eternity of the Trinity is essentially temporal. We will be looking at some of the "data" of such a research program, as it were, with their explication and analysis in chapters one through four. A broader discussion of the Lakatosian method will be conducted in chapter seven, too.

A more detailed preview is now in order. Chapter two begins with the core thesis that the eternity of the Trinity is essentially temporal. The concept of temporality will be elaborated upon by a review of the Christian interpretation of time and eternity. It will include some exposition on the concepts of time and eternity as they may be traced beginning with Plato, through Plotinus, Gregory of Nyssa, Augustine, and Boethius up to Newton. Attention will be paid, too, to Hegel. It is necessary that this discussion be conducted in general terms, though, as even a semi-exhaustive rehearsal of the literature on this topic within the Christian aegis alone would require a volume unto itself. Then I will take a "quantum leap" into the twentieth century to see how the thought of Karl Barth leads theologians to new possibilities of reflection about time and eternity, especially as he is interpreted by eschatological theologians like Robert Jenson, Wolfhart Pannenberg and Jürgen Moltmann. The purpose of this summary overview is to describe the contemporary renewal of emphasis on the temporality of God. This will conclude chapter two.

With chapter three I will turn to the subject of the doctrine of the Trinity and its contemporary interpreters. The current blossoming of reflection on this doctrine draws from and expands upon the assertion of divine temporality noted in chapter one. I will discuss how the doctrine, on the basis of Greek philosophical presuppositions, had lost its practical viability for Christian faith and receded from its rightful prominent position in Christian theology. The conclusion of the survey will show how the doctrine of the Trinity in its most Christian strains ought all along to have been understood in terms of an assumed temporality and world-relatedness of the Trinity, an insight which can be traced to the Cappadocians in the East and Hilary of Poitiers in the West. I have, of course, already alluded to this agenda in a somewhat homiletical fashion above.

With chapter four I will turn to consideration of contemporary data from the physical sciences. I do so with the admission that I am a theologian and not a scientist. While I am romanced by the beauty of the scientific enterprise, its discoveries, and certainly the world with which it courses, I am not at home in the mathematical language shared by that community. But I will do my best to interpret and assess what, within the domain of this book, some scientists are doing. It is my conviction that theological reflection must stretch to include such data and be open to the remonstrances of the experts when the naive imagination of the layperson stretches too far. It is not incautious, though, to assert at least that if the Trinity is to be regarded as temporal, and if it is indeed related to worldly life, then data from contemporary physics should have some import in our trinitarian reflection. This is not to say, of course, that other scientific data have no bearing on the question. The Christian theologian likely would admit that all data indeed do to some degree. A principle of limitation is required for an endeavor such as this. Thus I will mark off certain questions of current physics and related cosmological concerns as part of the particular domain of this book. I recognize that many related questions could be brought to bear. Perhaps they will become the subjects of further inquiry in another project.

While chapter four will be a summary view of some key themes of contemporary physics, in chapter five I will consider the thought of three contemporary, and quite diverse, physical cosmologists. These are Andrej Grib, Stephen Hawking and Christopher Isham. The point of assessing the work of these three scientists is to determine whether there might be any common themes that can be drawn from them, no matter their disparity. This commonality, or at least some common philosophical implications of their work, might parlay well into an eventual theological research program that attends with seriousness to the import of the natural sciences for theology. Thus chapter five will conclude with some proposed theses that gather up some of the metaphysical, philosophical, and theological implications of the material in both chapters three and four. These proposals, in turn, will show up again as part of the auxiliary theses in chapter seven.

Previous to that, however, in chapter six I will focus more explicitly on the thought of Jürgen Moltmann. Moltmann has been a key contemporary theologian who has been among the first to recognize the need to return to explicitly trinitarian theological reflection, and this with an eye toward issues of natural science, ecology, and justice. Moltmann has argued elegantly and persuasively for the recapturing of a genuinely biblical doctrine of God who acts in history. Moltmann's is a vision of God who is affected by that which God has created and yet is transcendent to it as the power of the future. That God experienced the death of his Son in the crucifixion, for example, is an assertion of temporality in God that could not be more profound. And with his development of a "spirited" view of God's trinitarian presence in the creation, Moltmann provides a vital alternative to the atemporal and *a se* god of the philosophers after the legacy of Plato and sustained by Augustine. In other words, Moltmann affirms, by way of the doctrine of the Trinity, just how temporal God really is. This affirmation would place Christian theology in a position to receive and adapt some of the perspectives about temporality and eternity shared in the scientific community. In that way we would be well beyond the diastasis of a (Newtonian) "Christian" point of view and a post-Einsteinian scientific perspective. The two parties could communicate and enter a new ecumenical age, distancing themselves from the legacy of *argumenta ad accordiam* which prevented until now any mutuality. Moltmann's attempt to make such a connection by way of his eschatological trinitarian theology is even aided by some reference to the scientific disciplines.

However, Moltmann's work does not go far enough. While his work has been influential, and represents a major development of Karl Barth's trinitarian thought, it has not been concerned with the philosophical and theological issues posed by current scientific research. It would benefit by attention to them. Moltmann errs, too, in identifying the nemeses of his trinitarian reflection. He unjustly charges that "radical monotheism" controverts trinitarian thought. I argue, however, that certain strains within process theology are more consciously aligned against both theism and trinitarianism, and so would more deserve Moltmann's criticism.[15]Thus, with chapter six, I hope to achieve three goals: 1) exhibit the broad lines of Moltmann's thought; 2) compare the development of his trinitarian thought to those positions described in chapter two; 3) show where his own program fails because it has been less than attentive to data from the natural sciences, even though he has stated the virtue of theological sensitivity to that domain.

The strengths of Moltmann's theology of the Trinity, then, will be combined with the implications noted in chapter five, so finally to initiate a research program model in chapter seven. With chapter seven, as I have already alluded, I will propose a number of auxiliary theses which address the issues posed by contemporary physical theory and serve as a protective belt for my core theorem. This Lakatosian model will be preceded by an excursus on the Lakatosian method so to set the rest of the chapter in context. The hope is that these auxiliary theses will also supplement Moltmann's suggestions and demonstrate the viability of the classic doctrine of the Trinity, however revised, as the core thesis which suggests how God in God's transcendence relates to the temporal cosmos. As Lakatos argues, if in and after this statement the corollaries are replaced, denied or reconstructed without change to the core thesis, and provide fruitfulness of further research as well, then one has a viable scientific research program. And, as Murphy argues, the same principle ought to hold for a theological research program.

There is at least one danger that is endemic to any attempted discussion between the domains of science and theology. That danger is that vocabularies, with their distinctive horizons of meanings, could be imported wholesale from one domain to another without acknowledgement that there could occur some shifts in meaning between the two. While neo-Kantians might refer to such confusions as "category mistakes," this is also the early warning issued by such as Stephen Toulmin and Langdon Gilkey.[16] Nevertheless, there are occasions in such a dialogue as I intend to pursue in which one can do nothing but be vulnerable to such possible confusions. For example, in auxiliary assertion 6.51 of chapter seven I suggest, "[the] ongoing work of the Trinity may be construed as the infusion of energy into a *system*, which, when described at the quantum level, is then appropriately labelled as an open system, consonant with the scientific use of that term." The assertion follows upon a criticism of Jürgen Moltmann's clear misuse of scientific terminology with respect to "open system." Yet it could appear that I here commit the same equivocation. Here I deliberately conjoin the theological concept of "Trinity" with the scientifc terms "quantum level" and "open system," as if to say that one category indeed does have something to do with the other. This is not a trivial matter. Of course, the very premise of this project is that possibilities for direct conversational exchange might be found without always having to spend time (or all of time) on the task of defining terms. Theological language, of course, does not admit the possibility of complete collapse with scientfic language, and vice-versa. But neither are they completely different. A "critical realist" principle here must be assumed to stand in the background of this entire project, so that neither a univocalist, fundamentalist mistake is made in adopting scientific terminology literally as theological theses, nor a mistake be made in throwing up one's hands, admitting that "all" language is metaphorical. Therefore, I beg the reader's indulgence when it seems that I might be committing either heresy. I seek to hold to the sharp and narrow middle ground. When I state something like the example quoted above, I am aware of the *apparent* category confusions and clearly do not intend them. But neither do I intend their separation. A defense of methodology, indeed an argument for the hermeneutical foundation of the very possibility of dialogue between the natural sciences and theology, is a project too big for this thesis to tackle. That problem is one better addressed in the ongoing discussion, for example, on the merits of a critical realist epistemology.[17]

To sum up, my chief intention with this project is to argue that the Christian doctrine of the Trinity is a theologically productive means by which to address the question of how eternity relates to time. That this is so may be a humble and helpful rehearsal simply for those within the Christian horizon. I also have some subsidiary aims. This project is also a methodological experiment in that the final chapter, particularly, may exemplify the style of a Lakatosian research program and thereby provide another instance of that for which Nancey Murphy argues, that theology's style should be like that of a scientific research program. However, this thesis itself by no means would exemplify a full blown research program. It would be but a tentative beginning. Furthermore, the appeal to Jürgen Moltmann as the central theologian in this treatment may demonstrate both the cogency and the misconstruals of his own systematic thought.

Notes

1. See Wolfhart Pannenberg, *Theology and the Philosophy of Science*, translated by Francis McDonagh (Philadelphia: Westminster, 1976).

2. Jeffrey Stout, *Flight From Authority—Religion, Morality, and the Quest for Autonomy* (Notre Dame: University of Notre Dame Press, 1981).

3. Andrew Dickson White, of Cornell University, characterized the relationship between theology and science as a "warfare," and this became the standard caricature. Of course, it was neither historically, theologically, nor philsophically accurrate. See *A History of the Warfare of Science with Theology in Christendom* (New York: D. E. Appleton & Co., 1896). A more balanced Evangelical Christian perspective, which is also an intentional correction of White, may be found in Karl Gilberson, *Worlds Apart, The Unholy War Between Religion and Science* (Kansas City: Beacon Hill, 1993).

4. Jean-Luc Marion, *God Without Being, Hors-Texte*, translated by Thomas A. Carlson (Chicago and London: University of Chicago Press, 1991).

5. There are too many authors writing now on this subject to cite here exhaustively. Among them, however, I certainly would want to draw attention and express my indebtedness to my teachers, Ted Peters and Robert John Russell. With Dr. Russell's leadership of the Center for Theology and Natural Science, accompanied by Dr. Peters, the convergence that has been initiated between the natural sciences and theology has been nothing short of remarkable over the past decade. They have also been integral, along with the staff of the Vatican Observatory, in the sponsorship of three international dialogues thus far, results of which the reader will find cited below. These dialogues have brought together noted representatives from all areas of the natural sciences, history, philosophy, and theology. Among them, special attention should be directed to John Polkinghorne, Arthur Peacocke, Ernan McMullin, Ian Barbour, Nancey Murphy, Willem Drees, William Stoeger, and Chris Isham. Of course, there are many others. These, however, have been most influential, directly or indirectly, in the course of my thinking about connections between theology and the natural sciences. I would direct the reader to the bibliography for specific references to their work.

6. Ronald Cole-Turner, "An Unavoidable Challenge: Our Church In An Age of Science and Technology" (Cleveland: The Division of Education and Publication, United Church Board for Homeland Ministries, 1992).

7. Augustine, *Confessions*, translated by R. S. Pine-Coffin (Middlesex: Penguin, 1961); Boethius, *The Consolation of Philosophy*, trans. by V. E. Watts (Baltimore: Penguin, 1969). The acceptance of the Boethian notion of eternity has been almost unanimous in both theology and science until today.

8. Thomas Kuhn, *The Structure of Scientific Revolutions*, 22nd edition (Chicago: University of Chicago, 1970); Michael Polanyi, *Personal Knowledge* (Chicago: University of Chicago Press, 1958). These are not the only influential writers in the philosophy of science, of course. They are central, though, in the recognition that subjectivity plays a role even in the most accurate of scientific analysis and theory development (Polanyi), and that "paradigm shifts" in the manner of interpreting data are integral in new theory development (Kuhn). It is commonly accepted now that "all data are theory laden."

9. Ted Peters has asked this question forthrightly in *God, The Trinity* (Nashville: Westminster/John Knox, 1993).

10. Karl Barth, *Church Dogmatics*, G. W. Bromiley and T. F. Torrance, eds.(Edinburgh: T&T Clark, 1975).

11. *In This Name, The Trinity in Contemporary Theology* (New York: Charles Scribner's Sons, 1952). Welch predicted herein that Trinitarian discussion, based on Barth, would become the wave of the future. While this indeed did happen, it did not occur as early as Welch had envisioned.

12. Especially *God in Creation*, translated by Margaret Kohl (New York: Harper and Row, 1985), wherein Moltmann devotes particular chapters to the understanding of time and space. Also noteworthy is Wolfhart Pannenberg. In his *Systematic Theology*, vol. 1 (Grand Rapids: Eerdmans, 1991) he attends to these issues; see also his *Metaphysics and the Idea of God* (Grand Rapids: Eerdmans, 1990) and "Theological Questions Posed to Scientists," *Zygon*, 16:1 (March, 1981). Indeed, Pannenberg has exercised more energy than Moltmann to come to terms with some physical description and attempted to include them in his theological reflection. Other than that, he and Moltmann are quite close in their respective approaches to the doctrine of the Trinity, as well as their whole theological program. While Pannenberg's work, of course, will not be ignored, primary attention will be given to Moltmann because, first, the inattention he gives to the sciences provides exactly that opportunity I desire to show how the attention otherwise could positively influence his theological program; and, second, economy: one must cut somewhere.

13. Cf. Imre Lakatos, "Falsification and the Methodology of Scientific Research Programmes," in *Criticism and the Growth of Knowledge*, ed. Lakatos and Alan Musgrave (Cambridge: Cambridge University Press, 1970), 91-196; reprinted in *The Methodology of Scientific Research Programmes:Philosophical Papers*, vol.I, ed. John Worrall and Gregory Currie (Cambridge: Cambridge University Press, 1978), 8-101. See also "History of Science and Its Rational Reconstructions," in *Boston Studies in the Philosophy of Science*, 8 (1971), ed. R.C. Buck and R.S. Cohen, 91-135, reprinted in *The Methodology...*, 102-38.

14. Nancey Murphy, *Theology in the Age of Scientific Reasoning* (Ithaca and London: Cornell University Press, 1990).

15. Moltmann believes that it is the "radical monotheism" of H. Richard Niebuhr that threatens authentic trinitarianism. It is, rather, the a-trinitarian revisionism of the process theological school, as represented by Moltmann's friendly critic, John Cobb, that would mitigate Moltmann's program.

16. Stephen Toulmin, *Return to Cosmology* (Berkeley and Los Angeles: University of California Press, 1982); Langdon Gilkey, *Religion and the Scientific Future* (New York: Harper and Row, 1970).

17. For example, see chapter 4, note 39, for initial citations relevant to this discussion.

II

The Christian Idea Of Time And Eternity

I propose that the eternity of the Trinity is the fullness of temporalities. One might first think I am posing a contradiction of terms here by relating temporality with eternity. This judgement would be correct if the judge held a traditional interpretation of eternity as timeless. I do not accept that interpretation. I will argue, rather, that temporality lies *within* eternity, while eternity is also more than temporality. In other words, eternity includes and transcends temporality. Eternity is the manifold of higher dimensionalities and includes within it our own narrower four-dimensionality.[1] Not unlike Hegel, but not wholly like him either, I submit that eternity is the transcendental ground of time. This is a correlate of the panentheistic position that places the relative within the absolute, and vice-versa. How my proposal resonates and dissonates from a moderate Hegelian argument I hope to make clear as this monograph proceeds. For now, I would only suggest that the ontological explication of the union of eternity with time is the doctrine of the Trinity, which part of the argument I will develop in following chapters.

As I alluded, the more common theological perspectives have defined time or temporality either as *opposed* to eternity, or else have claimed eternity—that realm of ultimate value and beauty—as the sole reality at the expense of temporality. This latter option has been the gnostic preference and faintly reverberates in the existential theology of Paul Tillich, for example. The former option has been exercised by those early Hellenistically inclined theologians who took seriously the problem of temporality, like Athanasius. The resultant problem, however, has been the continuing difficulty of describing how such an unrelated and apathetic divinity can relate to anything phenomenal and historical, much more cohere with the biblical description of a God concerned about the personal and historical vicissitudes of a people and a world. The understanding of eternity as anti-temporal exacerbates the problem of speaking about God and God's actions in any meaningful way. Yet this is the rubric under which most theological reflection has been conducted for almost two millennia.

There are strong indicators, however, that this has been only a majority position and not a unanimous one. Proponents from early on in Christianity's life have advocated a different sense of "eternal." The recapture of this sense is part of the current agenda in the dialogue, too, between the sciences and theology.[2] Ted Peters writes that the problem of explaining how an eternal God can act in a temporal world arises "when eternity is assumed to be a state of timelessness that contrasts sharply with the temporal world in which humanity and the rest of nature is condemned to exist." This assessment requires us to "modify our concept of eternity so that it is not thought to stand in exclusion of what is temporal. Eternity needs to transcend time, to be sure; but it need not cancel or annihilate time."[3]

My hope is to carry Peters's baton at least a couple of steps forward. The outline of my argument in this chapter includes several elements. First, the majority opinion in the western Christian theological tradition regarding time and eternity follows Augustine's classic discussion in his *Confessions*, and was fairly fixed subsequently by Boethius. The result was the long-lived popular understanding that eternity is timeless. My claim, of course, is quite the reverse. That eternity relates to time and that time issues from eternity may appear to be self-evident to a different or non-Christian mind in the late twentieth century. Support for this position is available from Paul Tillich through Charles Hartshorne. But the claim that time is immanent in transcendent eternity is by no means a traditional western Christian claim. Hegel's victory over Heilas is yet popularly to be won. A review of the theological and philosophical tradition of early Christianity, however, will expose possibilities within the tradition for countering the "traditional" concepts of time and eternity. Second, with a brief review of the biblical theological discussion on the topic, I will attempt to underscore the viability of my minority opinion. Finally, having slightly bowed in the direction of Hegel, a review of Karl Barth's treatment of the subject and his placing it within the context of God's trinitarian character will round out this chapter and provide a segue into a more expansive treatment of the doctrine of the Trinity proper in the following chapter.

Philosophical and Theological Precedents

It is part of Plato's legacy that philosophers and theologians have been disposed to thinking of eternity as opposed to temporality, as if eternity were but timelessness. Extending the platonic logic, Boethius went so far as to describe eternity as the full, simultaneous and perfect possession of limitless life.[4] Thereby he identified eternity with the divine life itself, the *summum bonum*, as Aquinas would put it. Such divine life is "perfect." It experiences no wrenching, disjointed transition from past to present to future. Divine life is whole, which Boethius thought to include the whole of past, present and future. Creaturely life, on the other hand, is hardly whole. It is imperfect: a pale, momentary reflection of the ideal. According to Boethius, creaturely life does not even have a past or future. Creaturely life has only the present; it is episodic, epiphenomenal. Boethius's notion of eternity was not properly anti-time, however. One could interpret his definition of eternity as an early lead in asserting a certain temporal quality to God's eternity. Inadvertently underscoring the ambiguity of his definition, though, the Christian tradition tended still to conceive of eternity as timelessness, even while adverting to Boethius's authority. Perhaps this was due in part to the fact that Boethius's notion of divinity was simple. It was not given to a trinitarian elaboration. His was a notion of divinity that carried forward Plato's influence.

Most philosophical and theological reflection upon time and eternity assumes or responds to Plato. While it is generally held that Plato ascribes eternity to his Forms in the sense of atemporality, there are those who argue that eternity for Plato is a matter of everlasting temporal duration.[5] Plato's work does appear to allow differing interpretations. He writes of Forms and other entities as existing always, yet Plato seems also to attribute timelessness to the Forms. For our purposes we hearken to the *Parmenides* and the *Timaeus*.[6] In the former, Parmenides suggests that the Subject to which is accorded all existence is paradoxical. On the one hand, it is commonly maintained that the One is not in time and has no share of time.[7] On the other hand, temporality is a predicate of existence. One exists only in time. Thus the paradox: the One cannot exist. Parmenides elaborates and deepens the paradox. The reason for saying that the One is not in time is that whatever is in time is always growing older than its former self, which means that the former self is becoming younger than the present self. Yet at the same time it must be of the same age as itself. But none of these things can be true of the One. The only answer as to the "age" of the One, so it would seem thus far, is that the One "exists" only atemporally; that is, the One is eternal. The same argument is found in the *Timaeus*, though it is connected with Plato's concept of the Forms, rather than Parmenides's concept of the One. Plato argues that the Forms cannot grow older or younger. However, the conclusion is not that they therefore do not exist, but that eternal Being is exactly what must be ascribed to them.[8]

Plato's conception of eternity suggests that the ideal Forms are eternal in the sense of being timeless, while the images of the Forms here in the material world mirror eternality imperfectly in the sense of duration through the measure of time.[9] Philo, too, argues that temporality is part of a created order opposed to the timelessness of eternity. Like Augustine later, Philo was bothered with the deism of some people "who, having the world in admiration rather than the Maker of the World, pronounce it to be without beginning and everlasting, while with impious falsehood they postulate in God a vast inactivity." Dependent also upon Plato's *Timaeus*, Philo asserts that time began either simultaneously with the world or after it. "For since time is a measured space determined by the world's movement, and since movement could not be prior to the object moving, but must of necessity arise either after it or simultaneously with it, it follows of necessity that time also is either coeval with or later born than the world."[10] The implications here are significant. We shall recall them later in our discussion of contemporary physics. Philo would appear to argue that the motion of things themselves determines time. Matter-in-motion possesses an ontological and causal status that is prior to that of time.

In his turn Plotinus discusses eternity based upon the agenda left him by the *Timaeus*.[11] For Plotinus, time and eternity are essentially two kinds of life: life of the divine Intellect and life of Soul. Eternity is "the life which belongs to that which exists and is in being, all together and full, completely without extension or interval." Time, on the other hand, is the life of the soul in movement.[12] In one significant passage, Plotinus resolves the ambiguity left him by Plato regarding the meaning of "always." Plotinus's point is that "always" simply denotes *true* being, as opposed to being as "coming-to-be." The term is to be understood as atemporal.

> If then there is neither any earlier nor any later about it [the divine mind], but "is" is the truest thing about it, and indeed is it, and this in the sense that it is by its essence and life, then again we have got the very thing we are talking about, namely, eternity (*aion*)...But although "being" is an adequate word for substance, people thought that *coming* to be (*genesis*) was also substance, and therefore needed for their understanding to add in the word "always." It is not that being is one thing and *always* being another...this is why we must take the "always" as "truly" being. The "always" has to be included in that unextended property which in no way needs anything beyond what it already possesses. And it possesses everything.[13]

Note Plotinus's further, and complementary, definitions. Eternity is a life which stays in the same state, always having everything present to itself, and not one thing after another but everything together. Again, eternity is not the possession of some things at one time and others at another, but a completeness without parts, and with everything together as if in a point before flowing out into a line.[14] Again, eternity is "a life concerned with being, residing in being, all together, not extended in any direction."[15] On the other hand, time is defined as a mere copy of eternity and is "a life of the soul subject to movement which progresses from one mode to another."[16]

Gregory of Nyssa (d. 394) would appear to follow the same neoplatonic line of thought when he denies duration in eternity.[17] But Gregory's denial of duration in eternity does not logically require for him a contradiction between eternity and time. Gregory's concept of eternity is, in fact, closely tied with his concept of God and his apophatic mode of addressing the topic of God. In other words, that which is eternal is that about which no boundaries of language may be fixed. For Gregory, the predication of God as eternal was a denial of temporality as a predicate for God, but not a definition of the eternal as timeless. As Robert Jenson argues, Gregory's use of the term "infinity" as a predicate of God is precisely meant to denote that nothing can be predicated of God, else we really would not be dealing with "God."[18]

This negation of temporality (*diastema*) for God, in Gregory's thought, applied as well to Christ, to whatever was "before" the creation, even to the "waters above the heavens." Such things were without duration or quantity. It would be wrong to apply beginning and ending, past and future, to divinity, because such qualifications imply boundedness. God does not leave a particular time behind God's self, nor does God progress to anything lying ahead. God's nature does not coincide with times, and is not in any company with past or future. Concomitantly, there is nothing which moves alongside God and of which part is past and part future. Note that Gregory's concern is to define the divinity of God, not to describe eternity. So while some readers at first blush might interpret Gregory to equate eternity with timelessness, the more direct concern is to underscore that God, as "Godness," is incapable of *any* delimiting description, else the transcendence of God is lost and the god of whom one would speak is not the true God at all.

This seems all the more cogent when one notes Gregory's position that time and space belong to the creation. Time and space, for Gregory, are "the background,...on this foundation [God] builds the universe."[19] Gregory then suggests that the eternal God who establishes this background is not unrelated to it. There is a sense in Gregory's thought in which God in God's eternality may be viewed as not limited by, but embracing of, the created order, including time and space.

> But the existence which is all-sufficient, everlasting and world-enveloping, is not in space, nor in time: it is before these, and above these in an ineffable way; self-contained, knowable by faith alone; immeasurable by ages; without the accompaniment of time; seated and resting in itself, with no associations of past and future, there being nothing beside and beyond itself, whose passing can make something past and something future. Such accidents are confined to the creation, whose life is divided with time's divisions into memory and hope. But within that transcendent and blessed Power all things are equally present as in an instant: past and future are within its all-encircling grasp and its comprehensive view.[20]

On "God's side," it is clear for Gregory that God's eternity transcends time and space while it also envelops time and space. Somehow, we are already given the hint, the temporal is internal to and affects eternity, at least insofar as that which is eternal has freely assumed temporality. Robert Jenson supports this. He interprets Gregory in a way that corroborates with the affirmation that God's eternity embraces temporality.[21] Nor is this theme peculiar to eastern Christianity. The same attribution of infinity as a predicate for God's unboundedness as inclusive of temporality is found in the work of Hilary of Poitiers. Hilary, like Gregory, asserts repeatedly that God's being, as well as power, is infinite and this infinity manifests itself in the fact that God embraces and suffuses all the cosmos.[22] In such a scheme as this, Hilary would seem to imply, eternity could not be construed as anti-time or alongside it.

On the created side, however, time is very much something which "moves alongside" the human being. When tackling the issue of time's relation to human consciousness, there is ample opportunity in Gregory, as with the above quote, to infer that the effects of past and future may be correlated with the mental states of memory and expectation. It is not entirely clear here that Gregory would interpret time as dependent upon consciousness, but we do see an early recognition of time as having a psychological direction. This, of course, is analogous to Augustine's discussion of memory, knowledge and expectation as related to temporality and trinitarian figuration.

Augustine's Argument

Augustine's examination of time is found primarily in Book XI of *Confessions*, and *City of God*, V. In the former, Augustine meditates on the miracle that God's Word was expressed through the motion of something God created, yet motion is subject to the laws of time. But God's Word itself is eternal, distinct from its expressions written in the book of nature. Why then did God not create something eternal if he himself were eternal? Augustine answers that the question makes no sense. "How can anyone ask what [God was] doing *then* [before time]? If there was no time, there was no *then*." In other words, time itself is a creation of God, and God precedes all creation, including time, but not in a temporal sense, not in the sense of an endless time. "Before" God created, there was no time. God is transcendent to time. How God might be "in and with" time is another matter for Augustine's sacramental theology and is not considered here. Regarding a formal definition of eternity, though, Augustine clearly understands it to be atemporal.

As for the timely side, Augustine's formal understanding also includes a delimitation of temporality. Of course, time is and can be divided into the characteristic categories of past, present, and future. But Augustine is careful to demonstrate that only the present exists, and that but for a moment. "How can...the past and the future be when the past no longer is and the future is not yet? As for the present, if it were always present and never moved on to become the past, it would not be time but eternity."[23]

Since human beings exist temporally, and cannot exist in an eternal now, the question of time's relationship to human consciousness must be broached. How do we know time? If all we know is its present, yet we are not as humans privy to an "eternal now," strictly speaking, how do we know of its passage? How do we *relate* to time? Augustine's answer is that we do not measure time itself, but the impressions left in our minds by events in time.

> It is in my own mind, therefore, that I measure time. I must not allow my mind to insist that time is something objective. I must not let it thwart me because of all the different notions and impressions that are lodged in it. I say that I measure time in my mind. For everything which happens leaves an impression on it, and this impression remains after the thing itself has ceased to be. It is the impression that I measure, since it is still present, not the thing itself, which makes the impression as it passes and then moves into the past. When I measure time it is this impression that I measure. Either, then, this is what time is, or else I do not measure time at all.[24]

In other words, the measurement of the time between two events is the measurement of the difference between two memory records of time. On the one hand, there is the record of the past (*memoria*); on the other an expectation (*expectatio*) of the future, which too is a kind of memory. Hereby Augustine rejects any notion that the past and future are unknowable and that time is an eternal now. The unity of the past, present and future comes about in their being held together in the mind: in memory, sight and expectation.[25] The salient point is that Augustine clearly introduces into the enumeration of times the perceiving subject of the experience of time, the human psyche. Human consciousness and time are inextricably related.

This is not to argue that time is entirely dependent upon human consciousness; nor the contrary. Though Aristotle was one to move in the former direction,[26] and though Augustine *prima facie* denies that time is objective, it appears that Augustine does not intend to make such an idealistic claim. He is descriptive only to the extent that time is part of the created order, of which part simultaneously is human consciousness. Still, Augustine is at least as suggestive, and likely moreso, as Gregory in the implication of time's arrow as part of the created order. Such is not to argue, however, that

God's eternity is subject to that same arrow. Rather, God's eternity would embrace and transcend all aspects of the created order, temporality included.

While Augustine analyzes time's arrow as pertaining radically to human consciousness, and that the conscious human might surmise thereby something of or about eternity, it is important to recall that for Augustine the unity of eternity and time is not found in a supposed Eternal Present, but in God's creativity. If the measurement of time is connected to consciousness, then the origin of time is connected to something transcendent to humanity. In this dialectical move, Augustine emphasizes theocentricity, which means that temporality is on the creaturely side of the relationship between God and creation. Everything that exists originates from and by the creative word of God. "Of course, the world is not created *in* time, but *with* time…For what happens in time happens after something and before something else. The time that lies behind is the past, the time that is ahead the future…But the world was created with time when once the movement of change was included in its creation."[27]

This brings us back to our first question with regard to Augustine. How does time as a temporal creation relate to its eternal creator? Is time's beginning in time itself, or in eternity? Augustine believed that the beginning of time is an absolute, therefore in eternity. Since time is in creation, God is "before all time the eternal Creator of all time…" Still, how can we conceive of an eternal creator and the creation of temporality without one cancelling out the other? One way is to propose again that eternity need not be understood logically as anti-temporal. On this issue, however, we receive no definitive help from Augustine.

Beyond Boethius's Eternity

As influential as Augustine was for the Christian tradition, he yet had not clearly defined his understanding of eternity. As I observed above, the classic and precise definition came from Boethius, and stands as definitive for consequent Christian theology. Boethius starts with the apparent conflict between Providence and free will, which is, of course, another way in which the problem of the relationship of eternity to temporality may be stated. Boethius argues that philosophy solves the problem of Providence and free will by distinguishing between simple and conditional necessity.[28] A consideration of God as eternal is foundational for this distinction. Thus Boethius's famous passage: "Eternity is the whole, perfect, and simultaneous possession of endless life."

The meaning of this statement can be made clearer by comparison with temporal things. Temporal things exist only in the now, in the present, proceeding from past to future. Temporal things never possess themselves wholly with a past and future. Even if their life be endless, as Aristotle considered the world to be, that is not the same as eternal.

> Therefore, only that which comprehends and possesses the whole plenitude of endless life together, from which no future thing nor any past thing is absent, can justly be called eternal. Moreover, it is necessary that such a being be in full possession of itself, always present to itself, and hold the infinity of moving time present before itself.[29]

While Plato too held that the world's life was endless, without beginning and end, this still is not equal to an eternity that lacks duration. The world may be perpetual, Boethius says with Plato, but only God is eternal.[30] In other words, infinity and eternity, or their adjectival forms, are not synonymous, the contemporary confusion of the terms notwithstanding. Infinity, properly speaking, involves endless duration, which is but an ultimate extension of temporality. Eternity, on the other hand, is at least the addition of "one dimension," if not more, so that what is infinite may yet be perceived as a whole. To paraphrase Boethius's definitions, we might say the path from temporality through infinity into eternity is an extension and erasure of limits of consciousness and apperception, which includes even awareness of one's own limitlessness, a kind of limit which can only be described as eternity.

More mundanely, perhaps eternity may be likened to a bookcase full of books, all of which are ordered alphabetically, but which are equally accessible to an "eternal observer" who stands apart from the books, i.e., is transcendent to the books. The creature who stands temporally within the collection of books could only access other books from within the sequence by reaching forward or backward; the whole collection is not simultaneously available to the temporal creature. Whether the book collection is finite or infinite doesn't change the limitations of temporality. An infinite collection would merely increase the temporal reader's frustration at not being able to check-out volumes with ease.

Eternity, then, is that transcendent manifold which is distinguished from the temporal, while all the components of temporality are yet equally and simultaneously accessible to the eternal. As for infinity, it applies to duration, or endlessness, and thus may apply properly to both temporality and eternity as a predicate. But the term substantively is not synonymous with eternity or the eternal. I believe these conclusions reflect Boethius's intent in further specifying the meaning of eternity, and that they ought to apply to Augustine, Gregory and Philo in a correct reading of them, as well.[31] However, that infinity might be the mediator here between time and eternity has not necessarily solved the question as to whether eternity is to be understood as allergic to time. While we have noted possibilities in Boethius's own prescription that could allay the allergy, traditional Western theology takes a narrower view of his writing in supposing that eternity is time's opposite. What we have noted of perhaps more positive value, though, is that Christian thinkers early recognized a connection of time with human consciousness simultaneous with the confession of time as a creation. If it may be said that consciousness can lead to any minute characterization of eternity, as did Boethius, then we must say that there is likewise some real connection between all three terms of consciousness, temporality, and eternity, with the priority given to the third term. This observation, is not one discretely noted within the developing Christian tradition itself.

After Boethius, Christian theologizing as to the nature of time and eternity is not substantially changed, except for nuances provided by Thomas Aquinas.[32] With Isaac Newton, however, we find the philosophical fix of time as an absolute which is effectively separated from human consciousness and the motion of matter. Immanuel Kant hesitates to affirm such objectivity for time, but in doing so separates critical reason from the possibility of rationally entertaining Boethius's eternity. Indeed, Newton reasserts the Hellenic position of time as "pre-existent" and Kant then says we can't give a meaningful metaphysical description of it. Both consequences strain against the Christian position I have just outlined. Both figures, even so, considered themselves to be within the Christian tradition.

Some have commented that the popular impact of what Newton theorized as to the so-called "container theory" of time has been more influential than what he actually said. Newton's definition of time is clear and concise.

> Absolute, true and mathematical time, of itself, and from its own nature, flows equably without relation to anything external, and by another name is called duration: relative, apparent and common time, is some sensible and external (whether accurate or unequable) measure of duration by means of motion, which is commonly used instead of true time; such as an hour, a day, a month, a year.[33]

Newton then adds that space is of a similar absolute character. The consequence is that absolute motion, as compared to relative motion, is the translation of a body from one absolute place to another.

It may seem incongruous for Newton to have introduced concepts of absolute time, space, and motion after having so strongly emphasized throughout the *Principles* the empirical character of the scientific method. But when it came to such "philosophical disquisitions," Newton thought it appropriate to abstract from sense experience to consider things in and of themselves. Why? Evidently, Newton was convinced that his "water pail" experiment demonstrated the difference between absolute and relative motion.[34] Newton interpreted the water's recession from the center of the pail and its concomitant increase in concavity as evidence for absolute rotational motion. He then surmised that if an object could have absolute rotational motion, there must also be an absolute space in which it moves and an absolute time by which the motion endures.

It appears, too, that Newton may have had a religious motivation to posit the unobservable existence of absolute time. Having been disturbed, it seems, by criticisms of this point, in the second edition of the *Principles* Newton added the famous *General Scholium*. Here he set forth his belief in an eternal, omnipotent and omniscient God who sustains the order of the universe. God is "not eternity or infinity, but eternal and infinite....He endures forever and is everywhere present; and by existing always and everywhere, he constitutes duration and space. Since every particle of space is *always*, and every indivisible moment of duration is *everywhere*, certainly the Maker and Lord of all things cannot be *never* and *nowhere*."[35] Religious faith for Newton provided the demand for absolute space and time, which Newton thought to be corroborated by his water container theory.

Newton's idea was in contrast to much that was theologized before. Newton's conclusions, when applied theologically, would imply that God created "in" time, that time itself was not a creation of God and was "coeternal" with God. It is unclear how Newton could or would have coordinated absolute time with the absolute God. Absolute physical time, one may argue, would be incoherent with an atemporal notion of eternity. Eternity itself would require the interpretation of "endlessness," too. Absolute time, space, and motion would be the standards by which all else is measured. Even so, Newton's argument for absolute time seemed to cohere with common sense.

Though Kant gave high regard to Newton's achievement, Kant sought to explain the nature of time in a much different way, such that it was compromised of its objective status posited by Newton. Kant argued, upon conclusions derived from the so-called "antinomies" posed with respect to whether the universe began in or outside time, that time, finally, is not a phenomenon alongside other phenomena of the universe itself. Time does not belong to any phenomena outside the human perception of them. It belongs rather to the mental structure which perceives the world.[36]

Time, as well as space, Kant asserts, is the framework in which the manifold of all sensation is arranged. Time and space simultaneously unify the indeterminate matter which are the data for sense experience. As such "ordering devices" time and space are a priori forms; they are the necessary conditions to bring sense experience into awareness. The ordering of experience is a condition of awareness, not a consequence. Thus, time is "the form of the internal sense, that is, of the intuition of ourselves and of our internal state."[37] This is not to suggest that time is merely an imposition upon the world; it is not "all in the head." Kant wants to avoid solipsism and aver some kind of objectivity by saying that time is real inasmuch as empirical reality is characterized by temporal relations. This is no circular argument. It is proper to say that appearances *are* in time. Because there can be no empirical reality apart from the forms of space and time, and because one would assume that empirical reality is real, then the forms themselves are empirically real. However, time may extend only to the phenomenal realm, only to things as they appear to us, and not to things in themselves. In this particular Kantian case study as to the problem of time, we see a good example of Kant's critical agenda; to wit, to make a "critical realist" advance upon, rather than simply a synthesis of, the options of either strict empiricism or strict rationalism left to him by Hume and Descartes.[38]

This "advance," though, is only in respect to the sphere of "pure" reason. Matters of "practical" life, that is, those matters which are bracketed off from phenomenal critique, such as components for the moral life, religious beliefs, and eternity, are not matters for critical philosophical concern. The practical effect of this divorce is to limit metaphysics only to the scientifically or critically describable. All else is to be discussed under the aegis of a different employ of reason: "practical" reason. Eternity does not play a significant role in Kant's philosophy, except that it seems to designate the possibility of an endless advancement in one's life toward moral or immoral dispositions. Eternity, as a nontemporal concept, receives no critical adjudication in Kant's philosophy, except as it may correspond to the noumenal, which is inaccessible anyway. In this respect, Kant's legacy entails a censure of intelligible discourse about the meaning of eternity, and ironically, relegates the topic to the practical relativity of individual experience and opinion.[39]

The Unity of Reason and the Actual

Nevertheless, one category of pure reason, the transcendental, was mined by Hegel to fruitful effect. Hegel's original fashioning of the Absolute and historical concrete as transcendental categories lent to time and eternity a stronger objectivity not entertained by Kant. Furthermore, the objectivity of time is included within the objectivity of the eternal totality of experience, the possibility for which is the transcendental condition, God. Hegel's huge contribution in this regard still inspires creative contemporary thinking.[40]

If God, however, with eternity has been opposed to time in much of the tradition, with Hegel appears the threat that God apart from time cannot exist. "Without the world, God is not God."[41] God is absolute reality (*Wirklichkeit*) only in and through the reality of the world.[42] But God is logically precedent to particularity as the ontotheological and ontological ground of all else. In the threefold figuration of history, God's action correlates to the trinitarian movement adumbrated in the Christian symbols, and Hegel understands them precisely as such symbols which, for Hegel, are more appropriately understood philosophically. First, as universality, God is eternity before creation; God is the absolute, eternal, logical idea. Second, God acts in particularity by creating the finite which is distinct from God; first by way of separation (symbolized in Adam), then by way of reconciliation of the separated (symbolized in the christ). Third, God is understood as Infinite Subjectivity or Intersubjectivity; God is the Holy Spirit present in community, bringing all things into union with God. Hereby God is enriched and is, much more, God.[43] The ultimate identity of this God who engenders, acts in and is constituted by the cosmos is God as Spirit. Thus Hegel's own description of this trinitarian process: "God in his eternal universality is the one who distinguishes himself, determines himself, posits an other to himself, and likewise sublates the distinction, thereby remaining present to himself, and is spirit only through this process of being brought forth."[44]

While Hegel's God is formally to be understood as the threefold working-out of the one absolute Idea, it would be a mistake to regard Hegel as a philosophical monist. Indeed, in the Hegelian trialectic, it is a social God who precedes and gives shape to social particularity. As Peter Hodgson recognizes, though Hegel did not use the terms *immanent* and *economic* with regard to the Trinity, he did have in mind that the immanent or logical trinity, with its own triune structure *ad intra* must be the logical ground for sociality *ad extra*. The distinction is important because it establishes God's transcendence over and God's dependence upon a world for self-actualization. "Hegel recognized that the divine differentiation *ad intra* is the condition of possibility for God's relation to the world *ad extra* and that the outward relations reenact the inner distinctions without simply reduplicating or repeating them — in effect a correspondence between, not an identity of, the immanent and economic trinities."[45]

In sum, Hegel's "doctrine" of the Trinity may be conceived as the philosophical statement of a wholistic process with real differentiation among its parts. The further elaboration of this process, as is Hodgson's interest, is to de-construct the *kindlich* terms of Father, Son and Holy Spirit so that the truth of the doctrine, concerning God's real relations internally and externally, may be retrieved. Hodgson prefers to employ the terms *God, World* and

Spirit (the name of the whole God) rather than the traditional personal terms, and this is faithful to Hegel's intentions. While this helpfully advances our discussion insofar as it clearly supports our contention that eternity is *cum tempore* and moves us further away from the neo-platonic paradigm, the question might be asked as to whether the depersonalization is too much deconstruction with no adequate, reciprocal, reconstruction. I will revisit this question in subsequent chapters.

Biblical Words For Time

Self-consciously Christian reflection of this century, though, has tried to address the legacy bequeathed by Newton and Kant, now qualified by Hegel, in an attempt to recapture the sense of eternity as transcendent-over-yet-immanent-in time, as well as its intelligibility. Among those in Biblical Theology who have attempted to derive a Christian conceptuality of time from word studies of the Bible, Oscar Cullmann's attempt has perhaps been the most noted.[46] Cullmann seeks to establish a Christian concept of time based upon a crucial distinction between Greek thought and "primitive" Christianity, and he believes that the clearest contrasts between the Greek world view and that of primitive Christianity concern their concepts of time and eternity. The Greek concept of time, Cullmann argues, is primarily circular. Events repeat themselves, as images of the eternal forms which move about as do the constellations of the heavens; they do not advance. This indeed is properly a platonic conceptuality. Consequently, eternity in the "Greek view" means not an endlessly extended time, but that which is outside of time.[47] This is, of course, precisely that definition I wish to argue against.

On the other hand, Cullmann maintains that primitive Christianity knew nothing of such timelessness and it viewed time as primarily "linear." Eternity, Cullman therefore argues, is within time as well. It is an infinite extension of temporality. It is "the endless succession of the ages." Eschatology, too, is a category within time, Cullmann maintains. The eschaton is part of time's progression. For Cullmann, the critical point of belief (and inspiration) for the Christian lies not ahead, not in the future, but in the historical victory of Easter. This is the "midpoint" which constitutes the essential linearity of time in primitive Christianity.[48]

Cullmann argues, in other words, somewhat against the mainstream. His claim is that the Judaeo-Christian tradition attributes temporal character to eternity. This temporal eternity constitutes the background for all God's creative acts, including creation of the universe and the "re-creation" of the

Resurrection of Christ. The Judaeo-Christian tradition, while certainly maintaining some cyclic rituals, nevertheless contributed to the world scene a conception of linear time theretofore unknown in its quality and nuances. This interpretation of time is evidenced in the Judaeo-Christian accounting of a historical relationship with Yahweh, who helped Israel *advance* its life. This series of interactions accumulated to form a succession of events from which no single component could be omitted and from which later the Israelite sense of linear time matured.[49] The same sense of directionality is carried over in Christianity in its followers' experience of Jesus of Nazareth, whose death, resurrection and promised return gave this sense of directionality an even more pronounced eschatological-future orientation.

In criticism of Cullmann, however, one would observe that Cullmann fails to appreciate the significance of the future when he attempts to found linear time only upon the historical occasion of the resurrection. The sense of expectation is a key psychological underpinning in the linear sense of time.[50] Expectation and its consequent sense of time's movement forward, is enhanced by belief both in an unrepeatable creation and some sort of redemptive end to come. Temporality is distinct, though not altogether separate, from human subjectivity.

Furthermore, Cullmann's conclusions are better justified upon historical rather than the biblical-lexical grounds upon which Cullmann claims to argue. James Barr's critique of Cullmann is convincing here.[51] After considerable review, Barr must conclude that nowhere in the Bible is anything said about what time is like, and this has forced exegetes to get a view of time out of the words themselves. The view Cullmann extracts indeed may be wholly inconsistent with the view that naturally would be held by early Christians. Their understanding of the Genesis story, for example, likely implied that they believed the creation of time to be simultaneous with the creation of the world, though Cullmann rejects this.[52] Augustine's observation about time as a created constituent of the natural order, as it were, is already embedded in the primitive Christian witness, Barr believes. This, allied with Cullmann's argument of the temporal character of eternity, gives some indication already that an understanding of eternity sheerly as timelessness is inadequate.[53]

It is also of concern, especially in light of Albert Schweitzer's "completed" quest just previous to Cullmann's work, that Cullmann neglects eschatology. He simply places it within the same expanding time line. A most significant development in the last several decades however has been the eschatologizing of the historical sense.[54] No treatment of a "properly Christian" view of time and eternity today can avoid the eschatological component. More shall be said of this below.

As for Cullmann's general characterization of Greek thought as "circular," opposed to the linearity of Hebrew thinking, Barr, for one, can find no evidence to support Cullmann's assumption. The Greek philosophers themselves belie Cullmann's claims.[55] Circularity may also be attributed to some aspects of Hebrew thought.[56] It is fairer to conclude that a cyclic view is not necessarily Greek, nor necessarily opposed to the biblical view. Indeed, Barr writes, the fairest conclusion is that there is no single biblical conception of time; there are several. It may generally be stated, however, that cyclical time is not as reflected in the biblical material as much as some form of linear time, and that form probably not in a modern sense.

While a variety of time concepts may be suggested by the biblical material, the same holds for understandings of the eschaton. These notions may refer to differing physical scenarios, too. The physicist Lawrence Fagg, for example, rehearses the many options for interpreting eschatology.[57] The point here is that the Bible can only serve as a starting point and can give no definitive view from within as to the nature of time. The work of developing any Christian doctrine of time belongs not to Biblical, but to Philosophical Theology, according to Barr.[58]

Barth Sets the Agenda

The theologian of this century who most exhaustively treats the problem of time and eternity within a systematic whole is Karl Barth. As with his doctrine of the Trinity, which shapes all his theology, Barth's comments of time and eternity are increasingly mined as a rich vein for further creative systematic construction.

Barth clearly maintains a temporal understanding of eternity. Combining Boethius's notion of eternity with the divine *experience* of time's flux, Barth holds that all moments in time are "simultaneous" for God.[59] But this does not mean that past, present, and future are collapsed all into one. God's eternity includes the "co-presence" of past, present, and future in their connectedness and disjunction, in the sense of our experience of the present as opposed to past and future and in the sense of "the fluid and fleeting" present. Barth calls this "pure duration."[60] In other words, as Robert John Russell observes, God's eternity is this duration in which "all moments of time are held together without their distinctions being erased."[61] In fact, Barth calls this sort of eternity "supremely temporal."

> Even the eternal God does not live without time. He is supremely temporal. For His eternity is authentic temporality, and therefore the source of all time. But in His eternity, in the uncreated self-subsistent time which is one of the perfections

of His divine nature, present, past and future, yesterday, to-day and to-morrow, are not successive, but simultaneous. It is in this way, in this eternity of His, that God lives to the extent that He lives His own life.

If this sort of eternity is supremely temporal, it could just as well be characterized as "supremely eternal" for Barth. For it is important to note that, for Barth, the meanings of both terms derive from God's overcoming of disunity notwithstanding the very reality of that disunity, as opposed to creaturely existence which can only live in such disjunction, in such "inauthentic temporality distinct from eternity."[62] The only authentic temporality is that temporality which is tantamount to authentic eternity. The dynamic of temporality is essential to the eternity of God, as Barth's doctrine of God would pose it.

It is unclear, however, how this authentic temporality is to be understood if it does not include temporal succession.[63] One wonders here whether temporal succession is trivialized and the notion of a God in history is undercut. One may also side with Moltmann in the charge that here is an instance when Barth betrays himself; that Barth shows true colors as an advocate of the philosopher's God whose "eternal" now of unchangingness once again breaks through the veneer of ephemeral time.[64] Robert John Russell, however, may have directed us to an appropriate answer by pointing once again to Barth's rejection of the "finite/infinite" distinction. As Barth finds this dichotomy itself limiting with reference to God, so also timelessness against succession may be an unwarranted understanding of Barth's sense of divine temporality. If "infinite" is opposed to "finite," that in itself is a boundary condition for God which Barth rejects. Likewise, then, "supreme temporality" need not mean the necessary exclusion of successiveness, but only the exclusion of "mere" successiveness as a potential boundary condition for divinity.

Still unclear, though, is Barth's intention in saying that "the future" is equally present to God as are present and past. This leads into the question of whether the future exists as something predetermined, or whether it may refer to the openness and directionality inherent in the experience of the present. I believe the argument weighs toward the latter and lies in Barth's conception of the Trinitarian nature of God. A brief word about Barth's trinitarian theology is therefore in order.

For Barth, the "root" of the Trinity is discerned analytically in the central fact of revelation.[65] To take revelation seriously, in no way can Christ and the Spirit be construed as subordinate to God. Indeed, the proper understanding of God as subject, object and predicate of revelation by which (Barthian) theology would be conducted implies that the act of revelation in Christ and in the Holy Spirit is equal to the revealer.[66] This, combined with the scriptural accounting of the word of Father, Son, and Spirit, necessitates a trinitarian understanding.[67] To take revelation seriously, then, as the revelation of who God is as the Trinity is also to say that our experience of the Trinitarian God is nothing other than the Trinitarian experience of God in God's self. God is the same, as Trinity, in other words, whether God be on the eternal or the temporal side.[68]

But this does not mean for Barth that the unity of the Trinity is simple. Similar to Hegel's argument outlined above, and with indebtedness to it, Barth argues that God is differentiated, though not tri-theistic.[69] There are three "persons" in the Trinity. Barth acknowledges, however, that the modern understanding of "person" as "ego" is not part of the patristic understanding of *mia ousia, treis hypostases* or *una substantia, tres personae*.[70] Barth thinks it more helpful to identify the Godhead as the divine person, and this by reference to *ousia* or *hypostasis*, and suggests, then, that the three hypostases be understood as "modes of being" (*Seinsweise*).[71] These very "modes of being" as the differences-in-unity of the Godhead are the very relationships which engender time's arrow within God, and thus, by God's trinitarian embrace of this world, bring temporality "outside" the divine life as well.[72]

What are the consequences of this Trinitarian theology for the conceptuality of time and eternity? Firstly, Barth posits a threefold character to divine eternity. It is pre-temporal, supra-temporal and post-temporal.[73] Here the prefixes bear an onto-logical reference rather than a sequential one. They are, in fact, essential for theology, and are closely related to the meanings of the three primary symbols of salvation history: creation, reconciliation, and redemption. By "pre-temporal" Barth means that way in which God precedes all creaturely existence. Supra-temporality designates how God relates to creaturely temporality. "Post-temporal," then, refers to that divine future in which all is in God and God in all; "Eternity is the goal and the end beyond which and over which another goal and end cannot exist. All roads necessarily lead to it."[74] In fact, God as this eternal "post-temporality" is finally understood as *the* very future toward which creaturely temporality is directed. God *is* the future. God is "the absolute, unsurpassable future of all time and of all that is in time." The "arrow of time," if you will, originates from God, is embraced by God and returns to God as the future. In this respect, the future does exist inasmuch as God exists. Further, though it is too complicated an issue to enter in on here, this future is tied to the doctrine of election for Barth. Therefore the future is "fixed" inasmuch as God's will for humanity is redemption. How God will achieve that, given that the exercise of human free will can and does frustrate the divine intent, means that the future is also open. Finally, it is most significant to note, too, that

Barth posits a kind of "time's arrow" in the very eternity of God. Barth says that within the divine eternity there is a "divine before" and a "divine after." Further, this eternity has a "direction." This very sequence is itself the ordering of temporal events experienced on the creaturely side. While this sounds Platonic (the world imperfectly "mirrors" the Ideals) it still clearly posits sequence—history!—in the divine life.[75]

In sum, we garner from the Barthian position that God's eternity is temporal, that temporality has a direction, and that the direction is toward an open future. The further implications, though I have not specifically referred to Barth's treatment of them, are that creaturely time is created by God, after the pattern of that temporality which is part of God. With Augustine, therefore, Barth affirms that time is created by God. In fact, he notes that it is "co-created" with matter. It may be helpful even to propose that creaturely time is created out of a "self-limitation" of the divine eternity.[76] In any respect, *all* time either adheres to God or derives from God as the defining source of time. Other than God, there is no beginning, no present and no future. Other than God there is no time, which means that one cannot pose, either, an "absolute time" against the reality of God.[77]

Barth's conceptuality of time and eternity has been immensely helpful. It has led directly to Jürgen Moltmann's description of God as "the power of the future"[78] and to Wolfhart Pannenberg's sense of the eschaton as the source and purpose of history; indeed, that God's eternity is "the power of the future over every moment."[79] The same conceptuality is found in the work of another Barthian protege, Eberhard Jüngel.[80] The thematization has insinuated itself into the work of contemporary philosophers, though they may not be directly aware of Barth's impact. J. R. Lucas, for example, argues for God's temporality on the basis of God as personal.[81] Moreover, defined as they are by the primacy of the Doctrine of the Trinity in Barth's work, the terms of temporality and eternity are seen by many now as inextricable from Trinitarian theology. We have already noted this in the trinitarian form Barth gives to God's eternity with his prefixed notions of temporality. Barth's affirmation that the eternity of God is temporal leads directly to the assertion that this dynamism is best expressed in the doctrine of the Trinity. And so it is fitting that we turn to the discussion of that domain in the next chapter.

Notes

1. This concept resonates very much with the current proposal of Michael Welker regarding the creatureliness of both heaven and earth. See Michael Welker, *God As Spirit*, translated by John F. Hoffmeyer (Minneapolis: Fortress, 1994).

2. Indeed, I admit some trepidation here. While I am certainly aware of the influence of my mentors, I have maintained the naive impression through the development of my research that I had recognized something new in this theme of eternity's embrace of temporality. In the course of this writing, my mentors themselves have written on this very same topic and have advised me to stay on this course. I am in their debt. See especially Robert John Russell's "Eternally Creating Time: The Theological Problem of Time and Eternity in Relation to Big Bang and Quantum Cosmology," (unpublished paper) and Ted Peters's book, *God As Trinity, Relationality and Temporality in the Divine Life* (Louisville: Westminster/John Knox Press, 1993).

3. *God As Trinity*, 219.

4. Boethius, *The Consolation of Philosophy*, trans. by V. E. Watts (Baltimore: Penguin, 1969). Also see John Whittaker, "The 'Eternity' of the Platonic Forms"; also F.M. Cornford, *Plato's Cosmology* (London: 1937, 98; 102) and W. von Leyden, "Time, Number and Eternity in Plato and Aristotle," *Philosophical Quarterly*, 14, (1964), 35-52.

5. All are cited in Richard Sorabji, *Time, Creation and the Continuum*, (Ithaca: Cornell Univ. Press, 1983), 108.

6. Here I follow the summary of Sorabji, 108-112.

7. Sorabji, 112.

8. *Timaeus*, 37C6-38C3. "[The father] tried to make this universe an everlasting (*aidios*) living organism as far as possible. Now the nature of this living organism is eternal (*aitonios*),...But he planned to make it a moving likeness of eternity (*aion*), as it were, and while arranging the heavens, he simultaneously made a likeness of eternity (*aion*) which stays still in unity, a copy of which moves according to number and is eternal (*aionios*), namely, that which we have called time...These are all parts of time, and 'was' and 'shall be' are the forms of time which have come into being. We are wrong when we apply them, without realizing it, to the everlasting (*aidios*) being. For we say that it was, is and shall be. But really only 'is' belongs properly to it. 'Was' and 'shall be'are appropriately said of becoming (*genesis*) which proceeds in time, for they are processes (*kineseis*)...These attributes have come into being as forms of time which imitate eternity (*aion*) and circles round according to number...Be that as it may, time has come into being with the heavens, in order that, having been created together, they may be dissolved together, if ever their dissolution should come about. And the heavens have come into being in accordance with the model of eternal (*diaionios*) nature, in order that they should be as like it as possible. For the model has being for the whole of eternity (*aion*), whereas the other has come into being and is and shall be right through the whole of time." Quoted in Sorabji, 112.

9. The ambiguity in Plato's approach is not thoroughly resolved insofar as Plato insists on using temporal qualifications (e.g., 'always'- *aei*) of the Forms. It is not clear whether Plato intended to ascribe the same atemporality to *aei* as he did to *aion*. However intended the ambiguity, it is left to Plotinus three hundred years later to make the significant distinction between the two senses of 'always.'

10. Quoted by Christopher Isham in Russell and Stoeger, eds., *Physics, Philosophy and Theology* (Vatican: Vatican Observatory, 1988), hereafter noted as *PPT*.

11. Plotinus, *The Enneads*, trans. by S. McKenna (London: Faber, 1969), III.7.

12. *Enneads*, 3.36-38; all of sections 1 through 6 are significant to the discussion. A perhaps surprising feature of Plotinus's concept of eternity is that he defines both time and eternity as two kinds of *life*. The idea is not original with him; it appears already in Philo, and Plato had identified time and eternity as attributes of living things. When Plotinus extends time and eternity from attributes of living things to the assertion that they are *lives*, he asserts that time is the life of the soul and eternity the life of the intellect. Here eternity and thinking come to be connected. That life which constitutes eternity, the life of the intellect, is a life of thinking. But just as eternity is understood atemporally, so also must thinking be viewed in such a special way. See Sorabji, 138.

13. *Enneads*, 3.7.6. In 3.7.2 Plotinus writes more curtly. "I mean not the 'always' in time [*en chronoi*], but the kind we think when speaking of eternity [the *aidion*]."

14. *Enneads*, 3.7.3.

15. *Enneads*, 3.7.3.

16. *Enneads*, 3.7.11.

17. Gregory of Nyssa, *Against Eunomius*, in *The Nicene and Post-Nicene Fathers*, vol. V, trans. by H. A. Wilson; Schaff and Wace (eds.) (Edinburgh: T & T Clark, 1988), 68-70, 97-100, 118, 201, 211. See also Hans Urs von Balthasar, *Presence et pensee* (Paris:1942), 1-10. Also Gregory's brother, Basil, *adversus Eunomius*, 1.20-1, in which Basil defines time as a *diastema* stretched out together with the holding together of the *kosmos*. A very helpful summary is found in Sorabji, 123.

18. See *Against Eunomius*, I:25.

19. *Against Eunomius*, I:26ff.

20. *Against Eunomius*, I:26.

21. Robert Jenson *The Triune Identity* (Philadelphia: Fortress, 1982). I will refer to Jenson in some detail in the survey of Trinitarian reflection below.

22. Hilary of Poitiers, *De Trinitate*, in Philip Schaff and Henry Wace (eds.), *Nicene and Post-Nicene Fathers*, Second Series, vol. IX (New York: Charles Scribner's Sons, 1899), 1, 6ff. See also E.P. Meijering, *Hilary of Poitiers On The Trinity, De Trinitate 1, 1-19, 2, 3* (Leiden: E.J. Brill, 1982).

23. Augustine, *The Confessions*, trans. by R.S. Pine-Coffin (Middlesex: Penguin, 1961), 11.14.

24. *Confessions*, 11.27.

25. *Confessions*, 11.20.

26. Aristotle, *Physics* 4.14, as included in *The Basic Works of Aristotle*, McKeon (ed.) (New York: Random House, 1941). "Whether if soul [mind] did not exist time would exist or not, is a question that may fairly be asked; for if there cannot be some one to count there cannot be anything that can be counted, so that evidently there cannot be number; for number is either what has been, or what can be, counted. But if nothing but soul, or in soul reason, is qualified to count, there would not be time unless there were soul, but only that of which time is an attribute, i.e., if *movement* can exist without soul, and the before and after are attributes of movement, and time is these *qua* numerable."

27. *Confessions*, 11.6.

28. That is, the "present awareness" of God, which is timeless knowledge, is simple;

it avoids the determinism (conditional necessity) of an attributed "foreknowledge." Cf. Sorabji, 256; Boethius, *Consol.*, 5.6f.

29. *Consol.*, 5.6.

30. *Timaeus*, 37.

31. It is noteworthy that Wolfhart Pannenberg recently has further substantiated this point in his discussion of the notion of "proper Infinity." Proper Infinity includes itself in, as well as distinguishes itself from, the finite. Thus it is a genuine *Aufhebung* which sublates both terms while also achieving the denotation of boundlessness intended by Gregory of Nyssa. Cf. Pannenberg, *Systematic Theology*, vol. 1, 397-410 and the article, "Problems of a Trinitarian Doctrine of God," *Dialog*, 26:4 (1987, Fall), 250-257. It is also noteworthy that Pannenberg suggests that the eternity of God is a quality of God's infinity.

32. For primary resources, see Aquinas, *Summa*, Pt. 1, X, 46 and Aristotle, *Physics*, IV.10-14.

33. *Sir Isaac Newton's Mathematical Principles of Natural Philosophy and His System of the World*, Cajori revision of 1729 tr. by Andrew Motte (Berkeley: University of California Press, 1947), 6.

34. I follow Benjamin's summary here. See J.T. Fraser (ed.), *The Voices of Time* (Amherst: University of Massachusetts, 1981), 18.

35. Fraser, 545.

36. Consider the assertion that the world began in time. In "proving" this assertion, Kant argued that no temporal series or succession of physical phenomena can be indefinite; no such series can transpire without a first member. This physical infinity (distinguished from a purely mathematical-conceptual infinity) is characterized by its endlessness. It can never be completed through "successive synthesis." So Kant asserts, in a seemingly tautologous fashion, that it is impossible for an infinite phenomenal series to pass away. Its simple endurance implies, therefore that it necessarily had a beginning. A beginning of the world is a necessary condition of the world's existence. Kant is not arguing about temporal concepts. He is trying to argue only about the occurrence of successive events in time, with no assertion about their future endurance. But that an infinite series of events could have occurred already is impossible. An "elapsed infinity of successive events is a self-contradictory concept." See G. J Whitrow, "Time and the Universe," Fraser, 566.

37. Fraser, 49. Note also Copleston's summary in *A History of Philosophy*, vol. 6 (Garden City: Image, 1960), 34: "All representations (*Vorstellungen*), whether they have or have not external things as their objects, are determinations of the mind. And, as such, they belong to our internal state. Hence they must all be subject to the formal condition of inner sense or intuition, namely time. But time is thus only the mediate condition of external appearances, whereas it is the immediate condition of all internal appearances."

38. See Copleston, 218-219. Kant was "faced with the problem of effecting a harmonization   between the world of Newtonian physics, the world of mechanistic causality, and the world of freedom....in grappling with this problem Kant submitted to critical examination both rationalism and empiricism and worked out his own philosophy, not as a synthesis of these two movements, but as a triumph over them. Empiricism, he thought, is inadequate because it is unable to account for the possibility of synthetic *a priori* knowledge. If we take scientific knowledge seriously, we cannot embrace sheer empiricism, even if we agree that all knowledge begins with experience. We must have recourse to a theory of the *a priori* formal element in knowledge...But at the same time

that this new science shows the hollowness of dogmatic metaphysics, it also shows the limitations of scientific knowledge. And for anyone who takes seriously the moral consciousness and beliefs and hopes which are intimately associated with it the way is left open for a rationally legitimate, though scientifically indemonstrable, belief in freedom, immortality and God. The great truths of metaphysics are then placed beyond the reach of destructive criticism by the very act of removing them from the position of conclusions to worthless metaphysical arguments and linking them with the moral consciousness which is as much a fundamental feature of man as his capacity of scientific knowledge."

39. See Kant, *Religion Within the Limits of Reason Alone*, trans. by Greene and Hudson (New York: Harper and Row, 1960), 61ff. Note also 129: "It is impossible to settle, *a priori* and objectively, whether there are such mysteries or not [mysteries of 'the holy']. We must therefore search directly in the inner, the subjective part or our moral predisposition to see whether any such thing is to be found in us." Also see his *Critique of Practical Reason* and *Fundamental Principles of the Metaphysic of Morals*.

40. Especially mindful of Hegel today is Peter C. Hodgson. Cf. his *God in History, Shapes of Freedom* (Nashville: Abingdon, 1989) and *Winds of the Spirit* (Nashville: Abingdon, 1994). Of course, most of the "eschatological trinitarians" I shall discuss in chapter IV are deeply in debt to Hegel. Cf. also, Michael Welker, *God As Spirit*, translated by John Hoffmeyer (Minneapolis: Fortress, 1994).

41. *Lectures in the Philosophy of Religion* (hereafter *LPR*), 1:308n.

42. *LPR*, 1:369, 373, 419.

43. For a much broader and deeper discussion, cf. Hodgson, *God in History*, 63ff.

44. *LPR*, 3:284-5.

45. Hodgson, 67.

46. Oscar Cullmann, *Christ and Time* (Philadelphia: Westminster, 1950).

47. Cullmann, ch. 2.

48. Cullmann, 61ff., 81, 87. "...for the believing Christian the mid-point, since Easter, no longer lies in the future." Easter is the mid-point of endlessly extended time for Christians, Cullmann maintains.

49. cf. Von Rad, *Old Testament Theology*, II; trans. by D. M. Stalker (New York: Harper and Row, 1960), 99ff. and Lawrence Fagg, *Two Faces of Time* (Wheaton: Theosophical Publishing House, 1985), 107.

50. People of other primal religions outside Greek culture believed themselves to live cyclically in their religious lives, celebrating seasonal events. For them, this cyclic time was the only "real" time; it enabled clean slates to be begun and tasks achieved by virtue of being wholly created anew, not simply regenerated, in the proper season.

51. The nuances of Cullmann's study need not concern us here, nor the details of Barr's criticism. Suffice it to say that Cullmann argues that *kairos* refers to a point of time, defined by its content, while *aion* refers to a duration of time. This distinction is wholly incorrect, however, as Barr argues. These words, as well as the many others that Cullmann marshalls as time referents from both testaments, are not as univocal as Cullmann would have one believe. All Barr need do, for example, is demonstrate that *kairos* and *chronos* are used interchangeably throughout the LXX and the NT, which he does. See James Barr, *Biblical Words for Time* (London: SCM, 1962), 32-48.

52. Barr, 75.

53. Barr is compelled in his response to Cullmann to lay some ground rules as to philosophical/theological statements about subjects such as time. Exegetical correlations

with theological-philosophical categories require careful justification. Cf. Barr, 133. One must be careful to distinguish between analyses based upon lexical stocks, broader biblical passages or Greek and Hebrew thought in general. So Barr suggests six categories by which to clarify one's hermeneutics,and one should take care not to confuse them with each other. These categories are: i) Statements about lexical phenomena; ii) Statements about morphological and syntactic phenomena; iii) statements about the meaning of larger biblical passages; iv) statements about the general thought of biblical writers; v) statements about the temporal implications of biblical passages which themselves do not contain explicitly temporal words, like 'time', 'eternity', etc.; vi) statements about a general world view of a group like 'Greeks', or 'Hebrews', etc.

54. Christopher Isham would add, with Langdon Gilkey, that the Hebraic view of Genesis and *creatio ex nihilo* expresses dependence upon one God who is purposeful and who, by acts of Creation-Incarnation-Resurrection strengthens the Hebraic concept of a purposeful and linear time via its temporal centering and ordering of BC-AD. This eschatological view of time replaces the string of events that make up the non-historical (and often cyclic) concept of time as portrayed in much Greek thought. "Of course, scripture maintains a clear belief in a creation and a Day of Judgement, but as to whether there was timelessness antecedent to creation, for example, or an endless flow of time preceding creation is not settled." See Christopher Isham, "Creation of the Universe as a Quantum Process," in *PPT*, 377. Also see Fagg, 113.

55. In Plato, for example, the circularity of time's movement is natural in view of the connection of the movement of the heavenly bodies as time's measure. But that does not imply anything necessarily opposed to progression and linearity in a historical sense. Aristotle's own doctrine of time arises from the perfection and uniformity of the circle and need not be concerned with any alleged circular disposition of historical sequences. Moreover, Aristotle's definition of time measured as "number" would tend to argue the more against circularity; a progression of numbers would seem to align more with a linear conceptuality.

56. Von Rad has argued that early Hebrew festivals were more than a reenactment; they were a repetition of a significant event (like the Passover). Qoheleth displays many examples of what might be called a cyclic view of time.

57. Options are, e.g., the older traditional view of the end time simply as a final consummation in the future; the "realized eschatology" of someone like C.H. Dodd; "existentialized" eschatology, in which time may not figure at all; or "proleptic eschatology," that mixture of present and future in eschatology so influentially argued by Pannenberg, Moltmann, Jenson, and many others. See Fagg, 113ff. See also Pannenberg, *Basic Questions in Theology*, II, trans. by George Kehm (Philadelphia: Westminster, 1971), 234ff.; *Jesus, God and Man*, trans. by Robert Wilkens and Duane Priebe (Philadelphia: Fortress, 1970), especially 192ff.; "Appearance As Arrival of the Future," *Journal of the American Academy of Religion*, 35 (1967), 107-118; *Systematische Theologie*, Band 1 (Göttingen: Vanderhoeck und Ruprecht, 1988), 433-443; Jürgen Moltmann *Theology of Hope*, trans. by James Leitch (New York: Harper and Row, 1967); *God in Creation*, trans. by Margaret Kohl (New York: Harper and Row, 1985).

58. Barr, 149.

59. Karl Barth, *Church Dogmatics* (Edinburgh: T.& T. Clark, 1960) (hereafter noted as *CD*) III/2/440.

60. *CD*, II/1, 611.

61. Robert John Russell, "Eternally Creating Time," unpublished paper.
62. Barth, *CD*, III/2/438.
63. Ted Peters asks the same question and argues for dropping the simultaneity of past, present and future that Barth maintains; *God as Trinity*, 190ff.
64. Jürgen Moltmann, *God in Creation*, trans. by Margaret Kohl (New York: Harper and Row, 1985).
65. Barth, *CD*, I/1, 307ff. "The statement...that God reveals Himself as the Lord, or what this statement is meant to describe, and therefore revelation itself as attested by Scripture, we call the root of the doctrine of the Trinity."
66. Barth, *CD*, I/1, 353.
67. Claude Welch reasserts this Barthian analytical approach. Cf. *In This Name* (New York: Scribner, 1952).
68. "Without ceasing to be God, He has made Himself a worldly, human, temporal God in relation to this work of His." *CD* III/2/457.
69. *CD*, II/1/297.
70. *CD*, I/1/351f.
71. *CD*, I/1/348f.
72. "In a bridging of the gulf (from God's side) between divine and human comprehensibility it comes to pass that in the sphere and within the limits of human comprehensibility there is a true knowledge of God's essence generally and hence also of the triunity." *CD*, I/1/371. I contend that the experience of temporality on the human side as Barth related it above is directly correlated with this position of our knowledge—and experience—of the Trinity.
73. *CD*, II/1/620. I am indebted to Robert John Russell for pointing this avenue out. "Eternally Creating Time," 7.
74. *CD*, III/1/629.
75. *CD*, II/1/593ff.
76. *CD* III/1/71; Russell, 10.
77. *CD* III/2/455ff. "Since God in His Word had time for us, and at the heart of all other times there was this particular time, the eternal time of God, all other times are now controlled by this time, i.e., dominated, limited, and determined by their proximity to it. This means positively that they are shown not to be mere illusions. The many philosophical theories of time which deny its reality and regard it as a mere form or abstraction or figment of the imagination can only be finally abandoned when we consider that God Himself once took time and treated it as something that is real. But it also means critically that there is no such thing as absolute time, no immutable law of time. Not even its irreversibility can be adduced as an inviolable principle in relation to the time which was once real at the heart of time as that of the life and death and revelation of the man Jesus. There is no time in itself rivalling God and imposing conditions on Him. There is no god called Chronos. And it is better to avoid conceptions of time which might suggest there is. On the other hand, we need not be surprised if the nature and laws of all other times, and all that we think we know as time, are seen to be illuminated and relativised by this time. Relativised does not mean discarded. Time is real and will always be so."
78. To be taken up in chapter 4.
79. With his earlier work, Pannenberg lays down the foundation for his own eschatological-theological program. In the Festschrift, *Ernst Bloch zu Ehren*, ed. Siegfried Unseld (Frankfurt, 1965), 209-25, Pannenberg writes already about the temporality of

God's eternity in the essay, "The God of Hope." His theme is similar to Moltmann's. "...everything that has come to pass, even in times long gone, has come about and also been changed again through this same power of the future which decides over the present just as it has brought it forth. Thus, reflection over the power of the future over the present leads to a new idea of creation, oriented not toward a primeval event in the past but toward the eschatological future...If God is to be thought of in this way as the future of even the most distant past, then he existed before our present and before every present, although he will definitively demonstrate his deity only in the future of his kingdom. He existed as the future that has been powerful in every present. Thus, the futurity of God implies his eternity. But it is one thing to conceive eternity as timelessness or as endless endurance of something that existed since the beginning of time, and quite another to think of it as the power of the future over every present." "The God of Hope," *Basic Questions in Theology*, 2 vols. Trans. by George H. Kehm, vol. 2 (Philadelphia: Westminster Press, 1970), 243-244.

80. Eberhard Jüngel, *The Doctrine of the Trinity: God's Being Is in Becoming* (Grand Rapids: Eerdman's, 1983).

81. J. R. Lucas, *The Future: An Essay on God, Temporality, and Truth* (Oxford: Basil Blackwell, 1989), 213. Similarly, Eric C. Rust attributes dynamism to God, arguing that "God is not a timeless being." "The Dynamic Nature of the Triune God," *Perspectives in Religious Studies*, 14:4 (Winter, 1987), 31-46. Arthur Williams, in "The Trinity and Time," *Scottish Journal of Theology* 39:1 (1986), 65-81, argues by way of a linguistic investigation of the term "Trinity" that it designates the assumption of historicity into eternity.

III

Contemporary Trinitarian Theologies

Among the most vigorous of systematic theologians today who are concerned with the question of the temporality of God's eternity in trinitarian terms is Robert Jenson. Jenson's elaboration of the themes of "God as the future" and divine temporality, intertwined with his trinitarian thought, make him a natural bridge from the discussion of temporality and eternity to a survey of the current status of trinitarian theology. Robert Jenson appropriates, though not entirely, the Barthian trinitarian scheme and concept of temporality. In a book devoted to the problem of stalemated ecumenism, *Unbaptized God, The Basic Flaw in Ecumenical Theology*,[1] Jenson argues that a wrong view of temporality is shared by both Protestant and Catholic Christianity. It is this shared, and heretofore unacknowledged presupposition, that has inhibited contemporary ecumenical dialogue from achieving the consensus toward which it has strained. This wrongful supposition also bears out the thesis—in reverse—that the Christian view of divine eternity ought to affirm its temporality. The basic flaw shared by these traditions is that time is thought to be external to events (or persons, or institutions), as well as external to God. Worse, theology has often proceeded from a univocal view of time to its doctrine of God, which subjects the doctrine to mistaken qualifications. Wolfhart Pannenberg has argued along the same lines.[2]

Jenson suggests these following suppositions, all erroneous, shared in the western Christian tradition.[3] First, time and personal being are external. Jenson affirms, rather, the Kantian view of time as the horizon of consciousness. To avoid the subjectivity of time, Jenson would posit an Absolute Consciousness. This is not to say, however, that time is only describable from the human side. The affirmation of Absolute Consciousness is not in and of itself an acceptance of Berkeleyan Idealism. It is, rather, an entree or bridge to the Barthian affirmation that the reality of time derives from the reality of God.

The second error is the "Christian" view that time is linear. While it is most certainly not circular in platonic fashion, linearity is not the only option, nor is it the definitive Jewish or Christian experience. Jenson here would agree, then, with the qualifications that Barr argued against Cullmann. Jenson prefers a phenomenological description of time. He argues that time is itself an "event;" it is "what happens when the Spirit 'comes'."[4]

Third, the western tradition has assumed even that time and events are mutually extrinsic; though events happen in time, they may or may not be carried along through time. Jenson answers this with the common sensical question, "if nothing ever happened, how can there be time?" Indeed, the ontological priority of events over time is quite thinkable, though Jenson does not see it in his perview to extend upon this remark. This would seem to cohere well with Augustine's and Philo's contention that time is created with the rest of creation; indeed that it is "co-created" or even a consequence of matter, as if matter/events enjoy an ontological priority over time. But the Augustinian legacy, especially with respect to the doctrine of the Trinity, is not appropriated wholly positively these days. Much contemporary review of Trinitarian doctrine, including Jenson's, is conducted in qualification of Augustine's doctrine of the Trinity in particular. It is helpful, then, briefly to turn back to review of Augustine's position before continuing with Jenson.

Augustine Revisited

After the hammering out of trinitarian dogma at Nicaea, the Greek and Latin reflection and systematization thereon began to develop in two different directions. With Athanasius, theology shifted toward ontology. The Cappadocians in particular, (Basil, d. 379; Gregory of Nyssa, d. 394; and Gregory of Nazianzus, d. 390) put trinitarian theology in its classic form of God as one nature in three persons (*mia ousia, treis hypostaseis*). They also better distinguished between "being begotten" (*gennesia*) and "being made" or "created" (*genesia*); to wit: The Son is begotten from the substance of the Father, whereas the world is created by the will of God. In this developed trinitarianism, God the Father is the "monarch," the unoriginate source and principal of Godhead (*fons et origo divinitatis*). The eternal being of God derives from the person of the Father. Every act of God in creation originates with the Father, proceeds through the Son, and is perfected by the Holy Spirit.[5]

We cannot say, though, what God is or what the divine persons are. Cappadocian theology advanced that "nature" could only be described in the sense of the divine persons' *relations* to each other and so began with the implicit recognition of three persons before speaking of their unity as the Trinity. This was a significant move. "Relationship" was the guiding interpretive principle. Thus, "Father" is the name of a relation, and so "the personal property of the Father, that which makes the Father unique, is unbegottenness (coming from no one); the personal property of the Son is begottenness (coming from the Father); the personal property of the Spirit is procession (coming from the Father)." As this theology developed, God the "Father" came to have two meanings: first, the one who comes from nothing and, second, the one who eternally begets the Son.[6] This expanded meaning of divine fatherhood eventually forced a significant adjustment in the Greek understanding of the monarchy of the Father. While it was still agreed that the Father was the principle of unity in the Trinity, the unity of God after the Cappadocian conception came to be understood more and more as the perichoresis of the three persons in each other, as so definitively summarized by St. John of Damascus (d. 749). Contemporary theologians like Robert Jenson wish trinitarian theology would have maintained this trajectory.

With Augustine (d. 430), however, Western Latin theology went a quite different direction. Augustine reversed what positive beginnings may have lain in the Cappadocian construction. Greatly influenced by the neo-Platonists, especially Plotinus, Augustine was concerned with expressing the doctrine of the Trinity by starting with reflection on the abstract idea of oneness rather than with the concreteness of the three persons.[7] In so doing, he identifies the Holy Spirit as the "bond of love" between the Father and the Son, rather than "bridge," as the Cappadocians imaged the relationship. While this identification helped to exclude Arian subordinationism, it also virtually collapsed the individual persons and their roles so that each is defined strictly in terms of the other; thus the Augustinian maxim which became so governing for consequent Western theology: *opera Trinitatis ad extra indivisa sunt*.[8] It is the Trinity which creates, the Trinity which redeems, the Trinity which sanctifies. Consequently, Augustine must resort to a doctrine of appropriations to reinvest the divine persons with distinctive attributes in order to maintain some distinction among the divine persons. The upshot, nevertheless, was that the collapse of the economy of the trinitarian persons into the *a se* identity of the immanent Trinity made it difficult, if not impossible, to know God by way of the economy. And if any knowledge could be derived from the economy, it itself was mitigated by the neo-Platonic delimitation of knowledge as analogical.

Augustine's posing of the unity of God entailed the assumption that there is no way in which God can be conceived by humans "in himself" (the atemporal neo-Platonic root assumption). Therefore, one must search for analogies to describe God, as they are the best approximations of the real we can find in the world. And so Augustine sought for the *vestigia Trinitatis* around him, and found the first analogy in terms of the "psychological" model of the Trinity.[9] Perhaps the triune dynamic of "lover-beloved-love" or "memory-understanding-will" could explain how one substance (soul) could exist in distinct representations or operations (knowing and loving) without sundering the substance (thus the knower and lover are same person). Augustine extended this psychological analogy to the Trinity: the one God exists in the generation from the Father of the Word and procession of the Spirit.

While this psychological motif may have been relatively modest in Augustine's theology, it came to bear a definitive status in consequent Western theology. Its innate dependence on Plotinus further rendered the God of his trinitarian doctrine as impersonal, as well as "timeless." As Catherine Mowry LaCugna would observe, "The changed metaphysical options for the theology of God changed politics, anthropology, and society as well."[10] Though much later Robert Jenson would agree with Augustine that it is the Trinity as a whole to whom we refer as "God," in whom relate the Father, Son, and Spirit, he could not accept the Platonic principles and consequences of Augustine's trinitarian position and its huge influence on Western life. Trinitarian theological revision would be critically necessary.

Jenson's Critique of Augustine

In a brief meditation on time and the Trinity,[11] Jenson adds further critique to the Augustinian legacy, this time with respect to Augustine's concept of time. A fallacious view of time has been the correlate to "a thoroughly unitarian interpretation of God" (what Moltmann would have labelled as monotheism). We have inherited this view from Augustine, who placed the past only in memory, while the present is both in and for the mind. Jenson argues instead that the difference between past, present, and future is "their difference *within* the mind of God and so within the created reality God posits."

In other words, because God is creator of all things, including time, (on this much Jenson agrees with Augustine), there is difference in created reality because there is difference in the source—the mind of God—and this source, of course, is the very unity of the difference. It is not a "transcendental unity of apperception" however, not a point at which lines of perception converge, and therefore not that eternity given image by the Platonic circle of time. The unity which God sustains is the trinitarian unity of "Father, Spirit and Son, in which the difference of source, goal and mediation is antecedent."[12]

This move is significant. Jenson argues, in sum, that we experience time because first there is (was) the difference-in-unity of the Trinity. The difference-in-unity of the Trinity is understood under the categories of person and relation. God is personal in the modern sense, but the person that is conscious, Jenson maintains, is not God as Father. As Jenson elsewhere argues, "The person that is conscious is the Trinity" and "only the Trinity as such."[13] The Trinity is God the Subject, within whom the three expressions of Father, Son, and Spirit express a differentiated relationship. Further, the quality of these differentiated relationships is so intimate and rich that they are inexhaustible unto infinity and communal unto unity.

Jenson suggests that these persons-in-relationship be termed "identities." God is thus identified by "proper name" as "Father, Son, and Spirit." As identities, the relationships carry the helpful anti-modalism inferences of Tertullian's phrase, *una substantia et tres personae*, without assuming the Greek philosophical baggage of those terms. Further, the *ousia* shared by the three *hypostases* — which originally were interchangeable terms, and eventually distinguished into "what an individual is" and "individuals" respectively — becomes in Jenson's thought the unboundable God and the identities, respectively, themselves. So there is a single divine subject, who happens as God in the inter-relationship of the three identities. Each identity has its unique role. Yet their intercourse with each other jointly realizes one divinity. Hence, Jenson argues against the Augustinian *ad extra* axiom. Augustine's confusion of the economies eventuates into a unity-with-no-difference and would thus mitigate the biblical revelation.[14] The acceptance of the Cappadocian position, rather, that God's relations are internal to him, could still guarantee the anti-modalism Tertullian desired and avoid collapse of the three persons into a functional unitarianism.[15] This position also would deny patripassianism, for example, in the insistence that it is Jesus who suffered and died, and that this suffering was experienced reciprocally by the Father. Hereby the unity and life of God the Trinity is thus all the more underscored.[16]

Now what do the triune identities have to do with time? As already noted with reference to Barth, the threefold structure of God is itself the ground for temporality. Jenson rejects any "linearity" in the relationships, however, and thus he is both anti-monarchian and anti-modalist. He does not conceive "God" as the Father, who begets the Son and sends the Spirit. Again, Father and Son in their reciprocity of Love are the (onto)logical source of Spirit, all three together of whom are God. And, of course, in the dynamism of their relationship, the identities are hardly static or circular. There is "surplus" to their intimacy. This results in acts of creation, reconciliation, and redemption, external works which are all necessarily related and equal to the energies of the internal relationships. In traditional terms, the life of the economic Trinity is reflective of the life of the immanent Trinity. When this life "happens," there is time.

> Time is because the Spirit is not the Father, and because both meet in the Son. Time is because God is his own origin and *as* such is *not* his goal because God is his own goal and *as* such is *not* the 'natural' result of his own being as origin; because origin and goal in God are an irreversibly ordered pair; and because

Father and Spirit meet and are reconciled in the Son. Time is what happens when
the Holy Spirit comes, from the Father and to the Son.[17]

Jenson, so to speak, has hereby cosmologized Rahner's Rule, that "the
economic Trinity is the immanent Trinity and vice-versa." The economic
Trinity is concerned with all the workings of the cosmos. Thereby it reflects
all the creative activity of the immanent Trinity, including the ongoing
creation of and accommodation to time that emerges as the very consequence
of the relationship between Father, Son, and Spirit.

Time and personal being are therefore very far from mutually external. Time is
the inner horizon of the life of that one in whom all things live and move and
have their being. Our time, we may even say, is the accommodation God makes
for us in his own triune life. Time is therefore at once a communal phenomenon
and the inner horizon of a personal consciousness: it occurs in that *meeting* occurs
in God, between Father, Son, and Spirit; and it occurs in that Father, Son, and
Spirit are the one God within whose creative subjectivity all things are posited.[18]

Time is neither circular nor simply linear, therefore. Because it is
constituted by the "event" of God, it is, so to speak, "implosive." The Spirit
opens every present reality with the posing of a future; that future does not
simply evolve out of the present reality, yet it is that present reality's own true
future. By such a construction Jenson safeguards the transcendence of God as
the world's future, while simultaneously underscoring the adequacy of that
future to the present situation. Conversely, the established present reality does
not oppress the next future moment, but is by the Spirit's setting now yet truly
that next future moment's past.

Within the Trinity, in other words, there is the givenness of past, present,
and future. They are given in their difference, yet held in reconciled unity, in
peace. Eternity, therefore, is the "grasp of past, present, and future in their
mutual giveness." In this respect, God has time. When Barth describes God's
particular eternity as the "pure duration," he means thereby this reconciled
time, in which there is but peace, not conflict, "between source, movement
and goal."[19] Thus the difference between time and eternity, and the relation,
as Jenson poses, according to the broader context of a doctrine of the Trinity
understood as essentially temporal. That the flow of time from the past
through the present to the future would be derived from reflection upon the
internal relations of the Trinity should give one a clue, then, as to how Jenson
would explicate God's relationship to the world in general.[20] Again an appeal
to the Cappadocians is helpful. Trinitarian dogma arose, Jenson argues, not
to explicate in Greek categories how one substance may be shared by three
persons. Its point was to elaborate how God's relations to humans are

precisely those which are internal to him. Furthermore, the occasions of God's entrance into such external relations mark the events by which is constituted time.

What sense does it make now to speak of God as event? How must reality be interpreted if its God is triune? Jenson refers to Gregory of Nyssa's doctrine of divine infinity and claims that Western theology would have been better served had it not preferred a Hellenistic interpretation over the Cappadocians.[21] The gospel's and Hellenism's interpretations of God clash. The enfeeblement of Western trinitarian theology may be traced to the gospel's defeat in this battle. Jenson advocates no abandonment to the Hellenistic categories, however, nor a simple "gospel" solution. What is needed is the creativity given precedent by the Cappadocian Fathers; "...the fault of Western trinitarianism was precisely a failure to carry on the metaphysical creativity begun by the Cappadocians and, so long as the Western church endures, it must be Hellenic."[22] Therefore, Jenson argues, we must begin to build a revisionist metaphysics.

> God—trinitarian identification of God, compelled us to say—is an event, and one, we may now add, constituted in relations and personal in structure. Our question must be: What sense can it make to call God an event? To say that an event "upholds the universe" or "speaks through the prophets?" Any properly formed sentence can of course be made to make sense by reinterpretation of "sense," that is, by revision of our grasp of reality. So our question becomes, "how must reality be interpreted if its God is triune? If he is the event between Father, Son and Spirit?"[23]

This segues to Jenson's rehearsal and interpretation of Gregory of Nyssa's doctrine of divine infinity.[24] Gregory applies the concept of infinity to God's *ousia*. An "infinite ousia" may appear to be an oxymoron, and this Gregory intends. An infinite "thingness" is rather hard to imagine. Thereby he challenges anyone to define or put ontological constraints on God. That is the point. God, as Gregory of Nyssa would apophatically define him, overcomes all definitions and is therefore infinite, while yet temporally active. And so Jenson:

> Infinite being is an odd sort of being. It cannot be anything other than its infinity, for there can be no infinite *some*-thing: a substance without clear boundaries could only be a wavery, insubstantial substance, and a substance with no boundaries must instantly dissipate. Just this notion was the starting point of Hellenic philosophy's analysis of the notion of infinity. An infinite something would always generate new characteristics beyond those that make its given self at any moment. Thus Aristotle: "That is infinite...which has always something beyond

itself." Therefore, an infinite something would have no "nature" at all, for a
"nature" is precisely what *defines*, that is, limits, the possibilities of an entity.
     The Christian attribution of infinity to God is thus in itself a radical reversal of
metaphysical values. And more in the direct line of our present argument, if
God's being is infinite, then divine being is nothing other than infinity as such.
What the three divine hypostases variously derive from each other, so as to be
distinguishably three and so that their joint act can be called "God" is sheer
unboundedness.[25]

     Jenson does allow that "infinity" to have any sense must be an infinity *of*
something. But God himself is no *some*thing. This is why early Christians
were called atheists. The divine *ousia*, rather than a substantiality, is the
infinity, and this is the sole characterization of what transpires between Jesus
and his Father in their Spirit.
     Consequently, according to Gregory, infinity is understood temporally;
God's *ousia* is temporal infinity. "God is not infinite because he timelessly
extends to all reality; but because time cannot exhaust or keep up with his
activity."[26] As Gregory writes, "The transcendent and blessed Life has neither
interior measure nor compass, for no temporal extension can keep pace with
it."[27] The eternity of Gregory's God is characterized in God's enveloping of
time. Thus, Gregory's God keeps things moving, while Hellenistic deity is a
motionless center in whom we attempt to ground moving things. Indeed,
Gregory allows the possibility that the "fundament" of time may be the future.
As God is the future for Barth, Jenson and others, so also Gregory would
suggest that "divinity" means always having a future.

> Therefore, we define Him to be earlier than any beginning, and exceeding any
> end...we express it by two titles; i.e., "Ungenerate" and "Endless" represent this
> infinitude and continuity and everlastingness of the Deity...these two titles equally
> help to express the eternity of the divine life...The two are conceptions of the
> same thing; and, therefore, either both should be admitted to the definition of
> being, or, if the one is to be judged inadmissible, the other should be rejected
> also...So let our thoughts upon the divine nature be worthy and exalted ones; or
> else, if they are going to judge of it according to human tests, let the future be
> more valued by them than the past, and let them confine the being of the Deity
> to that, since time's lapse sweeps away with it all existence in the past, whereas
> expected existence gains substance from our hope.[28]

     In sum, Jenson ups the ante. God does not have a future. God *is* the
future. What Jenson supposes Gregory and himself to mean by divine infinity
is that which always *is* future, which embraces and moves all temporality, and
is never exhausted by it. Jenson advances beyond Gregory of Nyssa by
maintaining that temporality is therefore controlled eschatologically. It is the
"object" of our *hope*, God the power of the future, who by entering into

relationship with the creation thereby creates temporality.[29] God relates to the creation as Trinity. We know and experience time because the Trinity is present to us and we are present in the Trinity.

Rahner's Rule

With Barth's affirmation that knowledge of the Trinity from the human side is a true (though not exhaustive) knowledge of the Trinity on the Trinity's side, we had some hint of what Karl Rahner would make explicit, and what Jenson explicitly affirmed of Rahner.[30] Commonly assumed now in theological reflection on the Trinity is "Rahner's Rule," that the "economic Trinity is the immanent Trinity and *vice-versa.*"[31] This may seem to collapse the distinctions, but Rahner insists that this is a necessary *epistemological* move, only by which can humans entertain any real knowledge of God's life. The rule is not meant to imply an ontological collapse of God's eternity into temporality. Nor is this a strict identification between the economic and immanent Trinity, as if A in one $= A'$ in the other.[32] Though it seems that many would interpret Rahner this way, and that many assume this for their own position, Rahner would not go so far. If so, the economic side would be but the mirroring of the immanent and would be emptied of historical content. Or theology could then focus only on immanent, or only on economic, which gets us back into skepticism about whether there are any real distinctions.

Rahner's Rule means to undercut the subjectivity of the human side; it precludes thinking that the threefold distinction exists only on the side of the creature. Rahner bases this on the logic of God's self-communication, as Barth, too, would have construed it. If the self-communication of God is truly a *self*-communication, then its mediation must derive from a real distinction in God, but a self-communication which is embarked upon in divine freedom.[33] In that sense, what "we" see of the economic Trinity is most certainly real in the immanent, but we don't see it all. Therefore, transcendence is still applicable to the "whole" Trinity. What the rule says positively, then, is that the persons of the Trinity are those whom we experience directly in their economies. We don't "know" or experience God as Trinity or as a unity, in other words. We do so in terms of the trinitarian persons.[34]

...in gratuitous grace in his own personal particularity and diversity...It is God's indwelling, uncreated grace...In other words: these three self-communications are the self-communications of the one God in the three relative ways in which God subsists...God relates to us in a threefold manner, and this threefold, free, and gratuitous relation to us *is* not merely a copy or analogy of the inner Trinity, but this Trinity itself, albeit as freely and gratuitously communicated.[35]

Like Barth, Rahner is uncomfortable with the ascription of "person" to any of the hypostases to whom creatures have economic access. Yet he does think it appropriate to speak of subjectivities if we are careful not to include therein the modern notion of person. So "subjectivity" as a category leads toward what Barth got out of "relations." Each person, what Rahner thinks is better termed as "distinct manner of subsisting," has a self-consciousness that elides with the self-consciousness of the other manners of subsisting. Therefore, there are not three ontologically distinct consciousnesses. "There is only one real consciousness in God, which is shared by Father, Son and Spirit, by each in his own proper way."[36] In this way Rahner would cast off the substantialist trappings of school theology and point a new way. Furthermore, by his emphasis on the realism of the economic role of the Trinity and the *distinctive* works which are charged to the different manners of subsisting, Rahner—like Jenson later—objects to the Augustinian minimalism; a minimalism that so sought for divine unity that it virtually denied the historical significance of the biblical revelation. It is *not* so that the Trinitarian works *ad extra* are indivisible. It is not so that the Father or the Spirit, in theory "could have" been incarnated, or even could have existed apart from the incarnation. And God "in general" is not how God is experienced. Were the Augustinian *ad extra* clause true, then nothing can be known assuredly of God. Were God known "generally," i.e., impersonally, then the history of trinitarian reflection has been a prodigal waste of time.

Such reflection would not be constructive about the human experience of temporality either. For implicit in Rahner's emphasis on the particular self-communications of God through the manners of subsisting is the supposition that the human experience of time is thereby given its shape and destination. The communication has an origin and aims at a future, which is also to say that transcendence and history are required such that no "imageless" mysticism is incurred. Indeed, the direction of the economic Trinity is from transcendence to history, so that the history of humankind may be embraced once again in transcendence. This is the future of humankind.

> If there occurs a self-communication of God to historical man, who is still becoming, it can occur only in this unifying duality of history and transcendence which man is. Further, if man is the one duality of origin and future, if humanity is history into transcendence, thus free, then God's self-communication also equals the difference between offer and acceptance of this communication. God gives the offer in such a way that the offer is accepted in freedom.[37]

In other words, though Rahner has not been explicit on this issue, the history of God's self-communication to and economic relationships with all creaturely life is taken up again into the transcendence of God in God's self. What happens in history, indeed, becomes part of God's very trinitarian life, which is, nevertheless, opaque to human knowing, and so is "internal" to God. In other words, human history constitutes—and is infinitely enveloped by—God's own life. There can be no discontinuity between God in God's transcendence and God "for us." From Rahner's trinitarian theology, therefore, we may adduce significant clues, quite similar to those garnered from Barth and Jenson, as to how to conceive of time's relationship to eternity.

Pannenberg and Reciprocal Self-Dedication

Another contemporary theologian who finds much consonance with Barth, Rahner, and Jenson, as well as Jüngel, is Wolfhart Pannenberg. With them, Pannenberg agrees that the revelation of God as Trinity must be established solely through God's participation in history, particularly in the historical person of Jesus. This is in clear opposition to any method which would derive from philosophical assumptions and agendas. Trinitarian reflection is, as it were, conducted from the bottom up; the economic Trinity is one's entry into the immanent Trinity. Rahner's Rule again is affirmed.

Particularly significant is Pannenberg's affirmation that the locus of revelation is history. Inasmuch as history is the arena of revelation and that revelation is therefore historically accessible, history is shaped by the transcendent source of the revelation. In other words, history anticipates the future to be eschatologically realized in the coming kingdom of God. The *sine qua non* upon whom we can base this anticipation is the person of Jesus. In his life, death, resurrection, and ascension we see prefigured proleptically what shall be for all of the coming kingdom, and we have therein the *sine qua non* for positing the Trinity.

The embrace of this eschataological-cum-historical position means for Pannenberg that he rejects any trinitarian theology that would start from the supposition of divine unity rather than the scriptural and economic experience of threeness. This puts him at odds with most of the western legacy from Augustine to Hegel, and with Barth as well. To begin with the premise of divine unity irrevocably means that one must start with a philosophical terminology that is not given historical access in revelation. With Augustine, this meant turning to the so-called psychological analogy with its consequences of subordinationism[38]; with Hegel, to a similar mental analogy.

Barth committed the same fallacy of collapsing the trinitarian relations into a single subject, Pannenberg (with Jenson and Moltmann) believes.[39] Further, this was tantamount to modalism, which isolates God from the vicissitudes of time. Any adoption of a philosophical foundation, it seems, would lead to such consequences. The philosophical questions can in fact be solved only from the other way around, from historical revelation.

> It remains a task for the Christian doctrine of God to show that the otherness of God as well as his unity cannot really be conceived within the philosophical formulation of the question, but can be comprehended only as the unity of the Father with the Son and the Spirit, so that the revelation of the triune God is what brings the philosophical question to a genuine fulfillment for the first time.[40]

Pannenberg is grateful for at least one fundamental philosophical proposal, though. That is Hegel's recognition that the "character of the person...[is to] relinquish its particularity, its particular personality...through being immersed in the other."[41] Hegel believed the essence of a person was for that person to exist in self-dedication to another. He extended this insight to the understanding of the unity of the Trinity "as a unity that only comes into existence through the process of reciprocal self-dedication."[42] Pannenberg sees here a vitality of insight as to the unity of the Trinity without loss to the threeness never before achieved, though there lay with Augustine, then with Richard of St. Victor, this possibility.[43]

Thus Pannenberg, too, regards relationality and the concept of personhood as much more helpful in the elucidation of the Trinity. What happens to one of the divine persons reciprocally happens to all. In the self-dedication of the persons to each other, they are thus mutually causative. This contrasts with the linear causation one is accustomed to seeing charted according to the Eastern view, wherein the line of causation runs from God as Father through the Son to the Spirit, or from the Father to both Son and Spirit. This is also to say, then, with the affirmation of revelation's historicality, that the immanent Trinity is at least in part dependent upon the economic. Or, as Ted Peters puts it, "The eternal nature of God is at least in part dependent upon temporal events."[44] In this sense, Pannenberg argues surprisingly, the very deity of God the Father depends upon his relationship to the Son. The events of salvation history are determinative of the divine life. Eternity must embrace temporality. God's eternity consists in his powerful presence to every time.[45] Indeed, Pannenberg rings quite similar to Eberhard Jüngel on this point.[46]

Pannenberg also argues for the temporality of eternity on more strictly ontological grounds. Pannenberg asks if certain phenomena, such as inertia, necessitate a search for a "God of the gaps" (as had been one means of theological response), or if we could relate such phenomena to a larger field which would allow for such conditions to exist.[47] He answers that Michael Farraday's concept of field theory may serve as a bridge to understanding trinitarian activity in creation. Field theory would help to re-explicate contingency, as well as the Christian doctrine of *creatio ex nihilo* and *creatio continua*. With respect to time and eternity, then, creation out of nothing would have an empirical meaning, conditioned by the context of a particular scientific theory of time. It would indeed refer to the *whole* cosmic process, not just the beginning. Thus, a deeper look at the issue, Pannenberg argues, would entail an understanding of eternity as the fullness of time. For eternity, perforce in this argument, would constitute the "field" or context for temporality.

Pannenberg also believes that the sciences posit contingency for each part of the world and within each level of explanation. The fact that the concept of irreversibility in thermodynamics has a limit, for example, requires that it be placed in a larger context of biology, which in turn will require its larger context in the spatio-temporal structure of the universe, i.e., cosmology. For the theologian, finally, to make sense of this, she must posit the "largest" field of the eschatological future. In content and form of argument, Pannenberg follows here both Kant and Plotinus in concluding the primacy of the future.[48]

> Eternity as the complete totality of life is thus seen for the standpoint of time only in terms of a fullness that is sought in the future. This was an important insight for Plotinus. When combined with the Platonic idea of the good and of striving for the good, it developed into the thought of eternity as the completed totality of life. The future thus became constitutive of the nature of time because only in terms of the future could the totality be given to time which makes possible the unity and continuity of time's process.[49]

All the more, then, Pannenberg substantiates his affirmation of eternity's temporality, having done so by appeal both to trinitarian thought and to philosophical consideration of the concept of eternity. If he has left any facet unattended, it might be the "practical" import of his musings. This is an area in which Catherine Mowry LaCugna aptly compensates.

LaCugna and the Unity of *Theologia* and *Oikonomia*

Catherine Mowry LaCugna is a contemporary theologian who has, perhaps, been the most prodigious researcher in gathering up the themes of God's relationality and historical involvement into a "practical" doctrine of the Trinity.[50] LaCugna believes that the division of the doctrine of the Trinity at Nicaea between *theologia* and *oikonomia*—what later came to be the split between the immanent and economic —removed the doctrine from that arena it was intended to govern and explicate in the first place: soteriology. At Nicaea it came about that soteriology was separated from the doctrine of God, LaCugna contends. The work, the economy, of God in Christ was disconnected from reflection about God proper, i.e., theology. In this way the internal relations of the divine persons were severed from relationships with the world. Theology after Nicaea clearly shifted toward ontology, and this in a philosophical milieu that took for granted the absolute transcendence of God. This sense of transcendence, furthermore, "precluded [on God's part] any traffic with temporal reality."[51] As a particular consequence, for example, the debate on patripassianism, conducted only within the rubrics of the First Article of the Nicaean Creed, was not informed by reflection on the economy of God through the human Jesus. Christian theology was thereby inhibited in the development of its christology and trinitarian theology because it had to accept without question the notion of divine impassibility implied in a self-contained—and graeicized—doctrine of God.[52] The consequences of practical irrelevance to the Christian life show themselves to this day.[53]

This division between the doctrine of God and the work of Christ had its precursor, too, in the difference of theological method between East and West. Both western and eastern theology affirm we cannot know the essence of an unknowable God. Eastern theology does so by way of apophatism— negation of all definitions. We saw an example of this method in Gregory of Nyssa's redefinition of "infinite" to mean that which defies definition and limitation. By emptying ourselves of expectations about what God is or should be or should be doing, apophatism means, we are freed to know and love the real living God instead of the God of our projections. When taken to extremes, however, the danger of this position is that it can evolve into an agnosticism, disregarding of biblical/historical revelation, which is quite comfortable with a separated and Hellenic doctrine of God. Positive, or kataphatic theology, characterizes western theology. But, again recognizing the essential mystery of God, it proceeds with language of analogy. A "kind" of knowledge of God is available, in other words, by attending to effects (*oikonomia*).[54] This, of course, is the premise of so-called "natural theology." When this method is taken to extreme, however, there is overconfident collapse between economy and theology.[55]

LaCugna argues that these modes need carefully to be used together, and together they constitute a more complete trinitarian method. Such a method recognizes again the connection between *theologia* and *oikonomia*. It also affirms that the "mystery" of God does not denote ineffability or irrationalism.

The interconnectedness of theology and economy, as with the knowledge of a human person by aid of that person's deeds, means that "mystery" is a predicate of personhood.

> To speak of God as mystery is another way of saying that God is "personal." An analogy can be drawn with our knowledge of other (human) persons...The more intimate our knowledge of another, the more we are drawn to that person's unique mystery and the deeper that mystery becomes. The same is true of God; God is not less mystery on account of God's radical immanence in Christ. Indeed, the God who is absolutely other, absolutely transcendent but also absolutely near to us—this God is absolute mystery.[56]

In LaCugna's view it is permissable, indeed required, that a trinitarian "science" employ analogy and differentiation in trinitarian reflection. The "mystery" of God as personal calls those who would be personally related to God all the more to the theological task. Thus "theology" and "economy" are united. Thus, too, it is no great step once again to affirm Rahner's Rule. LaCugna also provides its corollary; "Theology is soteriology and *vice-versa.*"[57] It is a given for trinitarian theological method.

The notion of God as being personal in relationship is a most fruitful one for LaCugna. When "personal" is applied to the three hypostases "within" the Trinity, it means that their unity is one of communion. As themselves they share themeselves. Affirming Rahner's Rule, she agrees that how the hypostases share themselves with each other in God is inducted by humans according to the works of the divine persons among us. This is also to say that that life shared in the Trinity is not isolated from human or creaturely life. The attribution of "personal" means that God's life *is* our life. Simultaneously, the attribution of "personal," insofar as it indicates mystery, does not exhaust the ineffability of God.

> The life of God is not something that belongs to God alone. *Trinitarian life is also our life.* As soon as we free ourselves from thinking that there are two levels to the Trinity, one *ad intra*, the other *ad extra*, then we see that there is *one* life of the triune God, a life in which we graciously have been included as partners.[58]

This life of God in which humans are graced to participate is comprehensive. Were one to image it in a diagram, LaCugna suggests the appropriateness of a parabola, both of which ends are "up." The life of God is likened to a movement from the Father to Son to Spirit, then to the world of time, space, and persons, back eschatologically into communion with God when God is "all in all." It is a movement *a patre ad patrem*, and therefore there is no need to single out any theological focus like pneumatology or christology as fixed or more important than another within this trinitarian sweep. All are co-equal, as the persons of the Trinity are co-equal, and all is consummated in the divine communion.[59]

This emphasis on personhood and communion with a soteriological point leads LaCugna to put as secondary the question as to what or whom to apply the term "person" in the Trinity. To whom the referents of *hypostasis* or *persona* are applied really does not matter. That "personal" be raised higher to include Trinity *and* the three, theology *and* economy, is LaCugna's agenda. Thereby the disjunctions of Nicaea, while recognized, can be overcome in the future project of trinitarian reflection. Nicaea's categories need not be the ultimate categories. In summary, she writes,

> What we come to in the end is that if we use the term "person" of God, whether in the singular or plural, we are not giving a description of the essence of God as it is in itself, but using a term that points beyond itself to the ineffability of God. Since person is the ecstatic and relational mode of being, then the proper focus of theology is the concrete manifestation of God's personal reality revealed in the face of Jesus Christ and the activity of the Holy Spirit. It does not so much matter whether we say God is one person in three modalities, or one nature in three persons, since these two assertions can be understood in approximately the same way. What matters is that we hold on to the assertion that God is *personal*, and that therefore the proper subject matter of the doctrine of the Trinity is the encounter between divine and human persons in the economy of redemption.[60]

Except by what we may infer, LaCugna has not given specific attention to our own immediate concern of the problem of time and eternity. The emphasis on and recovery of the "personhood" of God as catholic certainly has ramifications for this project, however. Further, the parabolic and eschatological trajectory of her description of the trinitarian life as *a patre ad patrem* is a movement through time to God's future. It may not be a picture which Jenson would adopt. He prefers the non-linear "event" mode of description for God's life. But the emphasis on relationality and, consequently, such movement, without loss to the transcendence of God, once again seems to lead one to a picture of eternity as the embrace of time. Indeed, the impact of economy on theology would seem to mean a concomitant impact of temporality upon eternity, perhaps to the point that eternity would be temporal.

That is an argument put forward by Jürgen Moltmann, who would heartily agree with LaCugna's emphasis on God's relationality. We will consider his thought in detail in chapter 6. It should be apparent now that key figures in contemporary theology have placed the doctrine of the Trinity back into mainstream reflection. They share the overall conviction that trinitarian theology calls for a revised understanding of the pre-supposed "timelessness" of God.

Process Theology and Divine Temporality

But these representatives, and this cursory summary of their positions, are not representative of all contemporary trinitarian theology.[61] That, of course, would be an issue far too broad, and finally irrelevant to my primary concern, for me to take up. Also, current theological reflection is not unanimous as to, first, the need for *trinitarian* construction and, second, the need to locate temporality in God. The first group would affirm the need to describe adequately God's relation to temporality, but without resort to the classic Christian theological locus. The second would still affirm, even with Augustine, a trinitarian construction that is in emphasis atemporal. Whereas both of these agendas would challenge the "protective belt" of a Lakatosian-style theological research program such as I have suggested, it would perhaps benefit us if we but briefly outline these positions before proceeding further.

One theological school of thought that has taken seriously the problem of temporality in God—concomitant with the problem of the one and the many—is that of process theology.[62] In the main, however, process theology is not characterized by the overt attempt to explicate the trinitarian symbols. Process theology has been particularly helpful in developing a metaphysics of relationality rather than substance. Indeed, Alfred North Whitehead noted that Eastern trinitarian reflection was the sole real advancement upon Plato. His metaphysical project was an attempt at synthesis, complete with a new nomenclature, of classic Platonism with the modern notion of dynamic relationality. The synthesis is evident in Whitehead's description of the bipolar nature of God as primordial and consequent; the first attribute refers to God's eternal will and creative access to possibilities that could fit with every occasion of actual experience; the second to the change in God wrought by the free responses of the entities involved in the actual occasions. Charles Hartshorne rephrased this bipolarity with the more descriptive terms of God's absoluteness and relativity. Consequently, in the general process description, the category of the eternal overlaps with that of the temporal.

It is quite beyond our purview here to describe the process program in detail. Pertinent to our discussion, though, is the observation that process theism has had difficulty cohering with the biblical symbols. One wag has suggested that process theology is a metaphysic in search of a religion. So, while process theology has been quite fruitful in elaborating a perspective wherein God is supremely related to and yet differentiated from the cosmos, which is the perspective of panentheism, only a few proponents have tried to develop this in an explicitly trinitarian context.

It is more the case that proponents of process theology have dismissed trinitarian language insofar as it is perceived to be substantialistic or politically incorrect; in any case, therefore, irrelevant.[63] At best, the effort to sustain traditional symbols may result in a binitarianism. For example, John Cobb argues that there is freedom to "reimage" the Trinitarian persons so as to be gender inclusive, which includes an absolute distinction between Jesus and Christ.[64] Cobb's suggestion that the "logos" be defined as "the principle of creativity" virtually identifies the Logos with the primordial nature of God.[65] The virtual result of this is a revisionist monotheism, which finds Jesus to be the supreme paradigm as to how an actual occasion may become fully "concrescent" with the divine. There's no need for a trinity in this construct. In fact, Cobb and David Ray Griffin confess that "process theology is not interested in formulating distinctions within God for the sake of conforming with traditional trinitarian notions."[66] While this process theological program seems not to attack the notion of temporality in our core thesis (indeed, it may be supportive), with its insoucience as to trinitarian construction it constitutes a parallel, if not competing, research program. I will argue in chapter six that Cobb's position indeed is the "radical monotheist" threat to which Moltmann should object.

Even so, as noted, there are some process theological writers who strive to be within a trinitarian domain. Lewis Ford, for example, likens the Father to God, who unifies within God's self the primordial nature (*Logos*) and consequent nature (Spirit).[67] Schubert Ogden, with his additional effort to attend to existentialist thought, identifies the divine essence as the Father, who incorporates the divine objectivity of the Son and divine subjectivity of the Spirit.[68] One who has written more concertedly is Joseph Bracken, S.J.[69] In his latest work, *Society and Spirit*, Bracken tries to bring together the doctrine of the Trinity and process theological themes into a cosmology informed by contemporary physical science.[70]

Bracken first explores the Whiteheadian notion of society, particularly as it is expressed in the thought of Hartshorne and Cobb. Bracken also seeks to put some distance between himself and these figures.[71] Bracken's aim is to overcome the deficiency of attention to "society" by Whitehead, especially as it would apply to a philosophical description of human communities, "complex" organisms, and the like. A wholistic understanding of communal intentionality, such as Bracken would pose, prohibits reduction to a descriptive level merely of atomistic actual occasions as the basic building blocks in the process cosmology. Bracken pronounces Whitehead guilty of this reductionism. Then Bracken proceeds to develop a concept of Spirit. He argues that "Subjective Spirit," especially as developed in the philosophy of Schelling, should be understood as "The Power of Radical Self-Determination." Bracken contends that subjective spirit would characterize every actual occasion (or energy event) in the universe, though this does not necessarily imply conscious intentionality. In other words, subjective spirit as the power of radical self-determination would be a fitting description of what Whitehead intends when he speaks of an actual occasion's act of "prehension." Then Bracken turns to Hegel's concept of Objective Spirit, synthesized with Bracken's notion of the Whiteheadian category of society, to establish the "world of intersubjectivity."

This possibility of a "society of spirit," both terms now having been redefined, sets the basis for a thoroughgoing cosmology. It is here where trinitarian reflection is invoked so that this cosmology is societal throughout. That is, God is understood as an intersubjective society of divine persons, who themselves are equally subjective spirits of radical self-determination. This divine society relates in authentic panentheistic fashion to the meta-society of the cosmos and its subsistent societies (physical systems, human communities, etc.), as well as to actual occasions, however episodic, in their dynamic processes of concrescence. Bracken articulates this relationship by speaking of a "field-oriented approach to reality."

> ...within a field-oriented approach to reality, each of the subfields is governed by its own laws and possesses its own relative autonomy even as it contributes to the larger field of activity that constitutes the greater whole. Applied to the God-world relationship, this means that the world of creation is a functioning totality within the field of activity proper to the divine persons. A strictly empirical or experiential approach to reality should therefore directly encompass the totality proper to creation with its laws and modes of operation.[72]

It is also noteworthy that within a "subfield" and its autonomous modes of operation one is only indirectly aware of the broader field. The presence of the divine persons in the larger field is mediated by the laws of structural principles appropriate to the subfield. Thus, agency may be said to be "top-down" in a mediate fashion, as well as "bottom-up." This also provides, Bracken believes, a helpful paradigm for the One and the Many, by which one can retain belief in a personal God.[73]

This model of mutual relationship leads into a revision of Whitehead's doctrine of panentheism. Here, with indebtedness to Marjorie Hewitt Suchocki,[74] Bracken levels a criticism against Whitehead and all "traditional" process theologians on this point, whether they follow Whitehead or

Hartshorne, which impresses this reader as devastatingly correct. When Bracken argues his position that entities and societies are radically self-determining and thus, in a certain sense, immortal, he presents this position as authentically panentheistic while Whitehead's is not. Those who are familiar with Whiteheadian categories know that basic to his scheme is the dynamic of an "actual occasion's" coming into being, its taking into itself a future possibility and, its consequent perishing, all "in a moment." The "past life" of the occasion as an objective fact is included somehow in the next occasion's epiphenomenal life, but it has no subjective reality. And all occasions, however distant, are included "objectively" in the life of God; they constitute the information by which God continually grows in terms of God's "consequent" nature. But they have no subjective spirit. If this is panentheism, in Bracken's eyes it is vicious and inert. God is the only one who remains at the end of the process, and whatever remains "other than" God that co-constitutes God is rather lifeless.

> Whitehead's doctrine of God is...not a form of panentheism either. For, in the end, only God survives. Finite entities are incorporated into God as soon as they acquire determinate being in the created order; hence they never exist independently of God, as a strict doctrine of panentheism would seem to require...God alone survives to feel those joys and sorrows in an enduring way. In the end, all creatures are nothing more than accidental modifications of the divine being.[75]

A healthier panentheism retains the subjectivity of all participants in the divine society. There is within such a spirited society both "top-down" and "bottom-up" agency, better modelled in Bracken's field-oriented approach.

In criticism, I would offer that Bracken's view of the Trinity as a wholly intersubjective society wherein no one person has a role disparate from another is carefully stated. It also is similar to the views of other theologians who affirm a social model of the Trinity.[76] Also, his suggestion that intersubjectivity as a *trinitarian* reality would be constitutive of "worldly" intersubjectivity is an advance in harmony with Barth. Though Bracken does not explicitly say this, it seems to be the consequence. Further, this mutual agency, as we will see, coheres nicely with the contemporary anti-reductionist view in physical cosmology. But just as philosophy requires no necessary reflection on the Trinity, I suggest that Bracken has finally proven no necessity of distinctly process philosophical categories for his intended Trinitarian metaphysic. Why adopt, after all, a process theological foundation, complete with its panpsychism, when there are quite viable alternatives, which attend to data of the natural sciences and which would well meet Bracken's criteria for a panentheistic, spirited, society?[77] Bracken succeeds admirably in demonstrating the symmetry of process theology with Hegel, Schelling, contemporary science and trinitarian thought. He demonstrates consonance and coherence.[78] More is required. Theological cosmology is more than synonymy. The next step is to prove the necessity of a process theological foundation. However, Bracken has already shown this to be a major challenge. Elsewhere he has even argued that a communitarian metaphysic more along the lines of a thinker like Josiah Royce, not Whitehead, was where more fruitful research and development might occur.[79] Royce's communitarian themes, I would argue, are even closer to the concepts of person and relationship posed by such as LaCugna than they are to Whitehead.

Nevertheless, the social conception of the Trinity bears much resemblance to the construals set forth by the "non-process" theologians above. Again, relationality and the concept of person play key roles, though Bracken does not want to identify the concept of person with "nature."[80] This implies a placement of temporality within the divine eternity, all the more supported with Bracken's appeal to current physical cosmology. Thus in Bracken's work at least the main beams of a bridge under construction are laid between process theology and more traditional trinitarian reflection. This can only aid in the support of our trinitarian "research program."

Finally, there are those who still advocate a timeless Trinity and would advert to Augustine for support. Brian Leftow finds it imaginable that God as a timeless being may possess consciousness, creativity, and exercise providence. In arguing so, Leftow removes language of temporal causality and argues that the only province from which God acts is the eternal; God acts not on specific moments in time, but only "in" the "time" of eternity.[81] I find it incongruous, though, that a "personal" being may somehow yet be immune to the confines of temporality. It seems that Leftow's agenda is in fact to keep God as wholly other, perhaps out of the salutary effort to avoid Ludwig Feuerbach's critique of theological anthropomorphism. The justification is similar for Paul Helm. He posits timelessness on God's part out of the "need to draw a proper distinction between the creator and the creature...[timelessness matters] as a necessary truth condition of all else that Christians want to say of God."[82] These are philosophical positions, however, that are made unnecessary in a strong doctrine of the Trinity that can replace the rationale for God's timelessness adequately with a notion of relational transcendence. The philosopher's distinctions need not be pressed to separations. Some sense of timelessness on God's part may be found, too, in those theologies which are still primarily existentialist. Moltmann, for example, finds the Tillichian description of God as the "ground of Being" and as "the eternal now" to imply a notion of a neo-Platonic God. Moltmann suggests even that Barth is not wholly unaffected by the same position.[83]

A Subtotal

No matter the existence still of similar arguments to the contrary, the clear thrust of contemporary trinitarian understanding is that the positive evaluation of God as both eternal and temporal need not be understood as self-contradictory. A trinitarian understanding, particularly by way of contemporary adaptations of Rahner's Rule, can describe God's eternity—at least partially—by way of God's economy. The theological emphases of personhood and relationality within contemporary Trinitarian thought underpin the concept that the eternal is approached temporally.[84] Indeed, an adaptation of Rahner's Rule together with the concepts of relationality and personhood would serve as helpful auxiliary hypotheses in a research program, the hard core of which is that the eternity of the Trinity is essentially temporal. That eternity may be interpreted just so, furthermore, was explicitly evidenced in the earlier section of this chapter. Those who made such explicit identifications were often those to whom we referred in the overview of trinitarian constructions.

The frontline of contemporary theology also agrees that the separation between the economic and immanent trinities should be rejected, as well as any separation of the doctrine of the Trinity *en toto* from the rest of the theological loci. Distinctions may yet be helpful, and so the terminology may be retained for more than the sake of historical continuity. The distinctions can be helpful in reminding us that that of which we attempt to speak cannot be fully comprehended. Thereby LaCugna reminds us how to perform the "science" of trinitarian reflection.

Distinctions notwithstanding, however, these theologians more and more are convinced that the eleatic philosophical attributes which accompanied an isolated doctrine of God are to be abandoned if such terms intend a god who is unrelated, impassible, therefore unspeakable, and who thus also would be incapable of receiving worship. Such is a god who, incidentally, is incapable of discussion by third parties who seek rapproachment between theology and the natural sciences. The Trinitarian God whom these representative theologians advocate, however, can receive praise, bridge discussion, and make further sense of the human questions about temporality, eternity, and purpose. These are conclusions, I think, in which they all would share, no matter their subtle variances on questions of how to describe and to whom to ascribe "nature" and "hypostases" and the like. They agree that there is no ground, biblically, theologically, or (even) philosophically, to continue the trinitarian discussion in terms of "substance," "nature" and so forth. God is in relationship; in relationship with God's self viz a vis the Father, Son and Spirit; in relationship and as consequence of God's self-relationship with the cosmos.

Thus I reassert my thesis. This means God is in time and time is in God, while God is not exhausted by time and promises eschatologically that time shall not exhaust those with whom God is in relationship. It is to that with whom and with which Christians believe God as Trinity is in relationship—the physical cosmos—to which we now turn.

Notes

1. Robert Jenson, *Unbaptized God, The Basic Flaw in Ecumenical Theology* (Minneapolis: Fortress, 1992).

2. See "Philosophical Concept of God," *Basic Questions in Theology*, II, 119-183. Indeed, Jenson's book could be read as a partial answer to Pannenberg's call that theology take up the task of demonstrating how the doctrine of the trinity answers the incompleteness posed in the mere philosophical understanding of God. Pannenberg writes: "It remains a task for the Christian doctrine of God to show that the otherness of God as well as his unity cannot really be conceived within the philosophical formulation of the question, but can be comprehended only as the unity of the Father with the Son and the Spirit, so that the revelation of the triune God is what brings the philosophical question to a genuine fulfillment for the first time." *Basic Questions...*, II, 182.

3. *Unbaptized God*, 110-111.

4. *Unbaptized God*, 111.

5. Thus Gregory of Nyssa's formulation, noted in LaCugna. See note 6.

6. Catherine Mowry LaCugna, *God For Us* (San Francisco: Harper Collins, 1991), 168-9. I follow LaCugna's excellent summary of the Greek/Latin trajectory here.

7. Augustine, *On the Trinity*, books 5-7.

8. *On the Trinity*: I/4,5,8,9; II/10; IV/21; V/14; Aquinas, *Summa Theologiae*, I,Q.39. It is noteworthy that nowhere in *de Trinitate* is the Augustinian maxim *as such* explicitly stated. The maxim is a synthesis of the above stated passages, later labelled as "Augustine's."

9. *On the Trinity*, books 8ff.

10. LaCugna, 101.; see also 97-100.

11. *Unbaptized God*, 143ff.

12. *Unbaptized God*, 144.

13. Robert Jenson, *The Triune Identity: God According to the Gospel* (Philadelphia: Fortress, 1982), 175; also 51, 89.

14. The consequence of the Augustinian confusion, as Jenson describes it, is as follows. For Augustine, "the three persons are not only equally related to the one substance, but *identically* related, so that the difference between them, that is, the relations, are irrelevant to their being God. But the original trinitarian insight is that the relations between their identities *are* their being God. When the Nicenes called the trinity as such God, they so named him *because* of the triune relations and differences; when Augustine calls the Trinity as such God, it is *in spite of them*....Augustine rejected the Cappadocian doctrine for the sake of his simplicity axiom, which indeed, as he says, makes absurd all talk about the identities only *mutually* being God. And Augustine's position remained axiomatic..." *The Triune Identity*, 118-9.

15. Modalism is the teaching that God himself is above time and that the distinctions of Father, Son and Spirit only appear serially in these roles to create, redeem, and sanctify. This had been standard theory since 190 in Rome. It was a direct attempt to keep God timeless. Its result is that none of the three is understood as God himself. Subordinationism, on the other hand, seems at least to identify "Father" with God; it also provided the hierarchical ranking so desired by Greek thought. In such a scheme Christ becomes merely the "halfway house" to heaven.

16. Christopher Stead observes that the "social model" of the Trinity itself goes back to the reflections of Gregory of Nyssa, particularly his *On Not Three Gods*. Gregory argues that as human life at its best evidences the unity of sociality, this indicates, by disanalogy, the mutual enjoyment and self-giving of the divine persons as authentic, concrete unity; in this way Gregory may affirm one God in three hypostases. For a summary of the argument, see G. Christopher Stead, "Why Not Three Gods? The Logic of Gregory of Nyssa's Trinitarian Doctrine," H. Dorrie (ed.), *Gregor von Nyssa und die Philosophie: zweites internationales Kolloquium uber Gregor von Nyssa* (Leiden: Brill, 1976).

17. *Unbaptized God*, 144.

18. *Unbaptized God*, 144.

19. Barth, *Church Dogmatics*, II/1, 685-6. The difference with *us* is that we have no such peace; we experience disruption by our location *on* the time line. "The extent of the specious present is not in our control; pieces of temporal actuality do get away from us altogether, pending the eschaton; and most of the past is indeed *fixed* most of the time, though grace, which *forgives* what has been and turns its curse into blessing, even now can repair this disruption." Cf. Jenson, *Unbaptized God*, 145.

20. In addition to the above references, also see Jenson's "The Triune God," Carl Braaten and Robert Jenson (eds.) *Christian Dogmatics*, vol. 1 (Philadelphia: Fortress, 1984), 79-191.

21. *Triune Identity*, 161.

22. *Triune Identity*, 161.

23. *Triune Identity*, 162f.

24. *Triune Identity*, 163-4.

25. *Triune Identity*, 164.

26. *Triune Identity*, 165.

27. *Against Eunomius*, in his *Opera*, ed. W. Jaeger, vols. I-II (Leiden: Brill, 1960), 1: 366.

28. *Against Eunomius*, I:42.

29. So Ted Peters also interprets Jenson's position. "The essential mode of divine temporality is unbounded futurity...This means time is neither linear nor cyclical and, therefore, we ought not to understand reality in terms of enduring substances. It is the oncoming of the future that creates time for us, because it forces the present reality to go beyond itself. It is the reality of the future that temporalizes us. It is the structure of the still outstanding eschatological future which determines the character of time and becoming in our present experience. What we experience as endurance is given not by persisting substances but rather by the reinterpretation which the future gives to all past occasions." *God As Trinity*, 163-4.

30. Karl Rahner, *The Trinity*, trans. by J. Donceel, (New York: Herder and Herder, 1970).

31. Rahner, 21-22. The term "Rahner's Rule" was coined by Ted Peters. See *dialog*, 26:1 (Winter, 1987), 44-48 and 26:2 (Spring, 1987), 133-38 and Peters, *God As Trinity*, 120n.

32. Yves Congar accepts this, but qualifies the "vice-versa" of Rahner's Rule by saying that there is an asymmetry between theology and economy when it comes to the self-communication *ad intra* and *ad extra*, simply because God's self-communication economically will not be a whole communication until the eschaton. Yves Congar, *I Believe*, 3:13-18. Rahner's principal on its own would not allow God to say "something new" in his self-communication, thus the need for asymmetry or, as I would put it, the need for the accent on transcendence. On this ground I would suggest Ted Peters overstates the case that

Rahner would "slip in" an "*a se* deity of the philosophers." (*God As Trinity*, 126). I think Jenson would agree with Congar. Indeed, Jenson is quite clear in his adaptation of Rahner's Rule that the immanent Trinity can be understood wholly as the economic Trinity eschatologically. The freedom of God, with its eschatological limit, is a legitimate theological reason for distinguishing between the immanent and economic; i.e., the immanent Trinity is the eschatological reality of the economic Trinity (*The Triune Identity*, 140). Walter Kasper makes much the same point in *The God of Jesus Christ*, 275-276; we must "take seriously the truth that through the incarnation the second divine person exists in history in a new way." Piet Schoonenberg also agrees: "In the economic self-communication, the intra-trinitarian self-communication is present in the world in a new way, namely, under the veil of historical words, signs, and actions, and ultimately in the figure of the man Jesus of Nazareth." Cf. his "Trinity, the Consummated Covenant," quoted, with Congar and Kasper, by Catherine Mowry LaCugna, *God For Us* (New York: Harper Collins, 1990) 176ff.

33. Hereby Rahner does not presuppose a "Latin" theology, but the biblical narrative, in which God is the Father—the unoriginate God—who communicates himself freely, and this does not threaten his integrity. How then are Son and Spirit understood as moments related in and yet distinct of the one self-communication of God? Rahner charges that traditional school theology is not clear on this; it cannot answer why Spirit could not have become human. Thus, systematic Trinitarian reflection must start in an opposite fashion by supposing that when God freely steps "outside of himself" in self-communication, it is and must be the Son who is incarnated and it is and must be the Spirit who brings about acceptance by the world in faith, hope and love of this self-communication; *The Trinity*, 86. Insofar as self-communication is free, the incarnation of Christ and the descent of the Spirit are also free, even though their connection is logically necessary. This agrees with the pre-Augustinian tradition. But if we even presuppose the self-communication as necessary and the other two events as free, then salvation history could say nothing about the Father, Son, and Spirit. The doctrine of Trinity then could and would only be a verbal accompaniment to a salvation history which would be no different had the Father or the Son become incarnate, Rahner argues.

34. Eberhard Jüngel, *God as the Mystery of the World* accepts forthrightly Rahner's Rule, too, and finds affinity between it and his own concept of "person." Earlier, in his *The Doctrine of the Trinity: God's Being Is In Becoming* (Grand Rapids: Eerdman's, 1976), Jüngel had come close to such an affirmation by arguing that there was a relation of analogy (*analogia relationis*) between the economic and immanent trinities. He posited, therefore, a principle of correspondence between our experience of God's work *ad extra* and God's life *ad intra*. Jüngel assumed, therefore, that for such a correspondence to hold, the way in which God is related to the world must be similar, if not identical, to God's self-relatedness. Critical to his argument is the idea, again, of person; a person is constituted by his or her relationships. "Personal means being in relationship! It must be emphatically maintained that person is a concept expressing relationship...and not as a concept of substance expressing the nature of a magnitude existing for itself" (Jüngel, 91). The dynamic of personal relationship within the Trinity, therefore, having correspondence to the relationships between the divine persons and creation, means that God cannot stay the same. God "becomes" out of the perichoretic dynamism of the three persons. Jüngel is not so helpful in the end, however, because he neither commits himself to an identification of personality to the three hypostases, which might risk the label of tritheism, nor to asserting such personality to the Godhead. While his agreement to Rahner's Rule may finally dismiss the need for any

analogia relationis on Jüngel's part, the emphasis on relationship over substance does allow for the temporality on God's part, which many later would affirm.
35. Jüngel, *The Doctrine of the Trinity*, 34-35.
36. Rahner, *Trinity*, 107.
37. *Trinity*, 90.
38. Pannenberg, *Systematic Theology*, 1:285-286.
39. "Die Subjektivität Gottes und die Trinitätslehre," *Grundfragen Systematischer Theologie*, II (Göttingen: Vandenhoeck und Ruprecht, 1981), 96-111.
40. "The Appropriation of the Philosophical Concept of God as a Dogmatic problem of Early Christian Theology," in *Basic Questions in Theology*, trans. by George Kehm, vol. 2 (Philadelphia: Westminster, 1971), 182.
41. Quoted in Pannenberg, *Jesus, God and Man*, 182.
42. *Jesus, God and Man*, 182.
43. *Jesus, God and man*, 181.
44. *God as Trinity*, 174. As Peters goes on to observe, the eternity of God is dependent in a very specific way upon the economic work of the Son, who through obedience will finally at the eschaton turn all things over to the Father. The Father's rule depends upon this. Indeed, the deity of God depends upon this (some day) historical act. See Pannenberg, *Systematic Theology*, 1, 313.
45. Clearly this relates closely to the problem of time and eternity. The flow of time is meaningless for that which remains ever the same. Pannenberg argues that the philosophical concept of eternity as separation from everything temporal intruded into the biblical idea of God's eternity as his powerful presence to every time; see *Basic Questions in Theology*, 173. "Thus Christianity was faced with the task of assimilating the concept of God who is static, a-temporal and by definition uninvolved with his world. This has had the devastating consequence of rendering inexplicable the biblical affirmation of the contention of God with man and of necessitating that every innovation in the divine-human relationship has to be sought as much as possible on the side of man."
46. In *God's Being Is In Becoming*, Jüngel, too, identifies time as a result of the triune differentiation. In this differentiation God's actions are the correspondence of God's being to itself. As the Father elects the Son from eternity, the Son elected himself in correspondence to the Father's will. This correspondence—or co-response—is both reiterated and advanced in Pannenberg's different terminology of reciprocal self-dedication (and distinction) of the triune persons.
47. Wolfhart Pannenberg, "The Doctrine of Creation and Modern Science," *Zygon* 23/1 (March: 1988), 3-21; "The God of Creation and Natural Science," *CTNS Bulletin* 7/2 (Spring: 1987), 1-10. A related discussion is found in his "Theological Questions to Scientists," Arthur Peacocke (ed.), *The Sciences and Theology in the Twentieth Century* (Notre Dame: University of Notre Dame Press, 1981), 3-16.
48. This extended quote from Pannenberg, therefore, is most noteworthy. "In the case of Kant's transcendental aesthetics—in the case of time as well as in the case of space—the infinite has priority over any finite part. In the case of time this brings Kant's argument into close contact with Plotinus's conception of time in distinction from that of Aristotle. Plotinus argued that only on the basis of the perfect wholeness of life is an understanding of the nature of time possible (Plotinus, *Enneads* 3.7, 3, 16-17; 2.7, 11). The whole of time according to Plotinus cannot be conceived as the whole of a sequence of moments because the sequence of temporal moments can be indefinitely extended by adding further units. Yet, in his view time and the sequence of its units are understandable only under the presupposition of the

idea of a complete wholeness of life, which Plotinus conceived under the name of eternity (*aion*). In his view the total unity of the whole life is indispensable in the interpretation of the time sequence because it hovers over that sequence as the future wholeness that is intended in every moment of time. Thus, the significance of eternity for the interpretation of time in Plotinus results in a primacy of the future concerning the nature of time. Not before Martin Heidegger's analysis of time in the twentieth century was this insight rediscovered, and with Heidegger it was developed only in a limited way, restricted to the experience of time in human existence." "The Doctrine of Creation and Modern Science," 16-17.

49. Pannenberg, *Systematic Theology*, vol. 1, 408.

50. The crown of LaCugna's work is *God For Us:The Trinity and Christian Life* (San Francisco: Harper Collins, 1991); see also "The Trinitarian Mystery of God," *Systematic Theology: Roman Catholic Perspectives*, ed. by Francis Schussler Fiorenza and John P. Galvin, 2 volumes (Minneapolis: Fortress, 1991); "Current Trends in Trinitarian Theology," *Religious Studies Review*, 13:2 (April, 1987), 141-147; "Trinity," *The Encyclopedia of Religion*, ed. by Mircea Eliade et al., vol. 15 (New York: MacMillan, 1988), 53-57.

51. *God For Us*, 167.

52. *God For Us*, 42.

53. "The Council of Nicaea determined the theoretical basis that would be used to work out this doctrine [of the Trinity]: Christ is *homoousios* with God with respect to divinity, that is, at the level of *theologia*. This created an obvious incommensurability with *oikonomia*, now identified specifically with the humanity of Christ. Given the trajectory set by Nicaea, in combination with the long-lasting controversies over Arianism and neo-Arianism, Christian theologians focused their attention more and more on the nature of *theologia* per se, that is, the interrelationship of the divine persons. While the motive was no doubt consistently soteriological, in time the economy became less and less decisive in shaping conclusion about the intratrinitarian relations. By the medieval period in both Byzantine and Latin theology, the divine persons were thought of as existing *in* God, in a realm cut off from the economy of salvation history by virtue of an unbreachable ontological difference. In scholastic theology, the doctrine of the Trinity was identified as the science of God's inner relatedness. The result of this was a one-sided theology of God that had little to do with the economy of Christ and the Spirit, with the themes of Incarnation and grace, and therefore little to do with the Christian life. Greek medieval theology took refuge in an exaggerated agnosticism that relegated the trinitarian persons to a region far beyond our capacity to experience or understand. Hence the defeat of the doctrine of the Trinity." *God For Us*, 209-210.

54. See, e.g., Aquinas, *Summa*, Ia, 12.

55. *God For Us*, 158.

56. "The Trinitarian Mystery of God," 156-157.

57. *God For Us*, 211.

58. *God For Us*, 228.

59. "The Trinitarian Mystery of God," 177. LaCugna's understanding of person as "communion" is like that of John D. Zizioulas. Each writer's theological anthropology depends on the concept of person as ec-centric, or, as LaCugna puts it, "catholic." A person—whether human or God—is irrevocably social. It would be an oxymoron to predicate "individual" of "person." See John D. Zizioulas, *Being As Communion, Studies in Personhood and the Church* (Crestwood: St. Vladimir's Seminary Press, 1985).

60. *God For Us*, 305.

61. Summaries of the current trinitarian scene are now being published. In addition to those already referenced, see John Thompson, *Modern Trinitarian Perspectivess* (Oxford: Oxford University Press, 1994); T.F. Torrance, *The Trinitarian Faith* (Edinburgh: T.&T. Clark, 1993) and Torrance, *Trinitarian Perspectives, Toward Doctrinal Agreement* (Edinburgh: T.& T. Clark, 1994).

62. The standard references now are almost legion. Among them, see, Alfred North Whitehead, *Process and Reality* (New York: Free Press, 1978); *Science and the Modern World* (New York: Free Press, 1967); John Cobb, *A Christian Natural Theology* (Philadelphia: Westminster, 1965); *Christ in a Pluralistic Age* (Philadelphia: Westminster, 1975); John Cobb and David Ray Griffin, *Process Theology: An Introductory Exposition* (Philadelphia: Westminster, 1975); Charles Hartshorne, *The Divine Relativity*; Delwin Brown, Ralph E. James Jr. and Gene Reeves (eds.), *Process Philosophy and Christian Thought* (Indianapolis and New York: Bobbs Merrill, 1971). Also useful as a secondary text for the subject of temporality approached from a variety of process philsophical perspectives, cf. David R. Griffin, ed., *Physics and the Ultimate Significance of Time* (Albany: SUNY, 1986). Finally, Ian Barbour has been a consistent proponent of the need to adopt a process theological metaphysic for the conduct of the theology/natural science discussion. See his standard, *Issues in Science and Religion* (New York: Harper and Row, 1966) and his Gifford Lectures, vol.1, *Religion In An Age of Science* (San Francisco: Harper, 1990).

63. E.g., John Cobb, "Reply to Moltmann's 'The Unity of the Triune God,'" *St. Vladimir's Theological Quarterly*, 28:3 (1984), 173-178.

64. Cobb, *Christ in a Pluralistic Age*, 259-264 and "Reply to Moltmann," 176.

65. "Reply to Moltmann," 176.

66. Cobb and Griffin, *Process Theology: An Introductory Exposition*, 110.

67. Lewis Ford, *The Lure of God* (Philadelphia: Fortress, 1978).

68. "On The Trinity," *Theology*, 83 (March, 1980), 97-102. John O'Donnell, who seeks a trinitarian confluence of process themes with Moltmann's eschatology, suggests that Ogden's program may be modalist. Cf. *Trinity and Temporality* (Oxford: Oxford University Press, 1983), 81. Ted Peters suggests that if this is so for Ogden, then likewise for Ford; *God As Trinity*, 147n.

69. *What Are They Saying About the Trinity?* (New York: Paulist, 1979); *The Triune Symbol: Persons, Process and Community*, College Theology Society Studies in Religon (Lanham: University Press of America, 1985); "The Holy Trinity as a Community of Divine Persons," *Heythrop Journal* 15 (1974), 166-82, 257-70; "Philosophy and Trinitarian Theology," *Process Studies* 8 (1978), 217-230, 11 (1981), 83-96; "Subsistent Relation: Mediating Concept for a New Synthesis?" *Journal of Religion*, April, (1984), 188-204; "The World: Body of God or Field of Cosmic Activity?", in *Charles Hartshorne's Concept of God*, ed. by Santiago Sia (Dordrecht: Klower Academic Publishers, 1990); and, most recently, *Society and Spirit, A Trinitarian Cosmology* (Selinsgrove: Susquehanna University Press, 1991).

70. The following comments are adapted from a more detailed review of the book I have provided in the *CTNS Bulletin*, 12:3 (Summer, 1992), 5-6.

71. Evidently, they regard him similarly. John Cobb implies in the foreword that the desire for some distance is mutual. Cobb comments that he does not always agree with the provocative advances posed by Bracken, but still affirms the book as "interesting" and worthy of consideration.

72. *Society and Spirit*, 153-4.

73. *Society and Spirit*, 152.

74. Marjorie Hewitt Suchocki, *God,Christ,Church* (New York: Crossroad, 1982).

75. *Society and Spirit*, 136, 139.

76. Again, Moltmann, *The Trinity and the Kingdom;* also Eberhard Jüngel, *God's Being Is In His Becoming*, et al.

77. There are many writers who would complement Bracken's agenda without appealing to process categories. In addition to Jüngel and Moltmann, cf. Peacocke, Arthur, *Creation and the World of Science* (Oxford: Clarendon Press, 1979); Polkinghorne, John, "The Nature of Physical Reality," *Zygon*, 26:2 (June, 1991), 221-236; *Science and Providence, God's Interaction with the World* (Boston: Shambhala, 1989). I would also recommend consulting Rust, Eric C., "The Dynamic Nature of the Triune God," *Perspectives in Religious Studies*, 14 (Winter, 1987), 31-46; and Pendergast, R.J., S.J., "A Thomistic Process Theory of the Trinity," *Science et Esprit*, XLIII/1 (1990), 35-59.

78. Ernan McMullin argues, for example, that consonance may be the limit of reasonable expectations with regard to the relationship of theology to natural science. See McMullin, Ernan (ed.), *Evolution and Creation* (Notre Dame: University of Notre Dame, 1985).

79. "Although disciples may quite well be able to adopt these concepts to an explanation of human behavior on the personal and societal levels, nevertheless it makes more sense to me to work with the categories of a process thinker who is specifically concerned with the interrelation of persons and communities. In this respect, I think that the work of Josiah Royce in *The Problem of Christianity* has been too little read and analyzed." Joseph Bracken, S.J., *What They Are Saying About the Trinity*. See note 67, 282.

80. He accuses Moltmann, Jüngel, et al., of doing just that, arguing that three separate persons are necessary to make up the divine person. The whole, as it were, is greater than its parts; none of the three are "God." Thus Bracken would charge tritheism of Moltmann, et al., although he himself may be bordering on quaternity, as Ted Peters observes (*God as Trinity*, 150n.).

81. Brian Leftow, *Time and Eternity* (Ithaca: Cornell University Press, 1991), 298.

82. Paul Helm, *Eternal God* (Oxford: Clarendon, 1989), 21-22.

83. Jürgen Moltmann, *God in Creation*, 80ff.

84. While they have not yet touched upon our metaphysical interests with this essay, Liberationist and Feminist theologies have stressed keenly the connections between personhood and relationality, even to the point of claiming them as their own insights. While I see nothing particularly "feminist" about the notion of person-in-communion, I am nevertheless in complete sympathy with the claim that such a notion is required to correct excesses of theological anthropology, ecclesiology, as well as trinitarian formulations of past years. See especially, Elisabeth Johnson, *She Who Is* (New York: Crossroad, 1993), and Leonardo Boff, *Trinity and Society* (New York: Orbis, 1991).

IV

Contemporary Physical Theory: Some Basics

Any theology which intends systematically and responsibly to explicate a contemporary understanding of time and eternity could hardly refrain from looking to the world that evokes the issue in question. And, insofar as there is currently the healthy attempt at a dialogue between theologians and natural scientists, there is all the more impetus to couch this discussion in the terms of the "one world" that we scientists and theologians quite fortunately share. As I also observed in chapter one, Christian thinking about time and eternity had remained rather consistent since, at least, Boethius. There are, unfortunately, some who prefer this outdated consistency still, in spite of the Einsteinian revolution in thought about temporality and the questions that have been forcefully brought to bear by the theories of quantum physics. Thus, it is not even any longer a question of "good" or "responsible" theology. Insofar as it desires to be systematic at all, Christian theology simply must give a careful reading and hearing to the discussion of temporality as that discussion issues from, at the least, physicists and cosmologists. Of course, there are many more natural scientists of other disciplines whose thinking would be important for us, too. Their contribution, however, would have to be taken up in a project much larger than this one. It is my intent to give that reading and hearing in this chapter, and, further, it is my hope thereby not only to be informed by the natural sciences regarding time and eternity, but to provide a Christian response of information such as might be found in the doctrine of the Trinity that we have just surveyed.

There is available now an ample store of comment upon the enormous revolution in physical theory which began with this century's birth.[1] With the first decade of this century, the quantum theory and special relativity theory virtually dismantled the foundations of classical physics, and with it traditional metaphysics. As for the concept of time itself as "established" by Newton, there could not have been a more radical change. It is not clear, though, that the upheaval experienced in this paradigm shift of physical theory necessarily entails an equal shift in Christian theological conceptuality. I wish to argue, rather, that a refocus on at least one classic Christian tenet, the doctrine of the Trinity, may provide a proposal by which the disparateness between the ideas of time and eternity in current physical and theological theory may be overcome. Furthermore, that the question of temporality's relation to eternity is further confused by the revolution in physical theory exacerbates the question of how a (once conceived) "eternal" God may relate to this temporal scheme in which we mortals find ourselves. In this chapter, however, it may be useful to summarize some essential features of relativity theory and the quantum theory, as well as those of thermodynamics and cosmology inasmuch as they impinge upon the construction of time.[2] Thereby I will draw out certain scientific themes that should serve a role in responsible Christian theologizing about time and eternity.

Relativity Theory

While a principle of relativity was accepted in standard classical physical theory, it held, however, that such relativity was the subordination of all matter and time to two absolutes: absolute space and absolute time. The principle stated that the laws of mechanics were independent of locality. The motion of a ball thrown vertically into the air and then caught would be describable in the same way whether the player was standing in place or in a train moving at a constant velocity. This principle was thought to apply to all mechanical phenomena; not so, however, for light or other electromagnetic phenomena. The intent of the Albert Michelson–Edward Morley experiment (1887) was to prove this inapplicability.[3] The celebrated surprise of its conclusion, however, led to the demise of belief in an absolute space or an absolute "container" of time against which all other velocities could be measured. Einstein was able to explain the Michaelson–Morley experiment with his Special Theory of Relativity, although the theory was based primarily on Einstein's concerns about the classical theory of electromagnetism and not about the experimental data. Thus, Einstein was able to develop a wholly relativized principle of relativity which stated that there exists no absolute frame of reference whatsoever; all inertial frames are to be regarded on an equal basis.

Put more precisely, Einstein's first postulate in the Special Theory of Relativity is that "the laws of physics take the same form in all inertial frames." And there are as many times as there are inertial frames in relative motion.[4] Hereby Einstein radically democratized the principle of relativity.[5] With the second postulate, Einstein showed that this principle applied to light and electromagnetic phenomena as well as to mechanical phenomena. "In any given inertial frame, the velocity of light 'c' is the same whether the light be emitted by a body at rest or by a body in uniform motion."[6] The measurements of the velocity of light give the same results regardless of the frame of reference in which the measurements are made. This fact makes Einstein's theory truly relativistic; there is no privileged frame of reference. Nevertheless, the theory provides the velocity of light itself as the standard against which all else is measured, which, in turn, enables all frames of reference with their "unique" times to be coordinated in a mathematical symmetry available already to Einstein in the Lorentz transformation equations. Interestingly, this consequence leads to some argument as to just how "relative" Einstein's special theory is. Some would claim that its aim was precisely to establish a standard reference with ontological status against which all kinematics can be measured. Others argue its implications as permission for a sort of anarchy of pluralism.[7]

The most significant result of time's inclusion in the transformation equations is that time and space become inextricably interdependent and interconvertible. Yet they are separately measurable quantities.[8] There are specific physical effects from this union. For example, if an observer in reference frame A compares herself to an observer in frame B, which frame is moving relative to A, she will see that a clock in B runs slower than one in her reference frame. The observer in B will notice an identical effect. A complementary effect occurs in measurement of lengths. Both observers will perceive a yardstick to be shorter in the other's frame, and by the same amount. Such space contraction and time dilation are not optical illusions. The fact of such results has been proven experimentally by comparing stationary atomic clocks on earth with ones flown around the world.[9]

Closely related to the interconnectedness of time and space is the relativization of simultaneity. Universal simultaneity is not possible because the time and space scales differ among inertial frames of reference in relative motion. Simultaneity can occur only within a particular frame, not across different frames in relative motion. What may appear to be simultaneous to one observer, say, the flashes of lightning bolts, will not appear to be so for another observer moving at a different velocity. This is the second major time-related characteristic revealed by relativity theory. Simultaneity is relative. But this does not mean that causality can be reordered within experience. More pointedly, the causal order of time-like events is invariant with respect to all inertial observers, when "time like" means capable of lying along the world line of an observer. Finally, as time approaches the boundary condition of the speed of light it approaches a stopping point and mass approaches infinity.

These two stated characteristics of time are revealed by the emphasis sustained on kinetics in Special Relativity. Einstein's General Theory of Relativity, with its concern of gravity upon observers, reveals a third major time-related characteristic, which is that there is an intimate relationship between time, acceleration, mass, and space curvature. Special Relativity dealt with "flat space" and ignored gravitational effect of mass-energy. General Relativity holds that the introduction of mass-energy into space-time results in a curved space-time. William Stoeger and George Ellis give a helpful example of a rubberized membrane stretched over a cylinder to form a drumhead. As long as nothing heavy is placed on the head, a light marble will role straight across it. Place a heavy object in the membrane, however, like a shot, and the marble will follow a curved path. The higher the mass, the steeper the curve; and the marble will not be able to hold a straight course unless it maintains a sufficiently high velocity. If it does not have enough speed, it will "roll in orbit" around the heavy object, as planets orbit the sun. "So the presence of matter distorts space, and particles and light rays now travel on curved paths in it. Gravitation is represented by this space-time curvature."[10]

The velocity of the object itself will influence space curvature, as well. For the closer an object reaches the upper limit of the speed of light, the more time dilates, and the greater the object's mass.[11] Consequently, space "bends" and time slows near higher masses or when subject to higher accelerations. As Christopher Isham notes, time may now be defined phenomenologically in terms of gravitational fields. This is one of the most fundamental features of general relativity.[12] In other words, there is no "pre-established" space-time with an invariant geometry, as Newton would have desired it. Rather, space-time and its geometry are determined by the distribution of mass within it. In turn, mass, like particles of matter and electromagnetic radiation, is affected by this geometry, "which determines the path it follows and the way signals are propagated in space and time."[13]

In sum, contemporary relativity theory overrules the absolutes of Newtonian mechanics, though Newton's formulae are still descriptively helpful for velocities far slower than the speed of light. Particles follow the curved paths of local spacetimes, rather than being influenced by a gravity once understood as some sort of invisible force of attraction.[14] Time and space measurement blend together as parts of a four-dimensional matrix, shaped by matter. Matter, energy, and spacetime, then, are the fundamental physical components of the created order within any view of the universe. Most certainly this should be so within a properly theistic view as well.[15]

Quantum Theory

The effects of relativity upon time apply when large-scale kinematics are involved. With the quantum theory describable effects are concerned with physical phenomena "in the small." Where Newtonian physics might have been generally descriptively helpful with macroscopic matters, it cannot cohere with the details of the world and their consequent implications as found at the atomic and sub-atomic level. It cannot cohere precisely because what once may have seemed to be paradoxical can actually be the case, such as wave/particle duality.

"Complementarity" is a pronounced theme in the quantum theory. The Principle of Complementarity, first summarized by Neils Bohr, is more general than and contains within it Heisenberg's Uncertainty Principle, which I will attend to shortly. The complementarity principle was first developed, however, in adaptation to Einstein's and Planck's discovery that light behaved as both a wave and a particle. Experiments by Louis de Broglie in 1923 proving the diffraction of electrons showed that wave-particle duality is exhibited by matter as well as light.[16] Wave and particle modes, as Bohr concluded, are mutually exclusive, but complementary. Each is necessary in rendering a complete description of microscopic physical phenomena. Further, if a given measurement reveals the wave character of the phenomenon, the particle character cannot be denoted in the same measurement.[17] Not only does complementarity apply to the physical form of a given phenomenon. In the microscopic world, there is a complementary connection between time and energy, and between location and momentum. One should be cautious, however, not to extend "complementarity" into a philosophical rationale for covering any sort of incompatibility.

> We can study in detail how the complementary descriptions of position and momentum relate to each other. On broader questions, like physics-and-biology, our understanding is considerably less and complementarity is in danger of becoming a descriptive catchword rather than an interpretive principle.[18]

This principle is related to the operation of another quantum rule, the Heisenberg Uncertainty Principle, which states that the exact location and momentum of a particle can never be known simultaneously. One measures the position of a particle with increasing exactness only at the expense of knowing concomitantly less about the particle's velocity and vice-versa. The Uncertainty Principle maintains further that no microscopic measurement may be taken which does not affect the phenomenon measured.

The Heisenberg principle has led to many controverted claims in physics and cosmology. According to many interpretations of quantum physics, this "observer-observed" complement is a result of the non-local, holistic character of sub-atomic phenomena. This is attributable to the influence of Bell's Theorem, which we will discuss below. But "where," or "how," or even "whether" reality is observed is open to controversy. The controversy seems to center around the "realism" claims an interpretation adopts. Were one to pose the general options for realism claims along a line segment, claims for realism might be placed at one pole, anti-realism at the other, and an agnostic or positivist instrumentalism might be posed between the other two.[19] Interpretations rarely, however, assume an anti-realist stance.

Neils Bohr represents the instrumentalist agnostic approach, which holds that an observer cannot ask whether an electron has position. Still, his view is, nevertheless, weakly realist, not anti-realist. Heisenberg, as another example, presumes an "ontology of indeterminism," which assumes something more of a realist epistemological stance, however critically qualified it is. Herein is at least the possibility that one can refer to the Aristotelian categories of formal and efficient causality, along with reference to substantial phenomena. This "school" of interpretation maintains that somewhere in the causal chain of observed-instrument-observer the observed comes into "reality." What path or history an electron, for example, might take could not be predicted with exactitude. The superposition of a quantum event must be interpreted probabilistically. Another school of interpretation, that of quantum logic, argues for a "lower level" or the "more primordial" existence of a non-distributive onto–logic. This argument holds that a particle is neither "here" nor "there" in the quantum world, but is "here" *and* "there" (or even "here and here" and "there and there"!). The "lattice" of an electron's path contains options which, within its logic, are non-commutable, in contrast to typical "human" Boolean logic, wherein the event coordinates are commutable. The very positing of such a lattice in this style of argument can press a distinctly realist position. From these interpretations of Heisenberg's Uncertainty Principle alone it is evident all the more that the quantum world appears to be counterintuitive to and taunting of Newtonian reality. The weight of preferred interpretation seems to bear, however, more toward the side of a qualified realism, known formally as Critical Realism.[20]

We must note that Heisenberg's Principle applies with equal force to any attempt simultaneously to measure time and energy. As with the Heisenberg uncertainty relation with respect to momentum and position of a particle, "the uncertainty in the measurement of energy of a particle times the uncertainty in the time it exists can never be less than Planck's constant."[21] Suppose, for example, that the energy of a nucleus is well known. Concomitantly, the period of time over which the nucleus might instantly decay is less known. The quantum theory exposes an intimate relationship between energy and time.[22] This leads us to a most nagging question of quantum theory. Clearly, no observer can be "objectively" detached from the observed; what is measured is nature exposed to our way of measuring (Heisenberg). The uncertainty is all the more radicalized when one acknowledges that the observer's measurements are but themselves electrons distorting the electrons of the object observed. This is unlike the degree of detachment which the observer may exercise in the macroscopic world wherein a sensitive enough instrument might have little effect on that which is measured. How then is something so unpredictable and unvisualizable, as well as so wholly other in its logic from human Boolean thinking, "found" or "realized" in the act of measurement? This is a particularly perplexing epistemological problem. It is exacerbated by the recognition that it is not only the quantum phenomena under observation themselves which contribute to the indeterminacy; the observer and the instrument for observation, too, are quantum phenomena which interact and confuse with the phenomena under observation. How is the observed connected to the observer and how does it finally achieve its "observability?" Where along the causal chain does the collapse of the wavepacket occur?

Knowing And Reality

Two famous "parables" have been handed down in this quantum era in the attempt to settle this question. They are the examples of Schrödinger's cat and Wigner's friend. With no animal rights movement as yet to demand sensitivity of the physicist, Erwin Schrödinger suggests the scenario of placing his kitty in a closed box. The box also contains a radioactive atom with a fifty percent chance of decaying within the next hour, thereby emitting a gamma ray. If this happens, the ray will trigger the breaking of a poison gas vial, which straightaway kills the cat. Now quantum theory would inform me that were I to open the box at the end of the hour the cat would be in the even-percentage state of being both "dead" and "alive;" the superposition of the gamma ray would seem to dictate such. So says the quantum theory, however counter common sense it should seem. The paradox is that upon my opening the box, the wave packet collapses and I will find either a cool cat or a peppy pussy. Normally we would answer that it wasn't the observation of the wave packet's collapse that brought about the collapse; especially if the cat were dead, I would claim I had nothing to do with it. The paradox is that the quantum theory, and many of its interpreters, could lead the Society for the Prevention of Cruelty to Animals precisely to the latter conclusion. Common sense would maintain that the issue was settled before I opened the box. But when? The quantum theory, rightly, tells us that we cannot say. "Along the chain of consequence, from atomic decay to my act of observation, things must have got fixed at least by the time that the cat's experience entered into it."[23] All of this means, in terms of the quantum theory, maybe I did kill the cat, maybe I didn't!

The story of "Wigner's friend" presses the question of the role of consciousness in such indeterminant measurement. Eugene Wigner's friend is conducting a common test; he is monitoring the electron being deflected by the magnetic field in the Stern-Gerlach experiment, listening to the Geiger counters at point A and point B to see which one clicks, thereby registering the electron's arrival at that point. The electron beam beforehand is unpolarized so that its superposition of "up" or "down" is equal; the probabilities of its hitting A or B are even. Now, in the midst of the test(s), Wigner asks his friend which counter just clicked. The friend replies "A." This means, for Wigner (not the friend!) that the electron's wavepacket then collapses into the state of an "up" spin. So would imply the quantum theory. But Wigner did not bring about this collapse by his intervention. He must trust his friend's experience as much as he trusts his own. It must have been settled at least by the time Wigner's friend heard the click that the electron's spin was "up,"[24] even though the quantum theory is open to a contrary interpretation.

Somewhere along the continuum from the unobservable object to my knowledge of it the actual result of the observation is fixed. Somewhere along the line the quantum rules have to change; the "spread-out" superposition must somehow turn into one unique reality. These informal arguments suggest what von Neumann demonstrated more exactly with his mathematics: "if the whole world is described quantum-mechanically, in terms of proxy waves, then somewhere between the quon source and final result a 'wave function collapse' must occur."[25] Some physicists go so far as to say that it is the observation itself which fixes the result. Others would say that the result is fixed somewhere along the chain before the actual observation of it. The intervention of consciousness is certainly the latest point possible. And, it seems, equally possible is the realization of the event at any prior point. I noted above quite briefly the general schools of agnostic instrumentalism, ontology of indeterminacy and quantum logic. John Polkinghorne is more refined in suggesting a taxonomy of four different possibilities of interpretation.[26] And Nick Herbert is more nuanced yet in suggesting eight.[27] I will outline four options in more depth and with additional qualifications.

The first option, consonant with agnostic instrumentalism, is to suggest that it is all a matter of epistemology. The wave function is understood simply as my description of it. I am not worried so much about the "deep reality" of the matter as I am with an adequate description of what is going on. If I cannot obtain a satisfactory measurement in one way, another way might do. It is a matter of my practice, as well as overcoming my ignorance. Any real change, therefore, will be in my mind, not in the measured reality itself. The disjunction between physical reality in the quantum world and my involvement in it is precisely my problem, according to this line of interpretation. Polkinghorne notes that this position is a kind of idealism. This is partly so. I would argue more that it is after the fashion of a sterile pragmatism, concerned not so much with reality as with results. In either view, the point of physics as inquiry into an "external" world is denied and ultimate inquiry is demoted to psychology or, at best, an anti-metaphysical epistemology.

A second answer, known as the Copenhagen Interpretation, presses just a bit further than the first. Copenhagenists (after Neils Bohr) believe that the Quantum theory does not permit the option of believing that unobserved entities possess their own attributes. In fact, they claim that such attributes prior to measurement are nonexistent. In such a way the Copenhagenists take as a central clue the Uncertainty Principle. Attributes are measurement-dependent. Therefore, whatever knowledge may be established about any microcosmic event, it is established at the stage of measurement, once the objects "get large" under the intervention of a classical measuring apparatus. The Copenhagen Interpretation cannot explain how the apparatus *chooses* one history over another; the best the Copenhagenists can say is that this simply happens. Ontologically, the implications are perhaps shocking. The use of classical instruments (which is our only choice!) divides the world into the "uncertain quantum world and the objectifying world of measuring instruments."[28] Indeed, Copenhagenists maintain, as it were, that the quantum world therefore is objective but objectless; the only "hard fact" is the measuring device itself.[29] This is the Copenhagen Interpretation at its most modest. There are, however, two interpretive positions which elaborate upon this.

A stronger Copenhagen view holds that it is not the apparatus which so defines the result as it is the observer. The end of wave-packet collapse is supposed here as the very observer who peeked into the cat's box. But this is also the intervention of an agency altogether different from the preceding possibilities. Proponents of this school of observer-created reality maintain that by one's choice of what attributes one looks for, one thus chooses what attributes a system may seem to possess. Eugene Wigner is a proponent of this view, as well as John Wheeler (though he has become a proponent of a stronger view yet). Observer-created reality may be capsulized in a maxim from Wheeler. "No elementary phenomenon is a real phenomenon until it is an observed phenomenon."[30]

When combined with a strong form of the Anthropic Principle (the scientific agreement that large-scale number coincidences within but seconds of the Big Bang can eventuate into only this kind of self-cognizing universe *vis-à-vis* humankind),[31] this observer-created reality position is stretched into a "consciousness-created reality" position, the philosophical consequences of which are even wilder. Those who maintain a consciousness-created reality stance differ from the observer-created reality folk inasmuch as an inanimate object—like a computer—rather than a sentient being may also be the observer. The observer creates the reality by choosing what kinds of attributes to measure. But "consciousness-created reality" goes a step further in arguing that it is consciousness which actually decides what game to play; consciousness "creates reality" by deciding "what particular attribute shall materialize."[32] This position maintains that when attributes are not observed they exist as an objective but objectless superposition of possibilities which acquire definition only when consciously observed. This quantum reality suggests that most of the universe most of the time dwells in a half-real limbo of possibility waiting for a conscious observer to make it fully real. John Wheeler has labeled the observer in this interaction with the observed in the microscopic realm as "participator." A striking consequence of this may be that we may be said, in a *specific sense*, to influence the primordial history of the universe by the way we presently measure the primordial photons from the Big Bang. Polkinghorne appropriately cautions against overexcitement with Wheeler's Participatory Anthropic Principle (PAP), however. The gap between asserting the precise location of an electron and the claim that an observer-participant is required to bring the electron into being is a chasmic claim, if not fanciful, indeed.[33] These positions of the observer-created and the consciousness-created schools have about them the undeniable air of Berkeleyan Idealism, as well as a self-confident anthropocentrism. One would think that careful attention to the implications would make it an untenable position, as many have noted.[34] We shall see some example, below, however, how it is yet a seemingly lively position, with much homiletical (if not truth) value, even when, as Polkinghorne states, "quantum theory does not approve the idea of an observer-created world."[35]

A final course of those interpretive positions that enjoy the most popularity today is the "many worlds interpretation" of Hugh Everett III. He proposed that of every possibility in an event's superposition ALL of them are made real, though only one observed, when the observation takes place. What is attractive about Everett's proposal is that it seems to solve the measurement problem with no "arbitrary canonization of the process of measurement." Indeed, there are no measurements at all, but only correlations between observer and observed world and numerous unobservable parallel worlds.[36] Of course, that this ever expanding thicket of conflicting possibilities and parallel universes may be described mathematically does not necessarily commend its practical value. It finally lacks the appeal of economy and elegance that adheres to sound science.

All of these positions, naturally, may be modified, particularly if they are blended with other quantum themes like non-Boolean logic and Bell's theorem of non-locality, which suggests that every electron's spin is connected however globally to the converse situation of another. With attention to such themes, many physicists argue the undivided wholeness of all the physical order, despite the incredible seeming discreetness of the quantum level. Others finally go the easy way and adopt a neo-realism, claiming that because every experiment must be described in classical language that reality itself is ordinary too.[37] And others, like Heisenberg, may assume the converse of neo-realism and say that unmeasured quantum attributes are just what they are, objective though unrealized possibilities. Those who would deny any deep reality were put on the defensive by the proof of Bell's theorem, however, so that most now do affirm an objective reality on a global scale, distinct—though not separate from—the cognizing observer. Despite the array of quantum interpretive options, this fairly settles the intelligibility of this "idiosyncratic reality,"[38] while equally giving evidence to the amazing openness the quantum world has within itself.

It would seem, then, that the most common epistemological denominator which can be employed to characterize the soft consensus just surveyed is Critical Realism, to which I alluded above. I take the term "Critical Realism" from Arthur Peacocke and numerous others who are comfortable in this station.[39] By it I mean to deny the viability of sheer Realism, on one hand, that would simplistically collapse our interpretations of an object with that object itself and deem it "real." Of course, it is a rare epistemologist since Kant who would hold to such a position. Nevertheless, I cannot affirm a realist position that removes the necessarily metaphorical character in our description of physical events. On the other hand, the option of Idealism seems ill-suited as a minority epistemological position, even if some writers like John Wheeler and Frank Tipler are emphatic in their arguing of it. For all practical purposes, Idealism implies that nothing is real until we subjectively make it so. Along the way instrumentalism (or pragmatism) is also avoided. Of course, there are more exacting ways to define the epistemological options, as Herbert has done, and these are not the sum of them. I paint here only the broad strokes. Critical Realism allows, first, that there is reality, and, second, that this reality is at least "something like" our most refined linguistic approximations of it. These approximations include recognition of the properties of objects and of the role of physical laws. Thus, temporality is included in a Critical Realist perspective as well. Faced with the alternatives of Realism, Idealism, Instrumentalism, or Platonism and more, it seems to me this is the most cautious, as well as common—and fruitful—way to go.

Further Implications of Quantum Theory

With but a bit more attention to the additional themes of wholism, temporal irreversibility and the novelty of the future, as suggested by quantum cosmology, we will have completed this brief and basic survey of contemporary physical theory and can finally turn toward general implications for the relationship between time and eternity which concerns us, and to consideration of the unique use of these themes made by three different physicist-interpreters.

I noted above that one clear consequence of quantum theory is that it posits an intimate relationship between energy and time. Does this mean that spacetime might be quantized in the microscopic world as are other energy "packets"? The possibility, though subject to much debate, seems not to be discounted.[40] However, one may only theorize; the instrumentation required experimentally and adequately to try the question is financially unfeasible to procure. There are some observable consequences of the quantum vacuum in atomic and nuclear physics, however, which may have some indirect bearing on the question. Many theorists posit a vacuum in this infinitesimal region which contains some minimum concentration of energy which might accumulate into short-lived unobservable particles. The energies, or masses, of these particles and their lifetimes must obey the Uncertainty Principle. Such behavior is called a quantum vacuum fluctuation. A strange feature of this fluctuation is that brief violations of the law of conservation of energy are allowed. A system's energy may briefly go "into debt" so rapidly that it could never be detected within the limits of the Uncertainty Principle.[41] These effects indeed are said to be quite significant in the very early universe. Wheeler gives these imagined phenomena the fanciful term of "quantum foam," and speculates there that the curvature of space-time can assume an array of weird shapes. The short distances involved (10^{-33}cm) in these tiny regions may finally render time in an ultimate sense to be a meaningless concept, where the concepts of "before" and "after" are totally broken down.[42]

Once again, though, it is helpful to invoke Polkinghorne's caution. "Before" and "after" do make consummate sense when one makes successive series of measurements, which is rather all one can do. The delicate unpredictability of complex dynamical systems is a fundamental and perhaps wonderful assertion about the way things are.[43] But one may also infer thereby–and this is most significant–that there is at the root of reality an openness to the future, and a future which is radically open.

The inability to specify beforehand the result of a quantum measurement implies an openness to the future built into the structure of the world at its constituent roots. In between acts of measurement a quantum mechanical system is represented by a smoothly evolving wave function, which is an expression of potentiality (that is to say, it contains within itself the possibility of various outcomes), rather than the specification of actuality (which would imply a precise and pictureable representation of where the system is and what it is doing). Thus quantum theory does not encourage the view that time is an illusion. Successive acts of measurement bring about genuinely new states of the system.[44]

Such openness at "the root of reality," so that genuine novelty can and does occur, is underscored by time's arrow and the creative function of chaos. Recent developments in the study of thermodynamics seem to underscore the ultimacy of temporal irreversibility. The work of Ilya Prigogine and Isabelle Stengers[45] suggests that as dissipative systems are driven from thermodynamic equilibrium new and more complicated states of order appear. Furthermore, Prigogine claims that new thermodynamical orders cannot be subject to a statistical reductionism of initial conditions. New and divergent physical systems may evolve from the same set of initial conditions and exhibit the irreducible character of emergence, of which Arthur Peacocke writes.[46] Clearly, new states of order do arise from dissipative systems, but one must contend yet with the overall correlative increase of entropy as new orders arise. This correspondence, nonetheless, underscores the sense of direction in time. Temporal irreversibility, consequently, cannot be explained merely as the product of human subjectivity. A consciousness-created world is all the more undercut by the laws of thermodynamics and creative dissipative systems. Nor, as Ted Peters observes, are we superimposing "a mental idea of time on an otherwise timeless natural world."[47] As Ilya Prigogine writes in a now famous quote, "We are becoming more and more conscious of the fact that on all levels, from elementary particles to cosmology, randomness and irreversibility play an ever-increasing role...*Science is rediscovering time.*"[48]

And while science is rediscovering time, it is also finding that the anti-reductionistic modes of explanation, such as sought by Prigogine and Peacocke warrant a principle of wholism. Of course, underlying processes of relativity and quantum collapses emerge into something no longer so discrete under the continuity enhancing rubric of the Schrödinger equations,[49] at least in principle. At the stage of continuity, then, experience is inadequately described when reduced solely to quantum mechanical description (which, of course, is motivation for searching for a grand unification theory). But as the chain of consequence grows into a thermodynamical system wherein chemical and biological laws are added, qualitatively new factors enter the picture, such that no explanation is adequate which refers only to the components of that new system. The whole system will have its own appropriate new level of description. It must be treated in terms of an understanding of "top-down" causation, or better, according to a principle of wholism. Furthermore, as Ted Peters observes, there is more than anti-reductionism being asserted here.

> Wholism recognizes that the higher levels of systems organization and even the level of individuality in living selves act *downward* on the lower physical processes, thus pressing these processes into the service of the higher level ends. Water molecules remain what they are even when whirled about by a vortex. Metabolism remains what it is, even though a person's decision either to play tennis or go to sleep will have an impact on its rate.[50]

We should note, too, that even quantum phenomena at their "own" level warrant wholistic description. Whereas it is so that quantum statistics call for a discrete style of interpretation, the interpenetrability of their fields of interaction and their cohesiveness also require a complementary wholistic description strikingly different from classical systems.[51] Robert John Russell observes that "nature reveals a highly non-local and wholistic character at the quantum level which is strikingly different from the separability of nature in our ordinary experience."[52] The wholistic principle, finally, will not be contradicted by component descriptions appropriate to lower levels of the system. They are complementary and valid at their own levels, as Paul Davies notes.[53]

Since we have been reflecting on wholism, we have yet to ask, finally, how these themes might come together in "the next level up." That is, what are the cosmological models that would include these (and of course more) concerns? The "standard" model, of course, of which many lay people are aware, is the model of an expanding universe which began with the Big Bang some fifteen billion years ago. There is much agreement, too, that the universe is like the surface of an expanding balloon, wherein all matter is rushing away from each other as well as away from its originating singularity. The Hubble redshift, the detection of remnant microwave radiation from the Big Bang and the recent COBE observation of gaseous residue at the "edge" of the universe seem to confirm this model. There are, nevertheless, other possible ways of construing the universe which must be taken into account. They ultimately impinge upon questions of causality, temporality, and eternity which concern us.

Robert John Russell lists eight types of cosmological models derived from General Relativity according to criteria of time, space, and topology (whether open or closed), and by them shows that no model but the standard closed (Big Bang) model would display both spatial and temporal finitude.[54] Yet even in the standard model, the possibility of universal collapse and re-explosion again suggests a cyclic infinity in which time would still carry on. Russell's point, however, is that no direct one to one correspondence can be drawn between finitude in physical models and finitude in theology. What is more likely achievable is recognition of some consonance, and not without dissonance, at a more abstract level. It is a warning that should be heard by physicists as well as theologians.

To conclude, in this chapter I have tried to summarize, however non-scientifically, relativity theory. Therein we rehearsed how interconnected are time, mass and velocity. We noted how space-time is conceived now as part of the four-dimensional matrix. With the quantum theory, I turned to its themes of complementarity, indeterminacy, observership and its differing interpretations, and quantum logic. Along the way I also noted the pertinent matters of the Anthropic Principle, Bell's Theorem of non-locality, and the problems inherent to an Idealist perspective in physics. We also discovered something about the micro-universe's seeming openness "down deep" to the future, and touched upon temporal irreversibility and wholism. Finally, I made brief comment about the variety of cosmological models available to us as descriptions of the universe.

In short space we have touched upon a great deal. It should also be clear that there are many ways in which physical cosmologists would gather this material into a particular metaphysical vision. This material is open to a variety of interpretations. The agenda for the theologian who desires to marshall this information responsibly into a resource for theology must be, therefore, to look for commonality. The novice cannot be too hasty in assuming what even the experts call premature.[55] With that caution in mind, then, I would turn now to the disparate interpretations given by three different contemporary physical cosmologists. In their varied use of the same data, as well as in their use of material that will be new to this discussion, we should be able to find at least some shared turf. My hope is that by finding some commonality of perspective with regard to time and eternity, we might then seek to incorporate that scientific commonality to inform a properly Christian theological interpretation in chapter 7.

Notes

1. Within this storehouse, I would draw attention to the following resources. Fagg, *The Two Faces of Time* (Boston: Shambhala, 1988); John Polkinghorne, *Science and Providence, God's Interaction With the World* (Boston: Shambhala, 1989); *One World–The Interaction of Science and Theology* (Princeton: Princeton University Press, 1986); *Science and Creation–The Search For Understanding* (Boston: Shambhala, 1989); *The Quantum World* (Princeton: Princeton University Press, 1984); Albert Einstein, *The Principle of Relativity*, trans. by W. Perrett and G.B. Jefferey (New York:Dover, 1952); Bertrand Russell, *The ABC of Relativity* (New York: New American Library, 1962); Holmes Ralston III, *Science and Religion, A Critical Survey* (New York: Random House, 1987); A.P. French (ed.), *Einstein - A Centenary Volume* (Cambridge: Harvard University Press, 1979); Ian Barbour, *Issues in Science and Religion* (New York: Harper and Row, 1966); Abraham Pais, *"Subtle Is The Lord"…,The Science and Life of Albert Einstein* (Oxford: Oxford University Press, 1982); Nigel Calder, *Einstein's Universe* (New York: Viking, 1979); Banesh Hoffmann, *The Strange Story of the Quantum* (New York: Dover, 1959); Paul Davies, *God and the New Physics* (New York: Simon and Schuster, 1983); Heinz Pagels, *The Cosmic Code, Quantum Physics and the Language of Nature* (New York: Simon and Schuster, 1982); Ken Wilbur (ed.), *Quantum Questions, Mystical Writings of the World's Great Physicists* (Boston: Shambhala, 1985); Arthur Peacocke, *Creation and the World of Science* (Oxford: Oxford University Press, 1979); John D. Barrow and Frank J. Tipler, *The Anthropic Cosmological Principle* (New York: Oxford University Press, 1986).

2. I am indebted here to the descriptions provided by Fagg; John Polkinghorne, *The Quantum World*, Princeton Science Library edition (Princeton: Princeton University Press, 1989); and G.F.R. Ellis and W.R.Stoeger, "Introduction to General Relativity and Cosmology," one of the contributions to Robert John Russel, Nancey Murphy and William Stoeger, S.J. eds., *Quantum Cosmology and the Laws of Nature* (Vatican City: Vatican Observatory, 1993), hereafter noted as *QCLN*.

3. Nigel Calder, *Einstein's Universe* (New York: Viking, 1979), 105-6.

4. Einstein, as recorded in Pais, 141.

5. Fagg, 12.

6. Pais, 141.

7. See Arthur Peacocke, "The Theory of Relativity and Our World View," *Old and New Questions in Physics, Cosmology, Philosophy and Theoretical Biology*, Alwyn van der Merwe, ed. (New York: Plenum, 1983), 733-752. Also helpful as differing examples of interpretation of relativity theory are Hans Reichenbach, "The Philosophical Significance of The Theory of Relativity" and Aloys Wenzyl, "Einstein's Theory of Relativity, Viewed From The Standpoint of Critical Realism, and Its Significance for Philosophy." Both essays are in Paul Schilp (ed.), *Albert Einstein: Philosopher-Scientist* (New York: Tudor, 1957), 288-311, 582-606.

8. Fagg, 15.

9. See John Boslough, "The Enigma of Time," *National Geographic*, 177:3 (March, 1990), 109-132.

10. Ellis and Stoeger, 5.

11. Fagg, 21. Also see Fraser, 475.

12. Isham, "Creation As A Quantum Process," Robert John Russel and William Stoeger, S.J. eds., *Physics, Philosophy and Theology* (Vatican City: Vatican Observatory, 1991), 391; hereafter referred to as *PPT*.

13. Ellis and Stoeger, 6.

14. Misner, as quoted by Robert John Russell, "Cosmology, Creation and Contingency," Peters (ed.) *Cosmos As Creation*, 182-3. "Space tells matter how to move; matter tells space how to curve." See Misner, Thorne and Wheeler, *Gravitation* (San Francisco: W.H. Freeman and Co., 1973), 5.

15. Arthur Peacocke, "Theology and Science Today," *Cosmos As Creation*, 33. "Time in modern relativistic physics is an integral and basic aspect of nature. Space and time have to be mutually defined in interlocking relations and both are related to definitions of mass and energy, themselves interconvertible. So matter, energy, and space-time constitute the created order. Hence, on any theistic view, time itself has to be regarded as owing its existence to God, something Augustine long ago perceived."

16. Heinz Pagels, 78-9.

17. This summary follows Fagg, 24-30.

18. Polkinghorne, *The Quantum World*, 53.

19. I am indebted to Robert John Russell for making clear to me in private discussion these distinct trends of ontological interpretation within the physicist community.

20. I will discuss the matter of Critical Realism more concertedly in the latter part of this chapter.

21. Planck's constant refers to the number which specifies the amount of discreteness of matter, i.e., the "size" of an electron.

22. Fagg, 31.

23. I am indebted to John Polkinghorne for his telling of the tale; likewise with the recounting of Wigner's friend. See *The Quantum World*, 62.

24. It seems to me, however, that one flaw of this story is that the addition of Wigner to the chain of consequence means that the wave packet collapse has Wigner's friend's involvement in it, which would seem to constitute a different "wave-packet." The sound of Wigner's friend's affirmation that the click was at A is added to the sound of the click at A. Nevertheless, the question as to where "judgement" is made is still well pressed by the example.

25. Nick Herbert, *Quantum Reality* (Garden City: Anchor/Doubleday, 1987), 151.

26. Polkinghorne, 63-8.

27. Herbert, 157-197.

28. Polkinghorne, 64.

29. Herbert, 162. Herbert provides the helpful example of a rainbow as something that is objective but not an object. The rainbow appears in a different place for each observer; each sees a slightly different rainbow. Yet it can be photographed. It is an objective phenomenon. An electron's attributes are said to be a similar illusion...until it is "photographed." In other words, "an electron's attributes do not belong to the electron itself but are a kind of illusion produced by the electron plus 'the entire experimental arrangement.'

30. Herbert, 164.

31. There are numerous resources available with reference to the Anthropic Principle. The magisterial primary source is John Barrow and Frank Tipler, *The Anthropic Cosmological Principle* (New York: Oxford University Press, 1986).

32. Herbert, 192.

33. John Polkinghorne, "The Quantum World," *PPT*, 341. "Quantum theory does not approve the idea of an observer-created world. To be sure, the quantum act of measurement involves a subtle, and incompletely understood, interaction between the means of observation and the system observed. The consequences are, however, strictly limited according to the potentiality available to be made actual. It is another example of the unjustified typing of quantum mechanical insight to proceed from this to extravagant claims such as John Wheeler's Participatory Anthropic Principle (PAP): Observers are necessary to bring the world into being. The gap between saying that the act of measurement determines whether an electron is 'here' or 'there' and the stupendous claim of the PAP seems to me to be quite unbridgeable. I cannot see any legitimate grounds for being as friendly toward this fanciful assertion as John Barrow and Frank Tipler seem to be in their discussion of the matter." See *The Anthropic Cosmological Principle*, ch. 7.

34. See Herbert, 193ff. Polkinghorne writes with characteristic forthrightness. "Are we to suppose that in the thousands of millions of years before conscious life emerged in the world—and still today in those extensive parts of the universe where no conscious life has yet developed—no wavepacket has ever collapsed, no atom for certain decayed? That quantum mechanics as we know it is a biologically induced phenomenon? That photographic plates stored away uninspected at the end of an experiment only acquire a definite image when someone opens the drawer to have a look at them? It takes a bit of swallowing." *The Quantum World*, 66.

35. "The Quantum World," in *PPT*, 341.

36. Herbert, 174.

37. Such is the attempt, though he clearly swims against the current, of G. Cavalleri of Italy, who claims that all relative motion and quantum phenomena can be adequately described in classical terms. Unpublished paper delivered at the European Society for the Study of Science and Theology (ESSSAT), Rome, Italy, March, 1992.

38. So Polkinghorne, "The Quantum World,"*PPT*, 341.

39. Much has been written on the theme of Critical Realism. See, e.g., the significant piece by Arthur Peacocke, *Intimations of Reality, Critical Realism in Science and Religion* (Notre Dame: University of Notre Dame Press, 1984), as well as most of Peacocke's other work. Especially helpful are the papers from the 1986 symposium on the Critical Realism of Arthur Peacocke, sponsored by the Center for Theology and the Natural Sciences, Berkeley, CA.

40. Fagg, 38.

41. Ian Barbour, "Creation and Cosmology," The McNair Lectures, Univ. of North Carolina, 1985, 14. Barbour lists quantum vacuum fluctuations as one of four theories; the others being the "many cycles," "many domains" and "many quantum worlds,"–which would explain the combination of constants favorable to emergence of life in the universe as stipulated in the Anthropic Principle. In any of these, whether cyclic or linear, time is imagined as of infinite length. Infinity is not, of course, the same as eternity, however.

42. Fagg, 31-41.

43. Polkinghorne, *Science and Providence*, 28f.

44. Polkinghorne, 78; see especially 77-84.

45. Ilya Prigogine and Isabelle Stengers, *Order Out of Chaos* (New York: Bantam, 1984).

46. Arthur Peacocke, *Creation and the World of Science* (Oxford: Clarendon Press, 1979) 92-103, 112-118.

47. Peters, *God As Trinity*, 161.

48. Prigogine and Stengers, xxviii.

49. In 1926 Erwin Schrödinger devised an equation that de Broglie's electron wave would have to obey if the electron were part of an hydrogen atom. This equation confirmed the light spectrum of hydrogen which Bohr had found earlier. Thus the notion that matter could be a wave was established. See Pagels, 79.

50. Peters, *God As Trinity*, 169.

51. See Robert John Russell, "Quantum Physics in Philosophical and Theological Perspective," in *PPT*, 345.

52. Russell, 348.

53. *God and the New Physics* (New York: Simon and Schuster, 1983), 62; quoted by Peters, 169.

54. "Cosmology, Creation and Contingency," in Peters, ed., *Cosmos As Creation*, 184-196. Russell lists 7 models which are consistent with general relativity. Model I has a finite past (fp), finite future (ff) and finite space (fs), called the "closed" (or standard) model. II , a closed "hesitation" model, is fp, infinite future (if) and fs. III, closed, is ip, ff & fs. IV, closed "turnaround," is ip, if & fs. V, open–standard, is fp, if & is. VI, open, is ip, ff & is. VII, open, if fp, ff & is. VIII, finally, Fred Hoyle's homogenous open "steady state" model, is ip, if & is. Willem Drees, too, *Beyond the Big Bang, Quantum Cosmologies and God* (La Salle: Open Court, 1990), surveys different current cosmological models, particularly by way of the research programs of Linde, Hawking, and Penrose. But his discussion is not as systematically focused as Russell's.

55. Christopher Isham issues such a warning in his "Creation of the Universe As A Quantum Process," in *QCLN*.

V

Three Cosmologists

There is no one orthodox philosophical interpretation of the laws of contemporary physics, as we saw in the previous chapter. While major themes, such as the so-called Big Bang theory, may be shared by distinct genres of interpretation, such themes assume distinctive colors when filtered through the lenses of each school of thought. The coalescence of Quantum physics and chaos theory in one epistemological school of thought, such as Instrumentalism, may lead to the conclusion that there is no such thing as an independent reality; in a school of thought that holds to the most thoroughgoing Idealism imaginable, one may find a "Many Worlds Realism" which has, quite literally, become the stuff of science-fiction.[1] This underscores the multi-valence of the major physical theories we have discussed. Simultaneously, we have spoken in generalities so far regarding the philosophical interpretation of the scientific themes that have emerged in this century. But must we suppose that the post-modern phenomenon of pluralism affects the natural sciences as much as it affects all other human inquiry today? Are we to concede that the impossibility of pure objectivity on the part of the sciences yields only the deconstructive and non-foundationalist claim that nothing is objective whatsoever? Clearly, that has not been my argument in the previous chapter. If even only of a straw poll character, the general agreement on Critical Realism emphasizes that the sciences assume more than a modicum of credibility in their claims to genuine referentiality.

But how far does agreement extend in the scientific community? What might the non-scientist presume were she interested in recounting the "scientific" picture of large-scale reality, especially were she interested in plumbing its implications for theology? As I have said before, one must always be careful in translating scientific discourse into a theological context of interpretation, not only because terms, of course, have their idiosyncratic assignments of meaning within given communities, but because the nature of the scientific enterprise itself is always tentative. Today's well-established theories can easily become tomorrow's quaint notions with but the discovery of one datum that counters previous thinking. A lay, and especially a theological, appropriation of scientifc perspectives, then, is always to be accompanied with some tentativeness. Theological proposals that incorporate scientifc concerns must themselves have a certain looseness about them if they are to be sustained. But that is not to discourage any attentiveness to the sciences whatsoever. It is, rather, to encourage theologians to attempt carefully to assay the commonality of interpretations among particular scientists themselves. We cannot, in other words, only look to general schools of interpretation of the sciences, such as we might find in secondary sources; we must look to their use by individual researchers as well, researchers whose own work has been held to more than occasional scrutiny by their own peers.

Such is the task of this chapter, though hardly so thoroughly as we would like. By attending to three different physical cosmologists, each indeed quite distinctive, we seek to note the common in spite of the differences. The first, Andrej A. Grib, is not well known to the West, and is also idiosyncratic in his own context of the Russian scientific community. But he has emerged as a fascinating partner in the explicit theology/natural science dialogue, tapped by the Templeton Foundation, as well as by other reputable groups, to speak on the connections such as we have been considering. His uniqueness is certain, but precisely because of that, what commonality we may establish between him and others regarding the philosophical and theological interpretation of physical theory marks him as a useful resource for our purposes. At the other end of a threefold spectrum I will engage is Stephen Hawking, the famous occupant of the Lucasian chair at Cambridge. His notariety in the popular culture, as well as in the scientifc community, commends him for our survey, especially as, at first glance, one might suppose that his agnosticism (if not atheism) would mitigate anything he might have in common with someone like Grib. I hope to show that the case is indeed quite otherwise. Finally, Christopher Isham, another British physicist of more moderate tones than either Hawking or Grib, may provide a careful underscoring of themes we find shared elsewhere. At the end of this chapter, then, I will propose tentative theses as to what theology might rightly garner from physics in general and these scientists in particular with respect to cosmology and the relationship of time and eternity.

Andrej A. Grib

One contemporary physicist who is concerned with describing a coherent relationship between eternity and temporality is Andrej A. Grib, director of the Friedmann Laboratory, St. Petersburg, Russia. His work exemplifies with mystical Russian Orthodox timbre a religious, radical Copenhagenist interpretation, which finally seems to adopt an Idealist philosophy. Because Grib's thought so clearly evidences his own religious passion, his work may appear the more peculiar within the specifically scientific domain and is thus likely to lead to some confusion—as some would perceive—of religious fervor with scientific rationality. Nevertheless, his is a unique voice in the theology-science dialogue. It serves, however unclear his argument may be, as a distinct mode of interpretation of commonly shared physical data and as an example of an attempt to pose science and theology as mutually informative. To be sure, this is not to characterize Grib's work as mostly subjective. Grib intends to develop an objectivist justification for his platform, though, for the above stated reasons, it is not yet altogether successful. It would be fairer, therefore, to describe his work as in transition, and to outline tendencies in his thought, rather than to treat it as a completed corpus and amenable to clear categorization.

Grib maintains that classical and quantum relativistic cosmologies have certain perspectives which invite new images of the relationship between eternity and temporality.[2] As a first consequence of the general and special theories of relativity, which establish the four-dimensional space/time matrix, Grib argues the existence of at least a "semi" block universe.[3] I attribute "semi" to his block universe because he claims a fixity only for the present and past. For Grib, the future appears to be at least undetermined, if not unreal. In a block-universe time/space events are, whether past or present, as it were, *real things* which still exist, even if unaccessible to present human experience. Grib believes this idea is already inherent in Augustine's argument that time is created by God. Grib argues this position by greatly emphasizing the fallaciousness of the alternative, as he sees it, of a "flashing universe," in which events epiphenomenally happen and then are annihilated forever, never to be retrieved. A flashing universe is one in which there is only the immediate present; we are surrounded by "nothingness." Past and future do not exist, except as illusion in the human mind. Descartes held a version of this, arguing that God recreated all the universe every moment so that it would "look" stable. In a flashing universe there would be all sorts of things that we should not see but still do, such as the light from a distant star. Thus Grib argues the non-viability of this view, even though there are many who argue for the unreality of the past (Bertrand Russell, Herbert Spencer, et al.). Relativity theory, Grib believes, abandons this point of view.[4] He adds that the moral implications of a flashing universe, in which there are no consequences to actions, are not acceptable, either.

So Grib argues for a semi-block universe. Space-time events are themselves created in such a way that the "past" exists in the same way as the present. Thus, physical description is given for what Augustine speaks of as the "present past," "present present," and "present future." But while Augustine was writing about the mind's role in the depiction of temporality, the suggestion here is that this is not only a concern of subjective consciousness. The upshot is that the past exists in a block universe in much the same way that Rome exists even if I don't see it. Again, looking at the stars is an apt example, for what we see there is the emanation of light from a source which may not exist at all in this present moment. We see only a star's history. Therefore, Grib argues, the prime implication of relativity theory is that a past event is truly a present event when an observer is able to stand within that event's light cone. But not only that. Grib clearly means to say, as well, that relativity theory implies a fixed matrix wherein space/time events are *always* situated, even when not observed. Relativity theory, for Grib, establishes an "eternal present." This "finite eternity," as he calls it, is the foundational metaphysical construct for his ontology.

So past events exist. The only difference from present events is that humans can exercise no agency over past events. They have special time/space coordinates which are no longer in the coordinate frame of the observer. Thus, *they are*. So Grib:

> All people whom we call *dead* are alive because this life being finite nevertheless is 'eternal' where 'eternal' means that events can't be annihilated. The four-dimensional Universe is full of smiles, cries, deeds, crimes which constitute an overgrowing 'event continuum' looking like a growing crystal with our movement towards the future.[5]

Grib here appeals to the Russian Orthodox theology of L. Karsavin to indicate how one might stand in a certain light cone, coordinated with all space-time events of his/her life.[6] If one could be so coordinated, that person would see all of her life as a kind of jet stream before her. This, declares Grib, is immortality. Of course, no one is able to be so coordinated. Therefore, human experience is of temporality, not eternity. Where, and how, one can stand in the light cone of one's life makes all the difference. The difference between temporality and eternity, in Grib's perspective, is one of place and observation. "Eternal," then, would signify that point of observation whereby the whole four-dimensional matrix would be seen all "at once" as an "all unity." This understanding, of course, aligns with Boethius's notion of eternity. From a relativistic point of view, then, human beings are four-dimensional creatures with a "jet stream" of past events trailing the moving frontier of the present. Grib could affirm, in other words, that Picasso's paintings of three headed people are realistic. To change the metaphor, events grow in time, like a tree. While observers at the top branches may see their world as only one branch, or even as only a budding leaf, all that they were in coming to branch and bud is still real, though unseen.

So why don't humans see this or feel this, except in subjective fashion and with, perhaps, an appeal to William James's concept of the specious present? First, Grib wants philosophically to argue—e.g., with Bergson and against

Augustine—that memory is not a consciousness of brain imprints, but of the events themselves as they are in four dimensions.[7] Secondly, we don't see the past because the universe is simply too large and too empty. The universe is composed of only a very small amount of matter (and invisible matter, at that. Grib does not take into account the contemporary arguments for dark matter, though they would seem to support his argument). So there are, practically speaking, no "mirrors" by which light rays might be reflected back into our line of sight.[8] "Again, it is the peculiar structure of our Universe (it is too large and too empty to reflect rays of our past) that we don't see our past. That is why we don't feel ourselves as four dimensional creatures with the 'jet of past events,' but only see three dimensional projections moving into the future."[9] Light rays from our past go into space and disappear into its "dark abyss."

So far Grib's universe blocks the present and past, and he seems to (or he wants to) give it an objective ontological status. But Grib gives equal weight to the role of the observer, and this mitigates the objective consistency he perceives in classical relativity. Two arguments derived from the quantum side of Grib's reflection weight him more toward subjectivism. They are his adoption of the strongest Copenhagen interpretation of quantum theory and the description of the logic of the quantum universe as non-Boolean.[10]

Grib begins with what he admits is a "trivial analysis" of quantum measurement. But the consequences quickly become epistemologically and theologically significant. He acknowledges, as we already well know, that one cannot speak about the existence of properties in a quantum system if they are not observed. It is still so, in the absence of measurement, that there is a deterministic evolution according to the Schrödinger equation, but from those determined parameters the actualized state of affairs brought about by a measurement is thus contingent; reality, out of its possibilities, is contingent upon observership. To put it otherwise, the wave-function collapse is due to the observer's making it so. At the collapse of a wave-function—i.e., by observation—history becomes real. This is the Copenhagen interpretation at its strongest. Though he is not explicit about it, Grib seems to adopt John Wheeler's Participatory Anthropic Principle here without compromise. Grib concludes that it is bad language to speak of a "self-originating Universe." Rather, the Universe is really 'created' from nothing (a vacuum state) by some external observer who made a 'choice' to measure this and not that of complementary observables. Arguing stronger still, Grib states that the contingency of the universe is properly a "subjective contingency." That is, its existence depends upon the agency of an observer.

One must be very careful with the phrase 'contingent Universe'. Although it is true that contingency in quantum theory is not due to lack of any information by the observer, nevertheless, it is not an *objective contingency* because it arises only from the act of making measurements. In the absence of any measurement we have a deterministic evolution, due to the Schrödinger equation. So it is not correct to say that the Universe could arise 'by chance' from some nothingness without any observer (or creator). In this sense, quantum contingency is subjective contingency.[11]

Grib finally moves to claim that in quantum cosmology the observer possesses an explicit creative agency. The observer is a creator by the very act of observing. This creates the new possibility of defining temporality.

The observer creates a quasi-classical wave function for gravity and for some fundamental matter fields (in simple models this is often taken to be some scalar field that can generate an inflationary expansion). Because of the quasi-classical nature of this function the possibility arises of defining time for the macroscopic universe and a classical evolution in this time.[12]

But the logic of the human observer does not cohere with the logic of the quantum world. Relying upon the subjective variant of the Copenhagen interpretation, and John von Neumann, Eugene Wigner and others as its proponents,[13] Grib claims that the observer gives a value to the observable not because of any physical interaction describable by the Schrödinger equation, but because of "a special property of consciousness." This special property is that it is distributive (Boolean). That is, observables, according to Boolean logic, are commutable. Boolean logic includes conjunctions and disjunctions that satisfy the law of distributivity. Thus, in Boolean logic, $a \wedge (b \vee c) = (a \wedge b) \vee (a \wedge c)$, where $\wedge$ is '*and*' and v is '*or*." But in a non-Boolean "lattice," in which a particle may assume any spin projection, '*or*' is not so distinct from '*and*.' Herein, $a \wedge (b \vee c)$ does *not* equal $(a \wedge b) \vee (a \wedge c)$. "And-or" is not the same as "either-or;" an electron has rather this or that "spin projection S_z" *and* a "definite projection of S_x," and is still only one particle. Boolean logic is incompatible with this kind of non-Boolean, quantum behavior.[14] The "logic of human consciousness is distributive and Boolean, while the logic of the Universe is non-Boolean."[15]

So how does the Boolean mind grasp a non-Boolean world? Time plays the consequential difference here, and one must "move" within it to ascertain non-Boolean reality.

A very important role is played here by time. A non-Boolean lattice is not isomorphic to a Boolean lattice. This is why, to get information about non-Boolean physical reality, the human mind must 'move' in time, so that at one

moment it sees one Boolean substructure (a set of commuting operators) and at
the next moment it sees another Boolean substructure corresponding to the
operators which did not commute with the previous ones. One could even say
that time is 'invented' by the Boolean mind in order to grasp non-Boolean
reality.[16]

The same procedure applies to noncommuting observables. The observer
again must "move" in time, and thus temporality, or irreversiblity appears.
Either way, the human agent renders the quantum world somehow
comprehensible. For this to be done, it must be translated from one sort of
non-Boolean universe into a space-time universe, and this can happen only by
agency of the observer's choosing to observe. This applies to all past events
as well as present. The past itself is the projection of a non-Boolean structure
upon the Boolean mind, which is to say that the continuity of the past is a
continuity because it is always "now" for each human consciousness when the
measurement (wave function collapse) occurs. Grib concludes,

If the Universe has a quantum non-Boolean structure it cannot be a universe of
space and time. Events appear only because of measurements. For example, the
Minkowsky spacetime of conventional special relativity has the structure of a
Boolean set. Without an observer there are no events.[17]

Thus, Grib wants to argue thus far, there is an objective ontological status
to the past and present. In fact, the logic of Grib's position drives one to
positing that there is no such thing as the past. There is only the present,
however unobservable. It "exists," however, in a non-Boolean state. It is
subjectivized into reality by the agency of the Boolean observer. In such
fashion Grib attempts to link a definite ontology with the tentativeness of
human experience, which, for Grib, is to discover the articulated connection
between classical relativity and quantum cosmology. It also seems to be the
explanation by which human beings render what "already" is "eternal"
(noncommutable) into the temporal (commutable).

Indeed, Grib agrees that the property of time as becoming is absent in
classical special and general relativity. It is when we turn to the quantum
world that we may describe the non-Boolean lattice of *'objectively existing'
potentialities*[18] as potentialities which "become" events by the translative
agency of the Boolean consciousness that gives truth values to elements of the
lattice. Time, therefore, is a human construct in quantum cosmology.
Quantum cosmology, Grib avers, has no time inherent to it; it is a kind of
"physics of eternity."[19] Yet, it is a matter of the observer's choice.

Quasi-classical wave function, being complex, leads to the possibility of defining
'time'. So 'time' is created by the Observer. The Hartle-Hawking wave function,

being real, doesn't lead to time and it must be 'collapsed' into a complex value
function after which time appears. This 'collapse' is due to the observation. Time
in quantum cosmology is some internal parameter of the block-Universe.
Different wave-functions lead to different 'times' (for example, imaginary) or no
'time' at all, when there are 3-spaces not ordered in time.[20]

So if the property even of "being in time" is created by the Boolean
observer in this block-universe, the question arises, when does this happen?
In Grib's program, as I noted above, the conjecture is made that the choice
is 'now;' it is a 'now' which is in eternity, and it is by this 'now' that we have
'becoming.' The difference between the past and the future, then, is that "the
past is defined as that Boolean set of events which can't be changed in this
choice of defining time, but the future is still open for choice." And what is
open for choice is that "objectively existing" set of potentialities in the non-
Boolean world.

It should be evident by this point that Grib has a particular agenda in mind
in his choice of the nomenclature of observership. Relying upon the Wigner's
Friend paradox in the Copenhagen interpretation of quantum cosmology,[21]
Grib agrees that the only means by which two different observers can see the
same quantum event is that there be posited the existence of some Ultimate
Observer or Ultimate Subject, who guarantees the continuity of the created
order. Thus, Grib argues, there finally really is "reality" to the quantum
order, as well as the classical relativistic order, because there is an agent
external to the whole process who by observing it guarantees its coherence for
those lesser observers who, like human beings, have at least a "co-creative"
status.[22] And that there be an agency external to the quantum system implies
the need for additional dimensions. Since additional dimensions clearly cannot
be material, Grib calls this ultimate observer "Spirit."[23]

Grib's conclusions may be summarized as follows. First, relativity theory
implies a "finite eternity" to this earthly life. Were one to stand "rightly" in
the light cone of life's events, one would see everything of that life present to
him or her.[24] Second, the special property of human consciousness, its
Boolean logic, leads to our movement in time from present to future and the
appearance of the irreversibility of time. This irreversibility is quantum in its
origin,[25] but it leads to the entropical arrow of time in classical physics.[26]

We may conclude about Grib, further, that time for him is not as
fundamental or even as real a category as eternity, inasmuch as it is Boolean
consciousness which imposes time order on a fundamentally non-Boolean
world. The Kantianism should be evident here. Grib conceives that one of the
transcendental conditions for human reason is a given perception of
temporality which does not exist in the phenomenal realm itself. The Kantian

transcendental condition, it seems, is Boolean, while the phenomenal *ding-an-sich* of the world is non-Boolean. However, Grib turns toward guaranteeing some kind of reality of time by reference to the Ultimate Observer—God—who guarantees such reality for the rest of us real creatures *de novo* and *continua* by God's presumably continuous act of observing. If Grib is philosophically disposed toward Kant, Grib is equally sympathetic with Berkeley.

At this point Grib perhaps betrays the inadequacies of the Copenhagen interpretation, as well as his own method. Stanley Jaki comments that "rank idealism" leads inevitably to the illocutions of solipsism.[27] There can be no genuine agreement within an epistemology—and so an implied ontology—wherein human or divine agency is tantamount to privileged causality. A Participatory Anthropic Principle of the strongest sort would necessarily have to give less logical and causal efficacy to any of those events networked within a particular event's horizon that could give rise, and even purpose, to that one event. Grib's error here, perhaps, is one of methodology. To assume a block universe, for example, as opposed to the only presumed alternative of a flashing universe commits the methodological fallacy of the excluded middle. It is an oversimplification to state that these are the only alternatives available to the physicist. The oversimplification leads Grib away from healthy attention to the possible mediatory role of natural laws. John Polkinghorne comments on the role of law in a weakened version of the Anthropic Principle. Polkinghorne rightly cautions hereby as to the excess of the PAP, an excess Jaki explicitly labels as "gross."[28] The open process of the universe is due not to observer agency solely. The Anthropic Principle recognizes an "astonishing potentiality with which the laws of physics are endowed."[29] Laws are real and have their own kind of agency external to the observer. Even a physicist somewhat more disposed to a positivist accounting of reality speaks positively about this middle-ground of scientific lawfulness. P.C.W. Davies writes:

> Unless one is prepared to retreat into the lonely fastness of solipsism, one has to concede that the discoveries of science reveal that there is *something* orderly about the world, something not totally the result of our imaginings. The very fact that our observations *can* be fitted into mathematical models and algorithms surely tells us something about reality that we had no right to expect a priori.[30]

Surely Grib does not disbelieve the existence and role of laws, but he has not yet provided an adequate accounting of their proper role in the complex dynamic between the observer and the observed. So far, Grib has cast the problem only in terms of the diastasis between the observer and the observed. One wonders whether Grib really intends to affirm such a radical pluralism.

The same sort of fallacy may be committed in Grib's posing of Boolean against non-Boolean logic. Indeed, discrete attention to the epistemological matter of levels of description may avoid reduction to such polar alternatives. Physicists, as well, are careful today even not to pose the epistemological question simply in terms of subject/object (or between the philosophical counterparts of idealism and realism). Deeper research has continually affirmed the gray area between observer and observed, so that the distinction is not so clear as once may have been assumed. On the other hand, one may argue certainly that there appears to be no third alternative to Boolean/non-Boolean logic, once one rules out intuition, and so we may be thrown back again to the fundamental question that evokes the Copenhagen interpretation: "what and where is the confluence of the observer and the observed?".

It may stand as a positive attempt, however, in the domain of the dialogue between theology and natural science, that Grib would offer some physical descriptions for classic Christian "core theories," such as the doctrine of resurrection, final judgement, etc.[31] The suggestions are so cursory, however, and so undercut, I believe, by the philosophical inadequacies of his position, that they cannot serve much further use directly in the project of this thesis. They also exemplify the search for that kind of direct correspondence between physical foci and theological loci that we have been cautioned against.

Nevertheless, the consequences of Grib's program, *as representative of a particular way of construing physical data*, i.e., the adoption of the strongest version of the Anthropic Principle aligned with an idealist philosophy, may bear on our core thesis that the Trinity is essentially temporal. In this respect, Grib finally asserts two seemingly contradictory concepts of time. He states that relativity makes temporality part of a fixed four-dimensional space/time matrix; that is, events are situated eternally within a semi-block universe. The fundamental affirmation therefore is that the universe is a "finite eternity." Second, Grib asserts that the *sense* of time's passage occurs at the quantum move, when the observer observes (when life is lived!). Temporality, then, is derived or "translated" out of the "eternal now" by the agency of the observer. For there to be continuity and coherence, finally, between different observers (like Wigner and his friend) there must by implication exist an Ultimate Observer, God, who as Spirit stands external to the whole process so as to render the process both real and meaningful for all its cognizing constituents. A doctrine of the Trinity which assumes temporality as essential to divinity will either, thus, dismiss Grib's argument because he places "God outside the system," or it will provide a more embracing context within which the polarities of Grib's accounting may be overcome. If the doctrine can achieve either of these aims without change to its hardcore, then we may judge the theological program, in this case, as viable. We shall pick up this theme again in chapter 7.

The Cosmology of Stephen Hawking

A famous cosmologist who also appears to construe temporality as fictional in a quantum universe, though with radically different consequences, is Stephen Hawking.[32] Where Grib poses a cosmology of a "finite eternity," it is justifiable to say that Hawking's is a "timeless quantum cosmology." Recognizing that relativity theory can apply only to an expansionary macro-universe and is not adequate to deal with the problem of an originating singularity, Hawking includes quantum mechanics in his cosmological proposal. In doing so, Hawking does not disavow the thermodynamical arrow of time; he understands it as internal to the system. He does, however, conceive it as local, while the macrouniverse need not display any such correspondence. I return to the banal example of a balloon to illustrate. Recall, as well, the principles of general relativity. If one were to identify one segment of the surface of an expanding balloon, if certain particles of mass on the balloon are not too heavy, those particles will be expanding with the balloon away from each other. But suppose, in another area, a singularity, i.e., a mass of great quantity, was pressing in on the surface of the balloon. Other lighter matter in the vicinity would tend to fall toward the singularity, all the more if that mass were enhanced by those particles falling toward and into it. "Time" in such a scenario, though on the same surface, does not correspond positively to "time" in another region. So it would be with differing masses, according to general relativity, on the surface of the universe. Furthermore, a quantum explanation is needed because of the high density of the supposed original singularity. Such an explanation must use the concept of "imaginary time" to cover global, and not just local, effects. This is Hawking's novel move.

Imaginary time does not refer to something fanciful. It refers, rather, to complex numbers that represent the superposition of all quantum phenomena. The use of imaginary time, in other words, reflects the "sum-over-histories" approach of Richard Feynmann. Imaginary time is likened to directions in space. If a person can proceed "forward" in one direction, she can turn and equally proceed "forward" in the other direction. This, of course, constrains what one might mean by "forward." Similarly, one could proceed in *any* direction in imaginary time, which constrains what one could mean by "future" or "past." One major consequence of the introduction of imaginary time into his cosmological scheme, an introduction which Hawking first intends as heuristic, is that temporal passage is now disconnected from the cosmos at the quantum level. To be sure, temporal passage remains physical; it is more than subjective (which seems to be an advance upon Grib). Hawking takes great effort to establish the consonance of the psychological, thermodynamical and cosmological arrows, with reference to the weaker version of the Anthropic Principle.[33]

Time, like space, is equal in all its directions; it is theoretically reversible. Thereby the distinction between time and space disappears completely. Time's direction, now conceived in Euclidean space-time, is no different from direction in space. When Feynmann's sum-over-histories is applied to Einstein's gravitational theory, "the analogue of the history of the particle is now a complete curved space-time that represents the history of the whole universe."[34] Hawking's model of the universe is one wherein internal time means that there is no sharp point (singularity) in the remote past (what is called $t=0$ in Big Bang cosmology). With the addition of imaginary time he "smooths out" the point of origination, and achieves a four-dimensional space with a single three-dimensional boundary.[35] The universe, in other words, is finite, but without an "edge." The only boundary condition of the universe is that it has no boundaries (except, of course, for this meta-linguistic boundary condition!).

After discussing the nuances of directions that an inflationary universe would take after the Big Bang, as supposed by a number of different proposals, Hawking suggests that there are only two combinations of the classical relativity theory of gravity by which the universe would behave. Either the universe existed for an infinite time or it had a singularity. But Hawking believes he has shown that the quantum relativity theory of gravity, now informed by imaginary time, offers his third possibility of a boundaryless finite universe.

> When we combine quantum mechanics with general relativity, there seems to be a new possibility that did not rise before: that space and time together might form a finite, four-dimensional space without singularities or boundaries, like the surface of the earth but with many more dimensions. It seems that this idea could explain many of the observed features of the universe, such as its large-scale uniformity and also the smaller scale departures from homogeneity, like galaxies, stars, and even human beings. It could even account for the arrow of time that we observe.[36]

In other words, Hawking argues for the possibility that space-time is finite but has no boundary, much like a balloon expanding has no edge and yet has a finite surface. The universe can be accounted for in this model as one epicyclically expanding and collapsing, or simply as always existing, thus necessitating no notion of any absolute beginning to Creation.[37]

> There would be no boundary to space-time and so there would be no need to specify the behavior at the boundary. There would be no singularity at which the laws of science broke down and no edge of space-time at which one would have to appeal to God or some new law to set the boundary conditions for space-time. One could say: "The boundary condition of the universe is that it has no boundary." The universe would be completely self-contained and not affected by anything outside itself. It would neither be created nor destroyed. It would just BE.[38]

The practical effect of this conclusion when posed against the classic question as to how God acts in the world is a deism. If God were required at all to get the spacetime continuum kickstarted, God would not be required for anything further.[39] Carl Sagan has added his voice to Hawking's in popularizing this point of view.

How might one respond to this "cosmologically proven" deism? One response is to challenge Hawking's singular view of time as cyclic-within-linear or cyclic with a direction, apart from asking about the transcendental conditions for it which are immune to experimental observation. That is, Augustine's view of time and eternity is not one shared by Hawking, though Hawking thinks otherwise. Augustine viewed the beginning of time as an event outside the scope of knowledge, an event which accompanied the creation of matter. Hawking understands a "beginning of time" to be "the beginning of a coordinate with reference to any special event, and without a breakdown of physical describability."[40] Rephrased in Gilkey's terms,[41] Hawking does not ask about an ontological contingency, which is the province of philosophical theology and not physical cosmology per se. Ted Peters rightly notes that Hawking rejects a god of the gaps notion of God. That which need not be explained by invocation of deity is quite self-sufficient and self-explanatory. By this approach, however, Hawking presupposes deism and denies the possibility of fruitful exploration of avenues of consonance between physics and theistic proposals. The implication is that Hawking is not as scientifically nor hermeneutically open as he ought to be.[42]

The Hawking model of course is of a closed universe type, but with no singularity. It resembles the standard Big Bang model with a finite past and finite future, except that the unboundedness variation suggests that spacetime, like the universe, simply "is," and is thus uncreated. Indeed, for the universe simply to "be," as Hawking avers, yet with an acknowledged direction of real time within its being, may suggest a consonance more with a proper definition of eternity than with infinity.[43] His universe, as Peters notes, looks like timeless eternity. "It transcends while enveloping regions of temporal passage. And it does so without God."[44]

But Hawking may also be disingenuous here. His argument could be summed to say that because there is no singularity, there is no "point" in the universe that requires explanation. Classically speaking, physical, philosophical, or theological categories were required to explain phenomenal curiosities (in this case, singularities). If in this case there is no need to explain inasmuch as there is no singularity, Hawking avers, then he may say that the universe simply "is." But this is in fact only to say that the universe at this point requires no explanation (at least from theological or other categories incompletely understood). To say that something requires no explanation is not, finally, to conclude infinity or eternity or whatever, nor to imply any deistic or anti-deistic consequences. Hawking's attempt to do the latter, in other words, is based on a fallacy of equivocation; he confuses the lack of need for explanation with deism. Properly and logically speaking, there are theological categories unexplored and not necessarily ruled out of order by Hawking's simple positing of the "being" of the universe. One has logical permission to explore other "explanations" or models.

However one would judge Hawking's work, again it is apparent that the themes of a "block universe" and a sense of eternity which transcends yet embraces temporality are two second order observations that could prove fruitful for the theologian, Hawking's deism notwithstanding. Hawking's view of quantum mechanics, which accepts the "simultaneous reality of all possibilities,"[45] could further define a view (or at least his view) of the meaning of "eternal." Hawking's sense of temporal passge is similar to Grib's, but it is also more objective. Nevertheless, Hawking also considers temporal passage to be a secondary concern. It is more a feature of realistic human description (not consciousness created!), but temporality goes wispily away when confronted by Hawking's ultimate quantum superposition. A theological doctrine of the Trinity, in answer to this view of time and eternity, therefore, will have to attend again to the transcendent character of atemporality in Hawking's program, recognizing that its primacy does not exclude, but embraces, any sense of temporality as construed by Hawking's affirmations of time's arrows. Of course, a specifically Christian Trinitarian concept will also speak of a God different from Hawking's deistic one. In doing so, it will not so much contradict as embrace and supercede Hawking's presumptions.[46]

The Third Construal: Christopher Isham

Our third representative, already noted many times in the above discussion is Christopher J. Isham, of the Blackett Laboratory, Imperial College, London. Not as well known as Hawking, but more so than Grib, Isham has already influenced the international dialogue between theology and science with two seminal papers. The first is "Creation of the Universe as a Quantum Process," to which I have already made some reference.[47] The second is "Quantum Theories of the Creation of the Universe," presented at the aforementioned second international conference on science and theology at Castel Gandolfo under the general theme of "Quantum Creation of the Universe and the Origin of the Laws of Nature."[48] Isham shares with our previous representatives the interest in describing a model of the universe at the quantum level. His results, however, are more cautious when theological implications are at stake. There are also some surprising areas of convergence between his and the others' work. He seems to agree with both that there is a kind of timelessness, if not finite eternity, at reality's depth. And, with Hawking, he finds a finite universe without boundaries to be acceptable. He also may be qualifiedly dissident against a critical realist interpretation of the universe, that position which has seemed to be the most agreeable among most interpreters.[49] Isham's first paper has been read as a challenge at least to classical realism, and so would stand apart from front-line critical realist observers like Arthur Peacocke, Stanley Jaki, John Polkinghorne, Ian Barbour, Ernan McMulin, Janet Soskice, William Stoeger and many others.[50] With such a prelude, I turn to a summary of Isham's work directly.

In both his papers, Isham considers the role played by the linked concepts of causality and time and then turns toward summary of the basic ideas in general relativity. He introduces some problems that are posed by quantum theory when general relativity is seen from a quantum framework. Here he finds time to have a significant phenomenological character. Isham reviews the Hartle-Hawking approach and their use of imaginary time which is critical to quantum theory. He also gives similar treatment to A. Vilenkin. Isham agrees with the Hartle-Hawking proposal that a radical reappraisal of "real" cosmological time is found to be necessary; rather than its being an *a priori* property of the background structure, it now becomes a phenomenological construct in terms of the gravitational and/or material content of the universe. His agreement notwithstanding, Isham in the earlier paper proceeds to assign a theological possibility of interpretation to the boundaryless boundary condition of Hawking. In both he assesses quantum creation of the universe, its achievements and successes, and finally some implications for theology. We look now in more detail at Isham's argument.

In rehearsing the logic of classical physics, Isham concludes that within that domain we can say nothing of a cause for the universe. The point is that if we start at a point "X," there is no way from within the model that we can predict which trajectory in state space the system will allow. The best we can do, with our knowledge of dynamical laws, is to compute the current state as the result of a deterministic universe, retroactively and then to say, in principle, what the state must have been at an earlier time. This, of course, is the fashion after which we are comfortable in stating that there was a Big Bang. However, "there is no way in which we can *predict* that this trajectory, rather than any other, is the history of our actual universe. In this sense, nothing can be said about creation itself."[51] That is, we can say nothing about the causality of the singularity according to classical constructions. Formally speaking within these confines, classical creation is acausal.

The problem is further complicated if one should desire to march against the bandwagon and posit a creation within the framework of a pre-existing spacetime. In this case physics would have to predict a plurality of originating points that could happen at "any" time within this manifold. Inevitably, the wave functions of the different "creations" would interfere with each other. We would be subject to interacting universes. Our experience, fortunately, doesn't allow this.[52]

Consequently, it is necessary to posit the creation of time with matter. Isham suggests, with Augustine, that time itself was created like matter along with matter. "What God was doing 'then'" is a question without meaning, since there was not any "then" if time was not existent. Scientists now use the same 'subterfuge', but still the suggestion that space and/or time were created entities raises questions about the ontological status of those entities. Isham quotes Philo who, like Augustine, was bothered that...

> There are some people who, having the world in admiration rather than the Maker of the World, pronounce it to be without beginning and everlasting, while with impious falsehood they postulate in God a vast inactivity....Time began simultaneously with the world or after it. For since time is a measured space determined by the world's movement, and since movement could not be prior to the object moving, but must of necessity arise either after it or simultaneously with it, it follows of necessity that time also is either coeval with or later born than the world.[53]

But Isham—quite constructively, I believe—suggests that time is not simply another created thing alongside other created things. Rather, enlarging upon Augustine's insight, but still in confluence with it, Isham suggests according to relativity theory that time is derivative from matter-in-motion.

Time in the contemporary physical view bears a phenomenological character. It also means for us, quite significantly, that "time" cannot bear the usual meaning conventional wisdom would ascribe to it the closer we get to the originating point. Indeed, according to quantum mechanical operations, once we get under the Planck time, 10^{-45} seconds, there may be no real sense to "time" at all.

The basic idea is that, rather than speaking of things moving *in* time, we should view time as determined *by* the motion of things. This gives to matter an ontological status that is prior to that of time—a reversal of the container image that would doubtless have appealed to Leibniz and which has a precise technical analogue in the current scientific theories with which we are concerned. Indeed, a critical ingredient in these theories is the replacement of what we normally call 'time' with a phenomenological construct in terms of the constituents (fields or particles) of the universe. This allows the possibility that as we approach the 'point' of creation (going backward in time), the phenomenological time will look less and less like the usual one, and in such a way that the problem of the 'beginning' of time is resolved with the realization that conventional 'time' is an inapplicable concept within the highly quantum mechanical, very early universe.[54]

When we turn to the theory of general relativity, it is a commonplace now to rehearse the fact that the background container model of Newton is now replaced by a four-dimensional spacetime. In special relativity, this matrix can be "sliced" any number of ways such that time is associated only with that slice. Different times accompany different inertial frames of reference. Like the spacetimes of Newtonian physics, special relativity time has the character of a fixed background structure despite the possibility of differing inertial frames. For any choice of frame, the solutions to their equations will be flat. When general relativity is introduced, however, there are many ways in which the primary four-dimensional spacetime in its entirety can be sliced into three-dimensional spaces. Each slice will represent a particular choice of "time" that need not be consistent with a different slice. Whether a four-dimensional spacetime be represented as a cylinder or cone (like the spacetime picture of the expanding universe), time can be defined only internally in terms of a particular property of the curvature of the three-dimensional character of that structure. Thus, time may, for example, be represented as the radius of the space, which radius will of course vary according to the distribution of mass and energy in that spacetime. Time has no privileged position. It can be described only phenomenologically. This will become a central implication of quantum cosmology as well in its attempt to combine this fundamental feature of general relativity with quantum mechanics in a description of the fundamental early dynamics of the universe.[55]

If time now is to be understood as internal to a system—say, as the volume of a curved space—then, when it comes to defining a quantum gravity state function, there need not and will not appear a time ('t') variable in the state function. The equation will be written with the terms of curvature, matter and volume. This may strike us as curious. It is difficult to see how a description of any temporal change can appear in such "frozen formalism." But that is precisely what time understood now as phenomenological means. This means that there are many possible choices for such a "time." The problem is that the results depend upon the choice made. Once again, as quantum mechanics inescapably leads us into paradox, the observer becomes the key player in the Heisenbergian question of "what time is it?". It is whatever one chooses it to be. More specifically, we realize again that in the quantum region phenomenological time will lead to an *approximation* of causality if we are working toward a quantum creation model. Many solutions will be admitted, even by a unique function, so that we once again are faced with the problem we encountered earlier; there is no way we can formally ascribe causality—or a time—to creation. How then are we to arrive upon, if at all possible, a genuine theory of origination of the universe, particularly if we are interested in creation from "nothing?" This leads us to the idea of "imaginary time," discussed above with reference to Hawking.

Isham finds that the Hartle-Hawking proposal is viable as a physical description. The use of imaginary time as a means to "smooth out" the conical singularity of an origination point, Isham believes, coheres well with the phenomenological character of time. One of the most attractive features of the Hartle-Hawking scheme, he believes, is that it describes the evolution of the physical parts of the system by use of this internal/ phenomenological time.[56] As we "go back in time" by way of this phenomenological time, we find that the underlying equality of space and time is increasingly asserted, such that finally (we know not "when"—this, is part of the measurement/reality problem inherent to quantum theory) time is imaginary as it is associated with its non-physical features. In this way Hawking can say that there is no "beginning of time."

Even so, Isham gives this a creative theological interpretation. Viewed from "the other direction," i.e., "since" the Big Bang, time as an imaginary number comes more into focus as the size of the three-dimensional surface expands. The singularity, it can be said then, wherein time and space are absolutely fused and so is imaginary, cannot be located on such a surface that is non-conical. Formally speaking, the originating point does not exist. Hawking takes this to mean that the universe had no beginning. Isham takes it to mean that creation literally came *formally* "out of nothing."[57]

The use of 'imaginary time' paths in the computation...has enabled us to use solutions to the classical field equations that are free of the conical singularity in the traditional picture of the Big Bang spacetime. The initial space from which the universe 'emerged' can be defined to be that part of the boundary of the four-dimensional space which is *not* part of the (later) three-surface. But this is the empty set, which gives a precise mathematical definition of the concept of 'nothing.'[58]

Isham evaluates this model positively because it is predictive and therefore capable in principle of experimental refutation, comprehensive, and elegantly fruitful in resolving traditional demarcation problems between four-dimensional "paths" and three-space state functions. Negatively speaking, the Hartle-Hawking proposal can lead to the positing of multiple universes, is likely to be mathematically inconsistent, and is not the only way of obtaining a picture of creation *ex nihilo*. Above all, however, Isham favors the implication that time can be interpreted as a genuine variable only well away from the quantum region. Our experience of time, or, better, the sense of classical time, unidirectionality, etc., may be construed as an "emergent" phenomenon. Likewise with quantum probabilities; "like the notion of classical time, probabilities may 'emerge' from the formalism and that, near the creation region [the wave function of the universe] may not have any direct physical interpretation at all! I rather like this view."[59]

In his "Quantum Theories of the Creation of the Universe" Isham expands upon his conclusions as to the phenomenological and imaginary character of time with reference to models other than Hawking's. He gives particular attention to Vilenkin. Based upon Vilenkin's model, and incorporating the Hartle-Hawking *ansatz*, Isham proposes the workable model of a universe that arises out of the "imaginary time balloon" of Hawking. In other words, he proposes the possibility that a real-time universe such as ours emerges from a primordial Imaginary-time four-dimensional sphere. What "once" was a Hawking universe without an edge may have evolved, in other words, into our universe with an edge. Thereby, imaginary time evolves into phenomenological time, which evolves into our real-time.[60] This may be both an intellectually and experientially satisfying way to describe the human intuition of temporality without harm to respectable theoretical scientific achievement. And whether it be this or other quantum cosmological models explored by Isham, all of which must be appropriated by the theologian with great caution, they all seem to agree on the idea that space and time emerge in some way from a purely quantum-mechanical region which can be described in some respects as if it were a classical, imaginary-time four-space.[61]

In sum, Isham is clearly humble about asserting any claims as to definitive models. He also continues to be concerned about the subject-object problem of observership in quantum theory, as well as with the meaning of quantum theory's probabilistic language. Such awareness on his part is helpful, I believe, in carefully advancing the project of developing a quantum creation theory. It makes all the more credible, too, those metaphysical assertions he would underscore as to the nature of time. For our purposes, this shows perhaps surprising convergence with those whom some would consider less cautious, like Grib and even Hawking. Isham does not erase temporality for the sake of eternity. But he does show that there is an arena in which time has no place; in which time may even be likened to timelessness. There are those who take this to mean that the fundamental structure of the universe is, in fact, "timeless."[62] I think this is quite erroneous and I will comment upon this implication shortly. One thing is clear, however. The theological implications of Isham's work are significant (even if he is halting about explicating them).

Implications for a Christian Concept of Time and Eternity

Many questions and implications should be raised by the survey above. Their import for a Christian concept of time and eternity, vis-à-vis the doctrine of the Trinity is significant. Indeed, they may surprisingly seem to attack our "hardcore" theory that the Trinity is essentially temporal head-on and thereby render it as a failed research program. To take seriously the data summarized above, together with the positions described of Grib, Hawking and Isham, constitutes what Willem Drees calls a "reverse eclecticism;" the method of taking that material which may be most damaging to one's own position and incorporating it positively, or at least neutrally, into one's scheme. Successfully to do this would make for real progress.[63] "Taking science where 'it hurts the most' offers the greatest challenge, but also the greatest profit with respect to credibility."[64] It is that spirit to which I aspire by posing, then, these following implications.

1. Time is a real property of reality.
    Inflationary cosmology, no matter the model of originating cause and inasmuch as it still affirms causality, provides evidence that time is unidirectional. Time has an arrow. No one who deals with physics "in the large" questions this assumption. Nor is the experience of temporality a matter merely of the mind. It is supra-subjective. This does not discount, of

course, the validity of the idea of psychological time, that time of personal experience.[65]

2. However, time as perceived through the theory of Quantum Gravity is not real.

At most, it is discrete and discontinuous, like quanta themselves. If one wished to maintain the Aristotelian sense of time as the measure between before and after, a quantum interpretation would be contradictory. Therefore, formally and practically speaking, there is no such thing as time as we know it at the most fundamental level of the universe. Hawking may have justified his initial appeal to imaginary time as a heuristic (he admitted it was a "trick"). But theoreticians like Isham and others are more honest in granting it even a "realist" position. Grib spoke of this era in the universe's "becoming" as an objectless object. However ambivalent the phrase may be, at the quantum level it appears Grib would have to agree, too, that temporality is not real, or more precisely, it is not an objective property.

3. The time of general relativity is phenomenological; it is part of the four-dimensional matrix itself.[66]

This zone between the quantum level and our common real-time level is contested. Grib poses a simple diastasis between the two, arguing that Boolean logic translates temporality out of the finite eternity of the primordial state. This is an intriguing proposal, but the jury is still out on this one. Hawking does not speak specifically about the matter, though it seems he would cast lots with Isham. Isham poses a phenomenological view of time. Time is internal to the system in question. Time may be construed as the volume (or radius, or whatever) of the system in question. It bears no privileged status of its own, and, consequently, it can be "sliced" or chosen in any way the observer sees fit. Time will progress or bend according to the curvature of the space on which the chosen world line is situated.

4. As a phenomenological construct, time can then be understood as derivative.

Time's value, indeed, its very existence, depends upon the mass and energy of the matter under observation. There clearly is no "background" spacetime for creation. Time, in this view, is a consequence of creation. Classic Christian thought is in consonance with the scientific view on this point.

5. Time is emergent.

The principle of emergence is hereby underscored. If there was a "space" when time was not, according to quantum theory, and a "space" wherein time is defined internally, there is also as a consequence of dynamical evolution a novel emergence of time as the experience of sequential temporality. There are new things under the sun which are epistemologically and ontologically irreducible simply to lower levels of meaning. Among these emergents is temporality itself. Paradoxically, we must speak not only in terms of the system's evolution which brings about this emergent. We must also "now" agree that time, at least, is complementarily real, phenomenological *and* unreal, depending upon which level of interpretation the observer wishes to employ. To speak of time as emergent does not mean, however, that we are now free to neglect certain qualifications. We must still remember that terms like "future" or "past" are limited to that region of spacetime that is far from "$t=0$", and that the problems of special relativity (like the impossibility of universal simultaneity) still obtain. Nevertheless, the implications of the emergent character of time have direct bearing on assertion number eight below.

6. The future is open.

On the face of it, this assertion may seem to be an oxymoron. How can one ascribe openness, indefiniteness or even infinity to something preceded by the substantive designation of "the"? Here perhaps even our scientific language begs for more metaphor than we would care to admit. What we clearly are comfortable about asserting, though, is that chance and indeterminacy play such a significant role in the small parts of the universe that anticipation, if not hope, may spring eternal. We simply do not know what "will" happen in the course of events. There are numerous possibilities that can only be anticipated probabilistically.

This is also to assert, as far as the evidence warrants, that "the future" does not exist in some sort of timeless Platonic world.[67] All of this sums to say, perhaps, should we want our language as precise as possible, that there "are" really only two components of time: the past and the present. Nevertheless, we are constrained to speak of the "not yet" in some fashion. It is, of course, also a convention to speak this way. Therefore, quite specific qualifications will have to be granted in use of the term "the future" as we proceed.

7. The role of observership is contested, but requires a critical realist approach.

As I have emphasized, it is unclear just where the collapse of the wave packet between the moment of potential and the moment of observation occurs. Further, it would be prudent to follow the conservative Copenhagen interpretation and agree that classical measuring devices play a crucial role in the realization of "larger" quantum phenomena. I also agree that the human observer is not *a priori* necessary for completion of the measurement, apart from the epistemic gain in the situation. We are left therefore, I believe, with a Critical Realist principle in the interpretation of quantum phenomena, as well as phenomena at the higher levels. A position of Critical Realism affirms, for example, the "packet-like" character of time inasmuch as it is *necessarily* connected with *any* mass and movement at the quantum level. It also affirms the complementary wave-like character of time inasmuch as it must accompany a *global* description of all particle events, according to Bell's theorem. This coheres with all human experience of mass, movement and time: we sense both its fluidity and its discreteness.

I am aware that with the term of Critical Realism I am re-introducing a concept that has received little direct reference in my survey of Grib, Hawking, and Isham. Still, I do not believe their positions would mitigate this assertion. Neither Grib nor Hawking have implied any direct concern about this or any other epistemological issue. Isham has done so indirectly by questioning the instrumentalist tone of the conventional interpretation of quantum theory and pleading for an approach that does not invoke the sharp subject-object dualism of observer and system.[68] Also, Isham adopts a cautious position as to the utility and meaning of probabilistic statements. He prefers the school of thought which maintains that meaningful probabilistic statements are those which affirm something with (or close to) probability one and this he identifies as aligned with a modest philosophical realism.[69]

8. This Critical Realist approach, combined with the recognition of the emergent character of time, requires wholistic explanation.

This assertion is warranted simply as a repetition of the general theme we surveyed in chapter 4 before attending directly to the work of particular scientists. It is all the more justified as a direct implication of the principle of complementarity and as a necessary consequence of critical realism. We can also at least say, with attempted modesty, that differing logics (as in Boolean and non-Boolean) may evidence the greater need for complementary explanations of phenomena pertinent to their own levels. Methodologically, wholism is required for appropriate systematic reflection in a "post-modern" world, as Ted Peters argues.[70]

9. This further implies the viability of a semi-block universe, in which past and present events are connected and growing in their nexus as they are informed by new events of an expanding cosmos.

This assertion can be problematic. A "block-universe" picture does pose problems "for any metaphysics which posits a simple total ordering of God's 'events/experiences': i.e., an ordering in which it is meaningful to say (and, indeed, necessarily true,) that for any two such experiences A and B either A 'precedes' B, or B 'precedes' A."[71] Thus I use the term "semi" for two reasons. First, "semi" designates that though the universe of which we speak displays, according to critical realism, serial order at the humanly observed level, "God's experiences" are not necessarily so. In this respect, the objection is theological, not physical. I still maintain, though, that events somehow are still involved in a nexus or network. Otherwise there is no way the past would pertain to the present. Second, "semi" designates that this particular block-universe does not have a fixed future; nor is it constituted by Parmenidean Forms or Platonic Ideals (assertion 6). Such a universe, in which spacetime is part of the fixed matrix, implies a kind of "finite eternity" if the universe is closed; an "infinite eternity" if it is open and expanding. A further caveat: methodology requires that I come not to the question of a block-universe with any preconceived notion, but that I may only draw upon the scientific research and speculation as a given.

Thus the import later of this assertion (9) may be that the core thesis of this project, that the eternity of the Trinity is temporal, is at least consonant with block-universe theory. In other words, I need not be committed to the truth of this particular block-universe theory; but if it is so, then all the better for my thesis. It is significant, though, that the debate over the block universe most recently seems to be weighted by Isham toward the reality of a fully blocked universe, suggesting even a Platonic Realism that could complement Grib's arguments. However, this matter is sheerly one for conversation only and not yet founded as fodder for further research.[72]

10. In either case, eternity is clearly construable as an "envelope" of temporality rather than opposed to it.

Eternity need not be opposed to temporality. It is not synonymous with timelessness. Here I follow the Barthian argument and assume its direct theological correlation to the physical construal. This is certainly contrary to Willem Drees's argument that a Platonic timelessness is precisely what needs to be reasserted in contemporary metaphysics.[73] Drees correctly comments that the consonance which authors seek between a theistic view of creation and Big Bang cosmology lies not with the interpretation of "t=0," but with the basic role of time as displaying a dynamic rather than static view of the universe.[74] Following Isham's work, however, Drees asserts that this temporality does not exist. Drees argues that since the quantum, "fundamental" level of the universe shows no temporality, the critical realists are wrong-headed. They are dealing with impertinent data.

> The still speculative ideas at the frontier of cosmological research, and even the standard theory of spacetime (General Relativity), thus suggest that the evolutionary presentation is one of limited validity, and not the most fundamental one. Hence, theological insights developed in the dialogue with the evolutionary understanding of the natural world are *not* directly extendable to the dialogue with cosmology.
> ...It seems as if the temporal critical realists have not been considering such a shift in conceptuality as a reason for caution.[75]

Consequently, Drees believes, theists for whom temporality is essential have a fundamental conflict with cosmology,...unless they were to accept a cosmological view of time as timelessness, after the fashion of Platonic realism, within which the common sense temporal view is embedded. Drees then proceeds to argue for God's timelessness and the possibility that spatial dimensions over and above the physical be added to cosmological models so as to allow for such a transcendence of timelessness.

I find part of Drees's argument to be helpful, particularly the echo of McMullin that we cannot directly extend theological dialogue with evolution to the dialogue with cosmology. Drees cautions, as it were, against a "category mistake." I question, though, the method by which Drees would remove temporality from the discussion. Drees identifies the "fundamental" quantum level as that which should be definitive for all of cosmology. It seems to me that this argument adopts a reductionism which a doctrine of emergence would proscribe. It also neglects the role of complementary and wholistic explanation that is prescribed by the quantum theory itself. It is curious, therefore, that Drees would reduce the argument in this way. Even a Platonic realist philosophical position would not remove the phenomenal for the sake of arguing the reality only of the fundamental. Furthermore, the disjunctiveness of timelessness *vs.* temporality, as Drees poses them, eventually would deny him the possibility of describing any *relation* of the two other than a negative one. The theological consequence will be apophatism,—certainly a distinguished and useful position—but it would and could be only that. As a head-on charge against the leading premise of this thesis, Drees could not be more direct. If Drees were correct, there is no denying that the hard core theory of temporality in the divine would be damaged. The requirement of wholism, however, makes his suggestion faulty.

One positive comment is timely, though. Though he allows for some physical problems, Drees has suggested that the addition of spatial dimensions over and above the regular physical ones might be useful. This approach has precedent.[76] The advantage is that it makes it possible to imagine transcendence; God hereby may be seen in this "supertemporal eternity" as "intimately close to all events without confining God to physical reality." And if the suggestion cannot overcome its physical problems (especially the contradiction of adding a time-like dimension to a matrix in which "t" has been removed), Drees allows, the regulative notion of transcendence as directing the understanding toward wider perspective is necessary.[77]

Drees's comment appears to be in fact a call for wholistic explanation, if not for a complete ontology. This leads to my final comment, which is more a suggestion than a direct implication drawn from the preceding sources.

11. Transcendence and eschatology may play a role as part of the wholistic and complementary explanation of eternity and temporality.

To put it otherwise, a semi-block universe requires much further description as to how it relates to its (or "a" or "the") future. One consequence of wholistic explanation is that a certain kind of transcendence is required to speak of causality. When one considers how the quantum world at its very roots displays an amazing openness to the future, together with how explanatory wholism and ontological wholism are required in the development of physical models, one may also finally be asking about a transcendent causality which is "top-down," or, theologically speaking, "future to present." Discussion of contingency and whether time be finite or infinite has been conducted so far in terms of origins. But what about the future? Might contingency be discussed eschatologically, as if there is purpose not deistically from the beginning, but from the future? While John Wheeler is among those who believe that time did not exist prior to the Big Bang, and that it will not after the "Big Crunch," he also believes with his concept of a Participatory Anthropic Principle that in some respect a future observer is required to empower a past genesis, and that this will involve some change in our understanding of time; "...observership allows and enforces a transcendence of the usual order of time [so that] the observer is as essential to the creation of the universe as the universe is to the creation of the observer."[78]

Again, this particular view of conscious agency is fraught with problems, as I suggested above with respect to Idealism. But Wheeler's comment as to how the future influences the past does set an agenda heretofore unexplored. That is, in what respect does the far future relate to past and present? Eschatology, in other words, asks not necessarily only for a description of how things will go down the line in terms of the universe's cooling off into an insouciant icy cosmos, or contracting into a furious inferno. It asks about hope and purpose, about contingency from the "other end." Freeman Dyson, for example, envisions an infinite future in which new forms of consciousness establish networks that finally embrace the universe, developing into a literal omniscience. Dyson argues, too, for scientific respectability as to such types of scientific theory.[79] Willem Drees agrees that "Science could help envisage" such a metaphysical conceptual space in which an eschatology that is appropriate to both scientific and theological concerns is intelligible.[80] As we shall see, there are numerous others who appeal to the open future as the eschatologically causal agent of present and past.[81] For these writers, eschatology is not only the arena of talk about the end of time, entropy, a cosmological big chill or big crunch. It is a fresh way in which one might speak of causation from the future; again, it is a kind of transcendent causative agency that works top-down in complementarity with the bottom-up processes of the universe.

With these observations I conclude this part of the argument. Any viable theological research program, I maintain, must incorporate, or at least not be mitigated by, these implications drawn from the survey above. Before making some constructive suggestions about such a theological research program, I would like to turn now to the work of one eminent theologian who has *not* incorporated these concerns into his program. Thereby we shall test the viability of his theological position, in the hope that it will parlay well into the proposed systematic constructions of a doctrine of the Trinity in chapter 7. We look now at the work of Jürgen Moltmann.

Notes

1. A much noted episode of *Star Trek - The Next Generation* adapted Hugh Everett's "Many World's" proposal into its plot, although it objectified the consequences of the rampant subjective Idealism that Everett proposes.

2. The following summary is based upon two papers by Grib, the first, entitled "Quantum Cosmology, The Role of Observer, Quantum Logics," presented at the research conference, *Quantum Creation of the Universe and the Origin of the Laws of Nature*, Castel Gandolfo, September 1991, sponsored by the Vatican Observatory and The Center for Theology and the Natural Sciences. This paper is published, with the other conference papers and responses, in Robert John Russell, Nancey Murphy and C. J. Isham, editors, *Quantum Cosmology and the Laws of Nature: Scientific Perspectives on Divine Action* (Rome and Notre Dame: Vatican Observatory and University of Notre Dame Press, 1993), hereafter referred to as *QCLN*. The second, similar, Grib paper (unpublished), "Time and Eternity in Modern Relativistic Cosmology," was presented at the Fourth European Conference on Science and Theology, *Origins, Time and Complexity*, Mondo Migliore, Italy, March, 1992. Hereafter I will abbreviate the first Grib paper as *QC*, the second as *TE*.

3. Grib, *TE*.

4. Grib, *TE*.

5. Grib, *TE*.

6. Cf. Karsavin, *Notes Petropolitana*.

7. cf. Grib, *QC*, 178-9.

8. Of course, the small amount of matter in the universe is also what counts for many theorists as an argument for a finite, but expanding universe; the gravitational force of the matter is insufficient to eventuate in the universe's collapse upon itself. It seems that this is, however, a minority opinion.

9. Grib, *TE*.

10. Grib, *QC*, 165.

11. Grib, *QC*, 173.

12. Grib, *QC*, 177.

13. Grib, QC, 175-8. John von Neumann is known for his proof against hidden variables in quantum theory, though John Bell proved its irrelevance to quantum theory. See Pagels, 166. London and Bauer defend, with the rest, the view that wave functions are collapsed by intervention of conscious observation. See *ACP*, 468-9.

14. Cf. B: Appendix, Grib, *QC*, 181-2. For an excellent description of the unique logic of quantum behavior, and consequently, a step toward logical description in chaos theory, see F.T. Arrechi, "A Critical Approach to Complexity and Self-Organization," (unpublished) presented at the Fourth European Conference on Science and Theology, March, 1992.

15. Grib, *QC*, 175.

16. Grib, *QC*, 176.

17. Grib, *QC*, 177.

18. My emphasis; see Grib, *TE*, 11.

19. *TE*, 11. Interestingly, Grib calls the Wheeler-DeWitt equation [the wave function "Planck's constant times psi equals zero"] the "main equation in quantum cosmology." Grib maintains that this equation describes the "physics of eternity."

20. *TE*, 12.

21. See above, chapter 4; also E.P. Wigner, *The Scientist Speculates* (London:W. Heinmann, 1961).

22. Grib, *TE*, 13.

23. *TE*, 13.

24. Grib suggests that this provides a physical description of what may be meant by the doctrine of the Resurrection of the Dead. It is a kind of repetition of this life's events in a new time order after the Big Crunch, due to the collapse of the wave function of the Universe. Only near the big crunch of a finite Friedmann universe of the closed type would we theoretically be able to see our pasts...or when one is "translated" into a perspective from eternity.

25. Once a wave-function is collapsed, it cannot be undone.

26. Grib, *TE*, 13.

27. Stanley Jaki, *The Purpose of It All* (Washington D.C.: Regnery Gateway, 1990), 108.

28. Jaki, 105-111.

29. Polkinghorne, *Science and Providence*, 37. Also, "If the Spirit is operating in the universe, part of his activity will certainly be through the scientific law which reflects his faithfulness and we do not have to picture him working against its grain." Polkinghorne, 38.

30. Davies, "The Intelligibility of Nature?", *QCLN*, 145ff. This particular quote was included in an earlier, unpublished, version of this paper. Davies is careful to avoid the positing of static "fundamental laws," however. He prefers to speak of the need for laws at all levels of description. Lawfulness, like the appearance of new events (or forms) themselves, is emergent; new laws come into play as the universe evolves to ever more complex states. Davies, 154ff.

31. For one to stand in a cone in such a way that one does see *all* of one's life before him or herself would constitute a kind of judgement, Grib believes. There is here an objective accounting of the past. Grib maintains, however, that an Ultimate Observer can in fact redeem this past, and so objective content is given to the copncepts of the resurrection of the dead and salvation.

32. *A Brief History of Time: From the Big Bang to Black Holes* (New York: Bantam, 1988).

33. The arrow of time, whether it be historical, psychological, thermodynamical or cosmological, maintains one direction with a past and a future. Hawking is thus interested in why there obtains a consonance between these "arrows," when the arrows were shot and when, if ever, they will fail (or return like boomerangs!). The explanation usually given is that reversibility is forbidden by the second law of thermodynamics; in any closed system disorder must always increase with time. He argues that "the no boundary condition for the universe, together with the weak anthropic principle, can explain why all three arrows point in the same direction — and, moreover, why a well-defined arrow of time should exist at all." The psychological arrow is essentially defined by the thermodynamic arrow. The same argument may be made with respect to the historical arrow. *Brief History...*, 145ff.

34. Hawking, 145ff..

35. Christopher Isham, likely with irony in view of Hawking's deism, is able to construct an *ex nihilo* interpretation of Hawking's model; see Isham, "Creation As A Quantum Process," *PPT*, 398ff). Because, ultimately, according to Hawking, no initial singularity can be established: "the initial space from which the universe 'emerged' can be defined to be that part of the boundary of the four-dimensional space which is **not** part of the (later) three surface. But this is an empty set, which gives a precise mathematical definition of the concept of 'nothing.'"

36. Hawking, 173-174.

37. Hawking, 116.

38. Hawking, 136.

39. "The idea that space and time may form a closed surface without boundary also has profound implications for the role of God in the affairs of the universe. With the success of scientific theories in describing events, most people have come to believe that God allows the universe to evolve according to a set of laws and does not intervene in the universe to break these laws. However, the laws do not tell us what the universe should have looked like when it started; it would still be up to God to wind up the clockwork and choose how to start it off. So long as the universe had a beginning, we could suppose it had a creator. But if the universe is really self-contained, having no boundary or edge, it would have neither beginning nor end: it would simply be. What place then for a creator?" Hawking, 140-141; see also 173-4.

40. Willem Drees, 55. Drees also quotes Hawking: "But time is defined only within the universe, and does not exist outside it, as was pointed out by St. Augustine (400)...The modern view is very similar. In general relativity, time is just a co-ordinate that labels events in the universe. It does not have any meaning outside the spacetime manifold. To ask what happened before the universe began is like asking for a point on Earth at 91 degrees north latitude; it is just not defined. Instead of talking about the universe being created, and maybe coming to an end, one should just say the universe is."

41. Langdon Gilkey, *Maker of Heaven and Earth* (Garden City: Doubleday, 1959).

42. Ted Peters, "Cosmos As Creation," *Cosmos As Creation*, 54-57. If fruitfulness (extensibility of application) be one of the necessary criteria (the others being simplicity, coherence and falsifiability) for a scientific model, it may be possible to criticize Hawking on this score. Cf. Barbour, *Myths, Models and Paradigms* (New York: Harper and Row, 1974). The recognition, too, that scientists do approach their work, as do all of us, with metaphysical assumptions requires now that they expose their assumptions to themselves and their public as much as possible, the more clearly to interpret the data themselves. In other words, that "all data are theory laden" is commonly acknowledged; what Hawking has not acknowledged are his own metaphysical theories which laden his data.

43. See Hawking, 133-141.

44. *God As Trinity*, 164-165.

45. Drees, 63.

46. Ted Peters thinks that Hawking's conscious deism—or religious skepticism—led Hawking to posit a universe with no initial singularity, and that therefore Hawking's science is tainted by his bias. I would not be so harsh. Numerous religious physicists have accepted Hawking's program as solid, and have, nevertheless, rendered it religiously

meaningful. Cf., C.J. Isham, in *PPT*, who gives a physical meaning to t=0 in Hawking's program, likening it to the doctrine of *creatio ex nihilo*.

47. In *PPT*, 375-408.

48. "Quantum Creation of the Universe and the Origin of the Laws of Nature," September, 1991, now published in Robert John Russell, et al. in *QCLN*, 49-89.

49. Cosmologists, by and large, usually work within a classical physics which can assume a realist language. As a quantum cosmologist, though, Christopher Isham allows that he cannot adopt realist language, convinced as he is by Bohr's argument. Isham does not solve the problem of realistic interpretation hereby, however. It means that he is rather hamstrung about interpretation at this point. Perhaps, at best, one might suggest that Isham interprets quantum cosmological description on the literal level as "kataphatic," but apophatic at a deeper level. I am indebted to Robert John Russell in private conversation for drawing out these observations.

50. So argues Russell, *PPT*, 354.

51. Isham, "Creation of the Universe As a Quantum Process," (hereafter *CUQP*) in *PPT*, 385. Isham argues that mathematical theories that attempt to provide solutions along the lines of "X → C →", when allowing for possibilities of collapse of the state space, must assume the form of "→ C → X — C'—"; that is, any variable could in principle have preceded the initial state 'X'. Furthermore, that the collapse of the state space could arise from different trajectories, that is, from an array of possibilities which are not equilinear with "X", means that there is no way by which one may deduce "retroactively" from "X" what an initial state was.

52. Isham, 387 and "Quantum Theories of the Creation of the Universe," (hereafter *QTCU*) in *QCLN*, 53-55. See also Drees, "A Case Against Critical Realism? Consequences of Quantum Cosmology for Theology," *QCLN*, 339f.

53. *CUQP*, 387.

54. *CUQP*, 388.

55. *CUQP*, 388-392 and *QTCU*, 58-63.

56. *CUQP*, 400.

57. It has not yet been noted, as far as I am aware, that the adaptation of imaginary numbers as a *formal* mathematical principle to posit no singularity is, in and of itself, not *necessarily* a material claim. This is a matter of logic, I think, which needs further elucidation. Hawking adopts a formal description, extracting from it the argument that there is no material singularity. The conclusion does not necessarily follow. Isham, on the other hand, is consistent in arguing that Hawking's formal description gives a *formal* meaning to "creatio ex nihilo."

58. *CUQP*, 401.

59. *CUQP*, 403.

60. *QTCU*, 71-74. Imagine that a cone, sans its point, is grafted onto a balloon. The top of the cone has an edge, while the whole system nevertheless has no identifiable origination point. In this fashion the original Hawking Universe retains its mathematical cogency and our current sense of temporality.

61. *QTCU*, 76.

62. Cf. Drees, in *QCLN*, 339ff.

63. *QCLN.*, 358f.

64. *QCLN*, 358, quoting Lindon Eaves, "Spirit, Method and Content in Science and Religion: The Theological Perspective of a Geneticist," *Zygon*, 24:2 (June, 1989), 185-215.

65. I disagree with the notion, however, that it is this psychological time that is more likely to be applied to God in fruitful fashion, as some have suggested in an unpublished "Collective Response to the paper of Chris Isham," April 13, 1991, assertion 2.2. This sort of claim would weigh the theological side of the discussion more toward sheer subjectivity than should be comfortable for those seeking objective or neutral ground. This kind of push has considerable history, for example, in the work of William James, who spent much space in his *Principles of Psychology* on the subject of time cognition. The consequence, I believe, is a supra-subjective metaphysic that can be judged only pragmatically or instrumentally, and always only in terms of fundamental personal experience. I don't see much fruitfulness from this kind of move. It would, I think, tend to reassert the neo-orthodox disjunction of a privileged scientific province (fact) and a religious-ethico province (value). Perhaps those who suggested this move have some instinct that this may be a problem for their position, as they qualify it with the recognition that "considerations of psychological time cannot be completely divorced from those of physical time since the former is presumably linked in some way to the physical processes in our bodies/brains." I agree. This also, however, raises the difficulty that the psychological sense of time, on one hand, can be reduced to a sheerly materialistic explanation; see, e.g., John Searle, *Minds, Brains and Bodies* (London: BBC, 1980). On the other hand, it raises the entire complex of issues related to the role of observership and Idealism again. In other words, to attempt to find in psychological time better theological and philosophical credentials advances the discussion no further than it has been conducted on physical terms; indeed, it is more challenging.

66. I agree with the comment in "Responses to Isham" (cf. above, unpublished) that the term "phenomenological" may be ambiguous in so far as philosophers and theologians often employ it in a different sense, e.g., as with Bergson. "Internal" time is better; it does make clearer that time is defined in terms of the system itself, so that the time variant label drops out of any equations, in contrast to a Newtonian sense or that of special relativity. For now, I shall with Isham simply accept this particular definition of phenomenological time and keep on with it.

67. I say this in agreement with "Responses to Isham," 3.1.

68. *QTCU*, cf. 86f.

69. *CUQP*, 403-404.

70. See *God, The World's Future* (Minneapolis: Fortress, 1992).

71. "Responses to Isham," 3.0. Cf. also C.J. Isham and J.C. Polkinghorne, "The Debate Over the Block Universe," *QCLN*, 135-144.

72. John Polkinghorne and Chris Isham have engaged this matter susubstantively and evocatively in *QCLN*, 135-144.

73. See note 52 above.

74. Drees, 332-3.

75. Drees, 343.

76. Drees has posed this possibility in an earlier unpublished version of the paper.

77. I accept that much of Drees's argument, short of his desire to connect God's transcendence with timelessness. Drees, 346-7.

78. Emphasis mine; quoted in Fagg, 69. Wheeler uses the strong interpretation of the Anthropic Principle, suggesting that "the universe could not have come into being unless it were guaranteed in advance to be able to give rise to life at some point in its history-to-be." This is also quoted in Fagg, 69...thus there is a very intimate connection between the presence of humanity—the participator—and the universe.

79. Summarized in Russell, *PPT*, 202-203. See also Freeman Dyson, *Infinite in All Directions* (New York: Harper and Row, 1988), and "Time without End: Physics and Biology in an Open Universe," *Review of Modern Physics*, 51 (1979), 447f., cited in Russell, *PPT*, 202-203.

80. *Beyond the Big Bang, Quantum Cosmologies and God* (LaSalle: Open Court, 1990), 121. See especially his section on eschatology, 113-154.

81. A notable exception, philosopher Milic Capek, writing on "The Unreality and Indeterminacy of the Future in the Light of Contemporary Physics," argues against any construal of the block universe. He presses the argument, though, that the future is both undetermined and unreal, claiming that other construals of some sort of future either determined or real are "needlessly generated by the invention of useless and fictitious entities" since Parmenides. "Conceptual analysis and all available empirical evidence both point to this conclusion." At base, and thus different from others we are consulting, Capek's is the contrary voice of the strictly empirical logical positivist. See *Physics and the Ultimate Significance of Time*, ed. by David Ray Griffin (Albany: SUNY Press, 1986), 297ff.

VI

Jürgen Moltmann On The Trinity And Time

Jürgen Moltmann, one of the leading eschatological theologians in the rich contemporary history of theology after Karl Barth, has deeply influenced several directions of thinking in current theology. Moltmann's *Theology of Hope* in 1964 was a clarion call to reflect, proclaim, and live the Christian faith within a new understanding of eschatology. The vital combination of biblical seriousness and revised epistemology in turn led to a renewal of concentration on the praxis of faith. It also led inexorably to the development of political theology in Europe and, consequently, liberation theology in the Third World.

This development has led many to think that Moltmann's primary interests were with a theology of history and the refinement of Christian political praxis. But this is clearly not so. Moltmann's primary concern has been to address the problem of suffering and evil in light of the holocaust. In doing that Moltmann has been driven to ask after the nature of God revealed through the suffering of the cross, and, subsequently, the metaphysical view of reality that perforce derives from a God who suffers, will redeem all sufferers—including God's suffering self!—and is trinitarian love immanent with and transcendent to all suffering.

While the tracing of Moltmann's right-headed concern with theodicy is not the focus of our discussion, the dialectic of resurrection hope and the *theologia crucis* leads necessarily to Moltmann's trinitarian constructions, and, consequently, to consideration in the latter part of his career of the *all* to which God the Trinity intimately relates, while yet maintaining the transcendence of God's eschatological future. Moltmann's overarching sense of time as eschatological has led him to conceive of the Trinity as constitutive of time and of creation as embedded in the Trinitarian-eschatological milieu. Thus, Moltmann's life has been devoted, too, to the explications of all the traditional loci of Christian theology and spirituality, including, for our immediate purposes, some thought on the place and import of the natural sciences in Christian theologizing.

The recognition that eschatology requires that theology address "the whole" means for Moltmann that the "two track thinking" of neo-orthodoxy must be abandoned. It was no longer possible to aver that the sciences had their domain of facts and theology its own of values. Even in 1966 Moltmann made the (even yet) radical proposal that theology belonged to the conversational domain of every science, natural or social.

Christian theology can no longer remain in a front line over against science; it
joins it on that front which we call the present, where the future is either won or
frustrated because the salvation of the world is hoped for and feared. Theological
considerations of this sort, therefore, do not belong in one particular faculty
among other faculties, but rather within the horizon of knowledge for every
science.[1]

So, at least formally, Moltmann from early in his career acknowledged the
necessity of conversation between theology and natural science. While that
conversation was finally resumed with energy a couple of decades later, it was
clear, with his publication of *God in Creation* (1985), that the conversation
was not as materially attentive as it may have been formally. It will be part
of my agenda in this chapter to show how this is so. Nevertheless, it is clear
that Moltmann's overarching concerns of eschatology and the doctrine of the
Trinity could be argued to lead necessarily and fruitfully to and beyond those
provocative constructions that he does pose. I would like to sketch those
primary areas of his thought and then show their bearing on our immediate
interest of time and eternity.

Moltmann's work of course, is well known. That which is most known
about his work, perhaps, is his methodology of eschatology, particularly as
announced in *Theology of Hope*. One cannot understand Moltmann without
understanding first the distinctive interpretation he gives to eschatology. What
many readers may not recognize is that throughout Moltmann's career the
understanding of God as Trinity is as important as his eschatology.
Eschatology and the doctrine of the Trinity are necessary, mutually informing,
binary concepts for Moltmann. It indeed may be the case that Moltmann's
doctrine of the Trinity was not as early refined as his eschatology.
Nevertheless, the sense as to its importance and requisiteness was there from
early on. In 1966, for example, in a series of essays written in preparation for
the *Theology of Hope*, Moltmann argued that a proper hermeneusis included
a trinitarian pneumatology. Further, only a trinitarian pneumatology could
establish the possibility for understanding revelation.[2] One may see here
Moltmann's trinitarian adaptation of Barth's principle that knowledge of God
comes about only through God's being present to the knower as both subject
and object. Furthermore, this God is not above time, but present to time in
trinitarian fashion as Christ, the Lord of the future.[3] When Moltmann's work
is viewed through the two lenses of eschatology and the Trinity, one may
apply his work to the question of time's relation to eternity. As we shall see,
Moltmann seeks to do this himself in his later work. Our focus first, however,
will be to explore his eschatology as the very theological method—some
would say that it functions even as a primary epistemology—by which all
other traditional loci are assessed and, if necessary, reconstructed.

It Starts With The Eschaton

Eschatology is not merely a locus of Christian systematic thought. It is rather the context and medium of Christian faith. Eschatology is not simply that locus of discussion about the end of time, nor the composite of *docta* of the last things. Eschatology for Moltmann is the very Christian symbol for divine transcendence and the "characteristic outlook" of Christian existence.[4]

To conceive of eschatology as the language for the transcendent means, for Moltmann, that previous notions of transcendence or otherness must be abandoned. This is virulently so with respect to use of Latin substantialist language and its Greek philosophical antecedents referring to God's unique otherness. With Ernst Bloch, Moltmann argued against the Parmenidean One in which there was identity of essence and existence. Entailed with this rejection is a rejection of the theological paradigm of knowledge as *anamnesis*, an epistemology taken over from Plato. There is no "primal essence" to which knowledge can return, no possibility of a *restitutio in integrum*. Rather, if one is to take seriously the phenomena of change and advance in time and history, as Bloch saw it, there must be a "category of the new." "Novelty," in terms of logic and experience, cannot be explained simply by reference to the past and present. Where could this "new" be if not in the past? It could be only in the future. However, where Bloch envisioned that this future would rise out of the *physis* of nature, Moltmann saw that for the new to be authentic it would have to lie outside of nature and history. The future thus came for Moltmann to be the symbol of transcendence. It is, indeed, the mode of God's being. It is the "paradigm of transcendence"; a transcendence which, as qualitatively and wholly other and new, alters the present.[5] The proper place for Christian theology to start, therefore, is not with the past, but with the future.[6] It is in this respect, Moltmann contends, that theological method is thoroughly eschatological.

The hermeneutical method therefore must be an interpretation of history conducted under the aegis of eschatology. A look at the alternatives to the agnosticism of the Hellenic metaphysical system further underscores this point. Were interpretation to be conducted from within the "anthropological turn," for example, the interpreter would be forced to admit that the context for disclosure of the world is the interpreter herself. Thus, one comes inevitably against one's "own limits and anxiety."[7] To accept these terms can, at best, result in a vision of history realizable only by humanity as the maker of history. And this is tantamount to a loss of the sense of transcendence. Under the auspices only of human (or natural) agency, there could be nothing new under the sun.

[Such a] definition, comprehension and understanding of history inevitably brings about at the same time an abrogation, a negation and annihilation of history. When the primary question is that of the origin, substance and essence of history, then the concrete movements, changes, crises and revolutions which constitute history are related to some factor that does not change, always exists and has equal validity at all times. The sciences and philosophy are here striving to combine the Greek logos with our modern experiences of reality, and our modern experiences of crisis with the Greek *logos*.[8]

But if there is recognized in the human reading of and response to history the implicit existence of hope, one must conclude that this hope cannot be located in the alternatives to the Greek *metaphysis* of anthropological or even existential understandings.[9] The source of hope itself is transcendent, if it is indeed hope.[10] It is also *extra nos* if existential meaning is based "on a truth which is found outside it and directed towards it."[11]

In other words, a proper hermeneusis construes history as meaningful finally only under eschatology. History is seen as the sphere of action of that revelation which derives from the future. Events can be interpreted only in terms of their meaning for the future. Thus, there is also future in the past. If the future is "causal," then the past "proleptically" anticipates the future. If this is a repetition of anything, it is a repetition of hope, a *spes perennis*. "Hope, as a waiting for history, enters, actualizing itself, into every new situation and, at the same time, still reaches out beyond every situation."[12] If the future can thus shape the past, as Moltmann imagistically puts it, then the believer's present is the "foyer" in the anticipated arrival of the future.[13] Christian faith is characterized by a particular sort of knowledge, though not in conflict with scientific knowledge. Christian faith understands that hope is realistic and so takes the possibilities of hope seriously. Hope relies on promise and promise can be understood and realized only eschatologically. Faith, insofar as it erupts into a search for understanding, is also an understanding, a knowledge, driven by hope; it is a *spes quaerens intellectum*, that *intellectum* of which is the very goal of hope (*spero ut intelligam.*).[14]

If history is to be understood in this way as the enactments of the future in the past, then certainly an initial piece in the understanding of God will include this understanding of transcendence, too. The future is the mode of God's being in history. God stands as the Lord of the Future transcendently over history, yet immanent to it in the prolepsis of historical events.[15] All history is "ruled" from this future. History takes its cues, as it were, from the image of the Kingdom of God to come. So Moltmann writes:

> A theological eschatology, if it is to remain eschatology at all, cannot develop the future and God's existence on the basis of the temporal concept of his eternity, or the impression of the sovereignty gained from the Christ event. It must rather

see to it that—just as the kingdom of God is not the mere "accident" of his divinity, or something added to it, but is that divinity's quintessence—so, the future too is the mode of his being that is dominant in history.[16]

The historical bases of Christian knowledge and hope are those acts by which God has revealed God's self indirectly in history.[17] All of these events bear the character of divine promise which calls forth hope for and toward the future. The central event of promise for Christians in history is, of course, the resurrection of Jesus. This is the proleptic event *par excellence* which discloses the future for humankind. It is an anticipation of the future of all creation, that the whole creation will be made new. The resurrection is a preview of what will happen according to the promises of God. It stands in contradiction to a world of crisis, decay and death. Thereby it calls forth the human response of hope enacted in praxis that lives in contradiction to the same worldly realities. One cannot gain sustenance for hope from knowledge based on anything other than the resurrection. But the universal and immediate revelation of God in all things and for all things can be seen when that knowledge is first enlightened by the resurrection of Jesus.

One may find here a helpful explanation of how "revealed" theology relates to "natural" theology. What really is at question, though, is how a new reality might be made known. Moltmann's argument is that the event itself—the resurrection, prefigured in the Exodus, etc.—creates a new eschatological horizon of understanding. That understanding is of "the universal future of the Lordship of the crucified Jesus Christ."[18] Thus the resurrection is the source and criterion of what can be said of God's revelation elsewhere. With this understanding we can hearken back to past events, seeing in them the history of promise which bears the future, seeing in them the future of the past. We also can look to present history and present nature, seeing the future of the present.

It should be quite clear by now that the priority of God's future over everything else gives to the historical/natural process an ineluctable direction that defies compromise. The natural order is subject to a purposefulness that is yet not wholly determined. The future is not closed. Moltmann's program is not a substitution of some sort of "eschatological determinism" (or teleological determinism) for a Lamarckian style of evolutionary determinism. While Moltmann maintains that this transcendent future of God exercises agency over present and past, it is also, precisely because it is transcendent, wholly open. The openness of the future is a theme to which Moltmann continually returns. The future is not fixed. Indeed, while we might learn its broad outlines from the beatific vision, there shall still be a future even when the *lumen gloriae* finally shines all in all. Freedom in and of the kingdom of

God will be the hallmark even of the kingdom to come.[19] Such openness is a
theme which Moltmann proclaims from early in his career.

> It might well be that once the promise becomes eschatological it breaks the
> bounds even of that which aetiology has hitherto considered to be creation and
> cosmos, with the result that the "eschaton" would not be a repetition of the
> beginning, nor a return from the condition of estrangement and the world of sin
> to the state of original purity, but is ultimately wider than the beginning ever
> was.[20]

This theme of openness is also clear in his later work.

> It is also even permissible to assume that in the kingdom of glory there will be
> time and history, future and possibility, and these to an unimpeded degree, and
> in a way that is no longer ambivalent. Instead of timeless eternity it would
> therefore be better to talk about "eternal time;" and instead of the "end of
> history" we should talk about the end of pre-history and the beginning of the
> "eternal history" of God, human beings and nature.[21]

However, we cannot and must not construe this history which awaits as
wholly positively along the lines of a triumphalistic theology of glory. The
question of God heretofore in the experience of history has always been
exacerbated by the facticity of tragedy. The experience of evil in the face of
presumed divinity contends with hope. It also eventuates into atheism or
fatalism if hope be not founded. Eschatology, therefore, if hope is to be
authentic, must take up into itself the question of theodicy. *Si deus, unde
malem?* That means for Moltmann that eschatological christology, whose
starting point is with the resurrection, must correlate with and never be
separated from christological eschatology, whose starting point is the
crucifixion of the one who was raised.

The Pauline *theologia crucis* is part and parcel of the theology of hope.
The cross and all that it symbolizes provides the historical context for hope
into which God entered. We understand the resurrection properly only from
within an eschatological horizon, but the hope thereby evoked is historically
anchored in the cross of Christ. The project of hope must always be subject
to the critique of the cross. Otherwise, hope dissolves into an abstract, deistic
or even humanistic utopianism (as in Bloch), or into triumphalistic
enthusiasm, occasions of which are documented from Corinth through the
montanists past Müntzer. This is the value of Moltmann's dialectic of
eschatological christology and christological eschatology; it evokes hope in the
coming rule of God out of the future, and yet ties it to the realistic, present,
suffering world signed in the cross. It affirms the divinity of God as the
"transcendent making real of all possibilities," and yet grounds the believer

in the present which yearns to be made adequate to the future, in which humanity, the *polis* and all nature will find their identities.

As the cross of Christ protects theology from vacuous utopianism, it also firmly roots all thinking about God's trinitarian being in God's historical accessibility at the very cross of Christ. The construction of a doctrine of the Trinity starts at the historical point of the crucifixion of Jesus. In this, Moltmann, like Pannenberg, is clear that trinitarian thinking, like Christology, begins "from below."[22] No other starting point could cohere with a theology based on the historical revelation of specific acts of God. One must begin with those specific acts and place them within the eschatological horizon of the history of promise if one wants properly to understand those acts. This means that the experience of the crucifixion of Jesus says something about the experience, reciprocally, of God and implies something about the mutual experience of the Father and the Son realized in the bond of the Spirit. The elaboration of these meanings is Moltmann's agenda in both *The Crucified God* and *The Trinity and the Kingdom*.

We assume that if God is indirectly revealed in history, then certainly what one might know about Jesus implies something about what one may know of God. In this respect, what we can know about divine reality begins with the scriptural accounting, and we do not need to resort to philosophical abstraction. The scriptural account speaks of God in Christ, reconciling the world to God's self. Thereby scripture speaks of the suffering of God in terms of the suffering of Christ.[23] But speculative metaphysics, such as those of Aquinas, could not allow for such a concept of God. Philosophical theism attributed to God the qualities of immutability and immovability; such a God was "apathetic."

> For metaphysics, the nature of divine being is determined by its unity and indivisibility, its lack of beginning and end, its immovability and immutability. As the nature of divine being is conceived of for the sake of finite being, it must embrace all the determinations of finite being and exclude those determinations which are directed against being...Death, suffering and mortality must therefore be excluded from the divine being...But Christian theology must think of God's being in suffering and dying and finally in the death of Jesus, if it is not to surrender itself and lose its identity....faith must take an opposite course and "understand God's Godness from the event of this death."[24]

Moltmann believes that this biblical understanding of God in *sympatheia* (a term taken from Abraham Heschel) with creation is the answer to theodicy. Rather than view God as separated from and immune to tragedy, sin, and evil, the biblical view puts such suffering in the very experience of God. The God who experiences suffering is in solidarity with those who suffer. It is the suffering of the world which God freely assumes out of love into God's self. But more helpfully, with respect to soteriology, as God then shows triumph over evil in the resurrection, so also genuine hope and praxis in contradiction to suffering is called forth and justified. The justification of the righteousness of God is achieved by a suffering God's victory in the resurrection, and will be validated for all in the eschaton.

The admission of a new metaphysic whereby God does suffer change and tragedy says something much more trenchant about the trinitarian nature of God. Moltmann contends that "if the cross of Jesus is understood as a divine event, i.e., as an event between Jesus and his God and Father, it is necessary to speak in trinitarian terms of the Son and the Father and the Spirit."[25] The cross of Christ demands trinitarian explication; only thereby can Christ's cross be adequately explicated. Any other sort of explication ignores and even does harm to the biblical/historical revelation.

> The reconciliation believed in as being in Christ has no meaning if God is not known as Trinity, if it is not recognized that He *is* but is at the same time the Other, the self-differentiating, the Other in the sense that this Other is God Himself and has potentially the divine nature in it, and that the abolishing of this otherness, this return, this love, is Spirit.[26]

This love can lead us into a dynamical description of the Trinity's relationship *ad intra* as implied from *ad extra*. This Spirited love of the lover with the beloved[27] means that there is an openness to suffering and change on the part of the lover. God, as the Father of the Son, is open to the sufferings of the Son. God experiences in grief the death of the Son. Reciprocally, and obversely, when the Son experiences the abandonment by the Father, the Son thus himself evidences openness to the Father's presence. To press further, the Father's experience of the separation of the Son and the death of the Son become a separation (Moltmann calls it a "nihil") within God's self. If the Father overcomes this *nihil* in an act of new creation out of his emptiness (a *creatio ex nihilo*), then God as the power of the future is open to the new life unto eternity of the Son. This new creation of resurrection and exaltation is analogous to God's first act of creation out of nothing.

And what of the Spirit's role in this dynamic? The Spirit of the Son sent by the Father in this new creative act now relates the Father and the Son. The Spirit also relates all creation, with which the Son is in solidarity, to the Father and the Son. This is the salutary and soteriological significance of the reconciliation achieved for us and all creation in the death and resurrection of the Son. The Spirit, in its action of relating, is then necessarily open too to the creation and to the Father and the Son, as they each are to the Spirit and the creation. In this way the persons of the Trinity are open to each other and the creation, while remaining sustainedly involved in the dynamic forging of history *ex nihilo, continua, et nova.*

This description of the Trinity "from below" ends in a fashion that is not possible through subscription to traditional philosophical theism. Philosophical theism, which starts from the concept of God's unity and essential unrelatedness to the created order, struggles finally to show God's relationship to the creature by way of a de-gradated sharing of the divine substance, if any real relationship is achieved in such a scheme at all. Moltmann admits that his approach, complete with the surrender of the Trinitarian persons to each other and to creation, could end with a panentheism. But it especially, like Luther with his notion of God hidden in the opposite (*Deus absconditus*), finds God in the humiliated and humiliation in God. Perhaps we can call Moltmann's concept more properly a "trinitarian-panentheistic theology of the cross."

> Therefore in communion with Christ it can truly be said that men live *in God* and *from God*, "that they live, move and have their being in him" (Acts 17:28). Understood in pantheistic terms, that would be a dream which would have to ignore the negative element in the world. But a trinitarian theology of the cross perceives God in the negative element and therefore the negative element in God, and in this dialectical way is panentheistic...To recognize God in the cross of Christ, conversely means to recognize the cross, inextricable suffering, death and hopeless rejection in God.[28]

But Moltmann also hedges on this call. We must be reminded of the eschatological caveat. The panentheistic character of the Trinity can be construed not in terms of contemporary proposals like those of process theology, which describe what "is." We can only interpret it with respect to the future. Only when God is "all in all," as the promise in St. John's Revelation holds, is history fulfilled and the Trinity completely immanent. Only at the eschaton will the justification of God be practically realized.

> As Paul says in 1 Cor. 15, only with the resurrection of the dead, the murdered and the gassed, only with the healing of those in despair who bear lifelong wounds, only with the abolition of all rule and authority, only with the annihilation of death will the Son hand over the kingdom to the Father. Then God will turn his sorrow into eternal joy. This will be the sign of the completion of the trinitarian history of God...[29]

If all human history is to be and is even now caught up in the trinitarian history, then Moltmann is proposing nothing less than that the process of suffering love and *creatio novum ex nihilo*, which characterizes the Trinity, is reality itself. The creativity of love constitutes reality. The fundament of all reality is the action of *real* love, exercised by real triune agencies. The point cannot be overemphasized. *Reality "happens" out of the economics of the trinitarian persons.* What "happens" in this triune reality is "God." So Moltmann: "Anyone who speaks of God in Christian terms must tell the history of Jesus as a history between the Son and the Father. In that case, 'God' is not another nature or a heavenly person or a moral authority, but in fact an 'event.'"[30]

This helps clarify what may have seemed to be an abiding ambiguity. It has not been clear until this point that "God" is the Trinity, and that the term "God" does not properly relate only to the term "Father," though that, of course, is the popular unreflective understanding, as well as one early Greek understanding. Rather, Moltmann is clear that "Father" denotes only the relationship of that divine person to the Son, and that humankind may refer to God as "Father" only insofar as we understand that our alignment with Jesus *within* the Trinity permits and asks for such address.[31] But more to the point, this understanding of God as "event," not unlike Jenson's concept as he adapted it from Peter Brunner, does not mean that the experience of God is episodic or occasional. The Triune God is also embracing. The divine reality is a continuous, accepting presence, encompassing all human history and all human inclinations. The divine reality is the very "situation in which man experiences, develops and shapes himself."[32] "[The Triune God] enters into the limited, finite situation of man. Not only does he enter into it, descend into it, but he also accepts it and embraces the whole of human existence with his being...without limits and conditions, so that each man may participate in him with the whole of his life."[33] The triune reality, in other words, is the source and sustenance, theologically *and* ontologically speaking, of all that is and can be.

A Closer Look at Moltmann's Trinity

We have already seen that Moltmann falls in line with the contemporary theological consciousness with regard to the non-viability of the Greek metaphysical understanding of God and God's attributes. What has not been noted is that Moltmann's objections to that understanding, as well as to others, are based upon his recognition of the Western world's changing view of reality. The classical cosmological proofs, for example, Moltmann argues, as modes of natural theological reason took their premises from the world in their arguments toward deity. They presupposed the world as an ordered cosmos.

The *de facto* contemporary presupposition about the cosmos, however, is one of chaos and entropy. "Violence, violence!" rightly cry the prophets. But the phrase is now recognized as more descriptive of how things are than as a judgement against them. The second law of thermodynamics speaks more than *nomos*; it undercuts future hope and, typologically, seems to predestine societies for dissolution and loneliness. Relationships between human individuals seem ever more transitory. Chaos means systemic imbalance, and entropy means death. If imbalance and death are precursors to life, as the post-Darwinian consciousness entertains, then life is but the arbitrary and purposeless rearrangement of ashes. Accidents do not just happen. They are the *norma normans sed non normata*, the norm which is itself unnormed, the foundation of all that happens. Such indeed would characterize the aspirited pathology of the contemporary deconstructed mind. While I have described the situation in non-Moltmannian terms, they cohere with his early recognition. Those who would cling to classical, or even neo-classical, scholasticism should take note. It is difficult to maintain the Aquinan proofs in *this* contemporary state of consciousness. Our changed view of reality mitigates the proofs.[34]

If there seems to be a lack of orderliness, Moltmann continues, then we tend to see ourselves as meant to tame the cosmos. Thus the cosmological proofs have yielded to a subjective proof, based on the presupposition that human existence and self-consciousness was the fundamental datum. This search for foundations was an advance over the classical basis. Its development is seen particularly from Descartes through Kant and Bultmann, in what philosophy has appropriately labelled as "the turn to the self." It also had its precursor in Augustine's method of starting with the *vestigia trinitatis* in human mental/emotional constructs. The intended end of this reflective process was the vision of God as the Absolute Subject. But Kant concluded (temporarily) that theological reasoning of this vein could achieve nothing more than a "practical" proof. On this subjective foundation, as Schleiermacher claimed, all statements about God are bound to be at the same time statements about personal existence determined by faith. So a Feuerbach quite rightly can ask where the self ends and God begins. Theology is but anthropology. The only "clear" answer is one that foregoes pure reason and adopts a Kantian legacy of pragmatic reason, in which moral monotheism is thought to provide the foundation for free and responsible conduct. As Moltmann sees it, this option reduces modern Christianity to "conforming" to Jesus. This is a truncated Christianity indeed. "The modern world's devotion to what is ethical and pragmatic has led to the disintegration of the doctrine of the trinity in moral monotheism. The reduction of faith to practice has not enriched faith; it has impoverished it. It has let practice itself become a matter of law and compulsion."[35]

The history of theology shows that we have been led to this conundrum. Christian faith ought to be lived with the vigor and spirit it has ever proclaimed. But modern consciousness is dubious about the possibility. On the one hand, there is no rational foundation for belief as there once seemed to be. On the other hand, the option of a pragmatic faith of moralism is bereft of the grounds for a doxology that could support the morally active life.[36] What road is there out of this impasse, short of fideism?[37] Moltmann suggests the way of Karl Barth. That is, take cues from Hegel and Fichte and start with God's self-identification through historical revelation. If God is God, then God must be the subject of God's own revelation and God's revelation can only be a self-revelation. There can be no talk "about" God unless God in God's revelation is the source of such discourse. Such a God is personally involved in revelation. So this leads to the idea of absolute personality, of God as "the personal God." This, combined with Ernst Bloch's concept of God as the principle of hope and power of the future,[38] blends happily with a biblically based account that assumes a personal God's involvement in, with, and over history. The problem now is how to describe this from a trinitarian perspective.

If it was a challenge to speak of God under the rubrics of supreme substance or moral monotheism, then it is likewise difficult to presume those rubrics as the background to the specific nomenclature of the doctrine of the Trinity. Moltmann is in league with others I have discussed in holding that natural theology's priority on the simple unity of God, expressed in school theology's *de Deo Uno*, has inhibited reflection on revealed theology's *de Deo Trino*. To begin with the abstract idea of unity of God *ad intra* made it most difficult to find the connection to understanding the threeness of God *ad extra*. Moltmann argues that the result is the posing of a double trinity, or, more commonly, abstract monotheism. "The representation of the trinitarian Persons in a homogenous divine substance, presupposed and recognizable from the cosmos, leads unintentionally but inescapably to the disintegration of the doctrine of the Trinity in abstract monotheism."[39] The understanding of God as Absolute Subject, however, as in Barth, has its own problematic and can lead to similar difficulties. The concept of person includes the concepts of relation and agency. If there is a prime "one" person posited as the unity of the Trinity, then the three divine persons are collapsed again into simple unity.

> [Here] the unity of the absolute subject is pressed to such a degree that the trinitarian Persons disintegrate into mere aspects of the one subject. But the special Christian tradition and proclamation cannot be conceived of within the concept of the absolute subject. To represent the trinitarian Persons in the one,

identical divine subject leads unintentionally but inescapably to the reduction of the Trinity to monotheism.[40]

Moltmann, therefore, will not construct a doctrine of the Trinity on the presupposition of the unity of the godhead. He would rather begin with the Trinity of the Persons as they are biblically revealed and then go on to ask about their unity. Then he would propose a concept of divine unity as the communion of the tri-unity. This has often been called a social model of the Trinity.

Moltmann readily appropriates the contemporary idea of "person" as a "field of relationships." Relationships, communities, social networks or fields are the common means of discussing "person" today. Quite helpfully, these terms supercede both "substance" and "subjective" thinking. Consequently, they must inform new trinitarian thinking. They also are in accord with the perichoretic paradigm of earlier trintarian theology.

> If we search for a concept of unity corresponding to the biblical testimony of the triune God, the God who unites others with himself, then we must dispense with both the concept of the one substance and the concept of the identical subject. All that remains is: the unitedness, the at-oneness of the three persons with one another...It must be perceived in the perichoresis of the divine Persons.[41]

Moltmann calls this an "ecological" conception of the Trinity. He also accepts that it is a social doctrine of the Trinity[42] and restates his conception in terms of communion and *koinonia*.[43] Perichoretic unity, after all, is an affirmation of differences-in-unity.[44] It underscores the distinction of each Person, yet describes their unity (not oneness).[45] And it poses trinitarian reflection in terms of the "openness" of the divine Persons to each other and to the world. These are significant terms, too, when Moltmann turns eventually to the discussion of temporality and eternity.

Moltmann's acceptance of the modern notion of person as constituted by relationality, along with his assumption of the historically revealed starting point—that is, the economics of the Trinity—lead him naturally to affirm Rahner's Rule.[46] In his reflection about the impact of the Theology of the Cross and the significance of the death of the Son for the Father, Moltmann felt compelled to surrender the traditional distinction between the economic and immanent Trinity. The relationship between the triune God to himself and to the world indeed must not be unidirectional, as from essence to manifestation or image to reflection. The relationship must be mutual. Nevertheless, the distinction between immanent and economic is useful insofar as the immanent Trinity is the purpose and end of doxology. This means, further, that statements about the immanent Trinity must not contradict statements about the economic Trinity, and statements about the economic Trinity must correspond to those about the immanent Trinity. Thereby Moltmann does not wholly conflate the distinctions. Indeed, he retains them for the same reasons Rahner intended. The immanent Trinity *will* be, however, the sole way of speaking of the Trinity and be revealed as such when the economic Trinity, complete with the history and experience of salvation, is "raised into and transcended in the immanent Trinity" at the eschaton.[47]

Throughout his trinitarian reflection Moltmann has posed "monotheism" as the undesirable consequence of alternatives to his mode of reflection. His assertions are often surprising and are not limited to his focus on the Trinity. He claims, for example, that the Orthodox dogmatic tradition protected the Trinity from the "danger of monotheism" and that monotheism "was and is the religion of patriarchy, just as pantheism is probably the religion of earlier matriarchy."[48] The lack of authentic trinitarianism in the early medieval church, Moltmann suggests, was due to the cultural embrace of "political-religious monotheism" and its attendant political form of monarchism. And, Moltmann says—clearly misunderstanding that which he quotes—"Christian faith is not 'radical monotheism.'"[49]

What may account for Moltmann's animus against monotheism? Theologically, Moltmann believes that a doctrine of the Trinity, again, which begins with "essence" or God as subject denies integrity to the second and third Persons of the Trinity. To start with the divine *monas* is also to assume monarchy. Monotheism and monarchy go hand in glove in Moltmann's reading of history. On the one hand, when the one God of Judaism is understood under the philosophical monotheism and monarchical concepts of Greek philosophy, the fusion is a Lord of all who is singularly unaffected by the subjects in his rule. On these grounds, a strictly monotheistic God can have no parts and must be immune to change. It "obliges us to think of God without Christ and consequently to think of Christ without God as well."[50] How may one conceive of Christ in such a monotheistic scheme? The answer is in Arius; Christ is interpreted in a christology of adoptionist subordinationism. As Moltmann writes, "Arianism is monotheistic Christianity in its purest form."[51] On the other hand, "Christian monotheism" can be the consequence of interpreting God's undivided unity as the One Subject. Herein, Christ is not subordinated so much as "dissipated" into the one God. This, of course, is the starting point for Sabellian modalism, in which the divine Persons are perceived merely as temporal appearances of the One God, first as Creator, then Redeemer, and finally Sanctifier.

The rationale against "radical monotheism" does not end here. Moltmann's criticism of monotheism based on the undesirability of falling into either of the classical anti-Trinitarian heresies is almost understandable, as far as it goes. But Moltmann is further repulsed because these forms of philosophical monotheism serve as the basis for oppressive political and clerical monotheisms as well. The image of "one almighty ruler" is mirrored both in the *polis* and in the *ecclesia*. The correspondence between political and cosmological ideas are early perceived, for example, in Aristotle. The rule of the many cannot be healthy when there exists the one, indivisible, immovable, impassible, and hence perfect deity. As the cosmos is hierarchically ruled, so also it must be on earth.

> ...if political rule was legitimated in the ancient world by an appeal to its correspondence with the gods, then polytheism corresponds to the multiplicity of cities and states, whereas cosmological monotheism calls for analogy in a universal imperium that unites the cities and states [thus God serves as the ground for the Pax Romana]. This is the only way in which the notion of the correspondence of political and religious ideas can be maintained and used as a legitimation of rule.[52]

If this is so in the political order, then likewise it has been copied in the clerical order. Cities and dioceses have their churches and their overseers, over all of whom must be the single overseer as the Vicar of Christ. That this is exacerbated by the Roman Catholic Church's insistence on male priesthood provides evidence that the conscious intention of the curia is to pattern its ecclesiology after such a "monotheistic monarchy."

Moltmann is not only critical of monotheism on these general grounds. He also points to particular culprits in his criticism of contemporary renditions of monotheism. In conscious opposition to aspects of their thought, he fashions his own position. Moltmann believes that Karl Barth and Karl Rahner fall prey to philosophical monotheism because they both begin with the image of God as the Absolute Subject. We noted earlier that Barth was uncomfortable in applying the modern notion of person to the three hypostases. Instead, after having initially posited the lordship of God, Barth proposed the formula for the Trinity as one subject in three modes of being. For Moltmann this is nothing less than modalism. No integrity is given to the divine persons. Rather, God "speaks himself" or reveals himself modalistically as a *repetitio aeternatatis in aeternitate*. This is only a threefold repetition of the "I" as subject; it is not a disclosure of the Trinity per se.[53] At base, Moltmann says of Barth, this betrays an Idealistic heritage. Barth uses a non-trinitarian concept of the unity of the one God to safeguard the lordship of God against a tri-theism that, Moltmann asserts, never existed.[54] Wolfhart Pannenberg agrees. In much the same sense as Moltmann, he writes that the weakness of Barth's trinitarian reflection is that Barth poses God's unity as the ground of threeness, rather than the result.[55]

Moltmann's brief is similar with respect to Karl Rahner. Rahner's resistance to attributing personhood to the hypostases and identifying them instead as "distinct modes of subsistence" leaves him wide open to Moltmann's charge of idealistic modalism. Rahner uses his terms so to avoid tritheism. But Moltmann argues that tritheism has never been a real danger. Rahner's application of the modern notion of personhood to the unique divine consciousness is but a retreat. In Moltmann's view, this falls back into an exclusivist understanding of God that denies access from *ad extra*. And Rahner's preference for the term "threefold God" (*Dreifältigkeit*) instead of the usual "triune God," the three-in-one (*Dreieinigkeit*) is "not merely modalistic, but also a bad German translation of 'trinitas.'"[56] Rahner is not only modalistic, he renders the doctrine of the Trinity as superfluous; the doctrine ends in "the mystic solitariness of God."[57] There is no greater danger than this, Moltmann concludes. The unity of the divine persons, understood as such, must be conceived rather in terms of openness, communicability, ability to integrate, and ultimately as perichoretic fellowship.[58]

Whether Moltmann's targets are theological positions or persons, his reasons do not justify his rejection of monotheism *per se*. Monotheism and Trinitarianism are not mutually exclusive. In fact, Moltmann's agenda is to demonstrate that the doctrine of the Trinity *does* show unity in diversity. And this unity is so characterized by openness to and empathy with the "other" within and without the Trinity that the union is palpable. Traditional Christian monotheism since Nicaea has this agenda precisely in mind; there is no God other than the one referred to as "Father, Son and Holy Spirit." If we seek to recapture the biblical understanding in the narrative of the one God who acts, as Moltmann would desire, consciously rejecting simultaneously the philosopher's god, then there should be no trouble, as Richard John Neuhaus writes, in calling ourselves "trinitarian monotheists and monotheistic trinitarians."[59]

For our purposes, perhaps it is enough to suggest that a different nomenclature is required for Moltmann.[60] His point in pressing the issue is pertinent, however, and thus we are justified in following the argument thus far. Moltmann's investment on this issue stems from the conviction that, first, the Trinity embraces all history, and, second, therefore all social and ecclesial structures are called too into the divine re-creation of this history. For Moltmann this means that there are tangible implications for the church, for human society, and for nature. If all creation, according to the doctrine of hope, is to proceed toward the divine future as glimpsed in the *koinonia* of the Trinity, creation too will anticipate this future by shaping itself in a non-hierarchical, de-centralized way. In numerous instances, Moltmann cites this way as synodal and voluntaristic with regard to the church, democratic-socialist and egalitarian with regard to society, and ecologically communitarian with respect to nature.[61]

The doctrine of the Trinity, therefore, functions as a systematic theological and a meta-ethical principle for the structuring of all Christian life and thought. It not only serves in this way. It also indicates in Moltmann's view that the primal Christian experience of God is an experience directly of the trinitarian Persons. Thus the primal Christian—indeed human!—experience is "proto-trinitarian." Trinitarian reflection is not only second-order. It is experiential and personal. The doctrine of the Trinity is a primary construction of primary experience of "God with us." In that, the doctrine is the first-order articulation of how the eternal assumes the temporal and how the temporal in quite "real" fashion influences the eternal. The human history of victory and tragedy is also God's history; likewise God's history is humankind's.[62] This is what Moltmann means to explicate in the doctrine of the Trinity. Finally, insofar as broken history demands healing and purpose, the doctrine of the Trinity indicates too, because it is a doctrine of persons who are *open* to each other, that history will be recreated, even out of its "nihil," through the power of the Trinity's future. At that time, the divine Persons will be truly "immanent," as God will be all in all and all will be in communion with God. So it is that the Trinity and eschatology shape the contours of Moltmann's theology from its beginning to its end.

"Monotheism" and Panentheism

Insofar as Moltmann positions his trinitarian theology over and against the foil of monotheism,—this term I have already argued is mistaken—the question arises as to what sort of theism Moltmann's theology affirms. Though Moltmann is unconcerned about the dangers of tri-theism, there are those who have charged that this is exactly the character of Moltmann's position.[63] It appears, however, based on our observations so far, that if one is going to land the charge of tritheism on Moltmann, then one had better paint the whole Eastern tradition with it, too. It is precisely Moltmann's appeal to the Eastern terminology of relation and communion that meets and overcomes the objection of tritheism. Yet there is still unclarity as to Moltmann's place. Carl Braaten notes that Moltmann repeatedly resorts to convention in use of the simple term "God" without trinitarian qualification, as if Moltmann falls on his own monotheistic sword.[64] It is also unclear whether Moltmann affirms a panentheistic perspective or is closer to traditional theism. I take theism to denote that God is distinguished from the world and yet involved in it. Panentheism denotes that God's being includes the created order but is not exhausted by it.[65] Though Moltmann observes that his thought tends toward panentheism, as we noted earlier, he nevertheless shows some discomfort with this and refers to examples that would underscore a more traditional theism.

For example, Moltmann eagerly refers to Isaac Luria's kabbalistic doctrine of *zimsum* to explicate how there might exist a "space" out of which God can create. He envisions that the omnipresent God's first act of creation was to will a self-contraction, an inversion of himself, so to make possible the existence of a world in a space no longer occupied by God.[66] This, then, is the world to which God relates as Trinity. The description is in accord with the definition of theism. But Moltmann proceeds to confuse the issue. He summarizes this particular discussion by saying that that panentheism is a trinitarian idea.

> The trinitarian concept of creation binds together God's transcendence and his immanence. The one-sided stress on God's transcendence led to deism, as with Newton. The one-sided stress on God's immanence in the world led to pantheism, as with Spinoza. The trinitarian concept of creation integrates the elements of truth in monotheism and pantheism. In the panentheistic view, God, having created the world, also dwells in it, and conversely the world which he has created exists in him. This is a concept which can really only be thought and described in trinitarian terms.

Elsewhere Moltmann identifies theism with the monotheism he resolutely rejects. Appealing to Whitehead, he asserts that theism is the idolatry of the philosopher's god, and he identifies this with the God presupposed in Aquinas's *de Deo Uno*.[67] In the same breath, Moltmann states that the proper view is like that of process theology, though process theology lacks the trinitarian terms.[68]

What is Moltmann's position? Were it panentheistic, it could almost be tautologous eventually to say that the eternity of the Trinity is essentially temporal. But it is not that pat, and Moltmann evidently does not know his own mind on this matter. Therefore a comparison of his overall eschatological trinitarian project with a panentheistic view may be helpful. Insofar as Moltmann has appealed to process theology for support, and insofar as process theology is the primary proponent of (a particular) panentheism, I shall refer to process theology as the point of comparison.

What are some points of agreement and disagreement between Moltmann and process theology? In general, of course, both theologies are concerned with theodicy. In every process theologian's view, God is related to the process but maintains the abilities to overcome its deficiencies.[69] For Moltmann, however, God overcomes all out of the transcendent power of the future. Inasmuch as the future is identical with absolute transcendence, God creates *ex nihilo et simul continua*. That is, for Moltmann, God always creates anew, and this creation, stemming from God's future, can and does change even the past. Just as the future saves the present, so also it redeems the past. Moltmann writes:

> Is there thus for Paul no continuity between history and this new future? Yes, even for him there is continuity. But it does not consist in some human or immanent factor in perpetual process; it is, rather, the faithfulness of God, who, in creating the new, remembers and brings back the old, which has turned away from him and has been lost. The expression "resurrection of the dead" means that God brings back the dead in his new creation and gathers up the lost. The new creation therefore takes up the old creation in itself, just as all historical continuity is created by the future which takes up into itself what has been lost. Thus historical continuity distinguishes itself in principle from an organic or ontological continuity. If God creates a qualitatively new future, then he is not only the future of the present, but also the future *of* the past and *for* the past.[70]

This is, of course, quite opposed to a process theology, in which the *becoming* of God—or, the fulfillment of the kingdom—is immanent in the natural and historical process. Process theology can admit of *no* final or transcendent end to history; likewise it posits no beginning. So Whitehead: "Neither God, nor the world, reaches static completion. Both are in the grip of the ultimate metaphysical ground, the creative advance into novelty. Either of them, God and the world, is the instrument of novelty for the other."[71]

Moltmann's eschatological theology, however, holds that the future event of history's "completion"[72] is not an inner worldly historical event. It comes to the world from without. "Only a future which transcends the experiment of history itself can become the paradigm of transcendence and give meaning to the experiment 'history.'"[73] Moltmann's theology can thus be characterized in its grammar as one always of future tense, while in a more naturalistically inclined theology eschatological assertions would refer to the present tense.[74] Only the transcendent future can remake what is and has been, as we have cited above. Such a future Moltmann has characterized not as the *futurum*, with its nascent blossoming seed of immanent process, but as *adventus*. If God is "becoming" at all, then, God becomes only insofar as God is "coming." Moltmann himself has noted this as an essential difference between process theology and his eschatological theology.[75]

A question arises as to the role of praxis in Moltmann's theology. The question includes, too, concern about the valuedness of nature and history in and of themselves apart from any role in the dawning of the eschaton.[76] Anyone familiar with Moltmann's work, of course, might find this to be a curious matter. Moltmann is well known as a political theologian whose work has been deeply influential for the early expositors of liberation theology. Even so, one might ask as to how any human action might contribute to the enterprise of the divine kingdom, if, in fact, that kingdom as Moltmann affirms comes *only* out of or from the transcendent future of God. Gerhard Forde and others today are fond of referring to the "eschatological limit" imposed by the otherness of God and the kingdom which is coming.[77] So, if the kingdom comes having had no immanental relationship with nature or history on this side of the eschatological divide, for what does human action or discrete natural process count? Do nature and human action on behalf of the coming kingdom have virtue in and of themselves?[78]

In his work before *Theology of Hope*, Moltmann gave much attention to the Calvinist theme of the sovereignty of God.[79] As sovereign, or "actor, producer, and director" in the salvation drama, God introduces the resurrection as the *novum primum*. The resurrection is the historical experience of the future, a prolepsis, which thereby engenders the hope that the tragedy of history will indeed be overcome. On the basis of hope, human action can contradict the present (and past) reality of the world. By way of the proleptic eschatological qualification of history, human action contributes to the kingdom of God. Indeed, it is the basis of Moltmann's political theology.

The role of human action in Moltmann's theology, then, appears to be a bit more circuitous than in process theology. In Moltmann's view, one might say human response is engendered and given integrity by God's acting from the future by way of past and present; similarly so with respect to the natural order. While Moltmann does not attribute conscious agency to the components of the natural world, he does argue that creation is an "open system" which bears "the prints of the triune God" and are "the real promise of the coming kingdom."[80] Thus the natural order too speaks more to the transcendence of God in Moltmann's view than in a process view.

A process theological view, on the other hand, would have God acting more unilaterally. God simply offers the initial aim to each and every moment. The aim is shaped according to the preceding circumstances of human being and cosmos. The human is free to respond or not, as one prefers. Indeed, the possibility is given that the freest of human choices might contribute to the divine enjoyment, and thereby the choice possesses value even apart from any prior judgement of adequacy on God's part. It would seem, in other words, that a process scheme gives more weight to human action than Moltmann's. In the process scheme, every act of God is contingent upon prior creaturely agency. Thereby God's initiatives are limited and God's power is qualified.

Moltmann's eschatological construction, however, would seem to be an attempt more to guard the transcendence of God without the sacrifice of immanence. We see this in Moltmann's affirmation that God as the power of the transcendent future can wholly redeem the past. "The resurrection of Christ is without parallel in the history known to us. But it can for that very reason be regarded as a 'history-making event' in the light of which all other history is illumined, called into question and transformed."[81] Human and natural agency are couched sheerly, it seems, in the prior initiative of God. But is such activity really so separate? Does it not contribute anything to history's future in at least some integral and reciprocal fashion?

Moltmann's answer ends in something like a "yes, but..." qualification. With reference again to I Corinthians 15, in answer to Peter Momose's posing of the same question,[82] Moltmann observes that there is continuity and discontinuity in human history. The continuity is that it is this world which shall be redeemed. But the redemption comes only from God's side inasmuch as there is the breech of death on the human side. No praxis can cross that boundary. If the dead have a future, it is a future which can come not as *futurum*, again, but as an *adventus*. Because of the reality of death, in other words, human and natural agency is limited in what it can contribute to God and history.

It should be noted that this difference implies a deeper difference between Moltmann's and process programs. For our purposes, at least, this difference is more significant than the difference between advent and future. That death plays a key role in both programs is hardly arguable. But death's—let us say *temporality's*—significance is unequally weighted in these programs. In the process scheme, temporality's significance is understood existentially. It is absorbed, so to speak, into the experience of God, and thereby it is made meaningful for the temporal being. Further, integral to the process understanding is the continuity of temporality; "death" is repeatedly necessary to the experiential continuum. Thus death is translated into liveliness and is, paradoxically, necessary to divinity's and creation's continuity. Not to put too fine a point on it, it would seem to some that process theology trivializes temporality. Temporality is but an ongoing experience for the eternal God, in whose eternal memory the transitoriness of temporality is overcome. Death need not be feared because it has been removed from human experience and remembered *in the divine life*. But one wonders how consoling this is for those who still experience temporality and whose end is but temporality. This turns on its end what sense of value there might have been to the freedom of human choices in the process theological scheme, as we discussed above, for it seems now their end is but to feed the experience of the subject God. There is no objective value, however, for the human subject as far as the human's consciousness is concerned.

This is not the case in Moltmann's program. Temporality, implicitly, is given great integrity and is the stuff of tragedy. This is the grand lesson of both nature and history. Temporality, understood not existentially, but with absolute natural and historical force, ends not in continuity, but in nothingness. Consequently, a divine transcendence that can create *ex nihilo* is required. Such transcendence, logically, is one which can come only from the future. It should be clear at this point also that any trinitarian characterization of God must overcome this very caesura implied by temporality and incorporate it into the experiences of the persons of the Trinity. One might conclude thereby that the meaning of the death of Christ, if his relational identity to God is affirmed, requires a radical trinitarian doctrine, a third qualification, as it were, so to deal positively with the nihil between God and Jesus. A process scheme, generically conceived, could not admit such a caesura between Jesus and God insofar as his death is his "fusion" with God's consequent nature.

But let us explore the nuances of these two programs regarding the doctrine of the Trinity *per se*. It is not enough, I believe, simply to hold that a doctrine of God is a doctrine of the Trinity, and *vice versa*, as John O'Donnell argues.[83] Of course, the doctrines are necessarily related. But a doctrine of the Trinity must account for particular themes in the history of theology, which accounting need not be so with a more general doctrine of God. And the argument could be made that a doctrine of God, within a certain neo-orthodox perspective, for example, is not even "more fundamental" than a doctrine of the Trinity. For Moltmann, the doctrine of the Trinity is the entry into a more thorough-going doctrine of God, and that starting point makes all the difference in comparison to a process theologian. At least once Moltmann has been clear that process theology can never be an adequate Christian theology precisely because it is not trinitarian. "Christian theology cannot develop (as is often done in process theology) a bipolar theology of interaction between God and the Spirit in man. It must, for the sake of the crucified one, intentionally become a trinitarian theology."[84]

Furthermore, if a process theology were to assume a trinitarian structure, it would have to be modalistic, rather than the communitarian structure which Moltmann affirms. Indeed, in his christology, John Cobb propounds a Logos Christology wherein Christ is identified with the Logos as the Principle of Creative Transformation. With this construction Cobb contends that the Logos is fully God and that there is no "ultimate difference between the Logos and God."[85] Cobb interprets that this is in accord with the official doctrine of Nicaea and thus goes along with the modalist view (which he also regards as the "official" view), "placing the emphasis upon the unity of the persons."[86] If any contemporary theological project short of deism could be closer to what

Moltmann regards as his nemesis, i.e., "monotheism," it is hard to find. Cobb also stops short of identifying Jesus with the Son, and would argue rather that the historical Jesus discovers his unity with God by way of his openness to the Logos. But this does not make Jesus the member of any trinity. Jesus, rather, through this obedience exemplifies what is possible in principle for any person or other actual event. The Logos is distinctly not the historical Jesus. It is a modalistic aspect of God, of whom Cobb finally would prefer no trinitarian description whatsoever.[87] Yet, of course, Moltmann would insist that it is the historical event of Jesus that gives God trinitarian character; it is through Jesus as part of the divine economy that we come to know the immanent Trinity.

Process theology also goes further to attack the communitarian model of the Trinity which Moltmann proposes. Lewis Ford explains why.

> This latter, social, interpretation is precluded in terms of Whitehead's categories because of the intrinsic connection forged between substantial unity and subjectivity. The denial of vacuous actuality entails that every substantial unity enjoys its own subjectivity, and no meaning can be attached to a subjective process of becoming which does not terminate in some sort of substantial unity. Thus while "person" as "center of subjectivity" may be distinguished from "substance" as "substantial unity," the two are in strict correlation. Three persons entail three substances, while one substance entails a single person. Moreover, substance in the sense of a divine substratum in which the three persons inhere is just that sort of vacuous actuality devoid of its own subjectivity which Whitehead rejects. "Person" in trinitarian formulations must mean rather a formally distinct aspect or principle or mode of functioning for a single, unitary actuality, that which Whitehead termed a "nature" when speaking of the primordial and consequent natures of God.[88]

Indeed, the claim of "modalistic dissolution" which Moltmann brings against Rahner and Barth must apply to a process theology doctrine of God as well. "The reflection Trinity of the absolute subject has only the appearance of a doctrine of the Trinity in itself, but in fact this doctrine is the monotheistic dissolution of the Trinity. This happens—as always—by the introduction of *modalism* (the three persons are three ways of the appearance of the being of the one God)."[89]

If modalism is unacceptable to Moltmann, then certainly any scheme, process or otherwise, which literally de-personalizes God is equally unacceptable. John O'Donnell argues, nevertheless, that there exists a deeper bond between Moltmann and process theologians, i.e., their common conviction that God's being lies in his becoming, which is also God's history. I would counter that this bond is equally illusory. Again, in no way would or could Moltmann agree to the term "becoming." The future comes from ahead; it does not grow from the past. This presses the difference, finally, between a process orientation and an eschatological one, as of Moltmann. Each has a quite different manner by which to relate God's transcendence to his immanence. It would seem that Moltmann on his own terms would better be described not as panentheistic, but as theistic. If the traditional term still does not fit comfortably, perhaps the best descriptive then is "eschatological theism."[90]

Finally, it seems also that Moltmann himself has come to a belated understanding of how different his eschatological program is from that of process theology. "Der Graben zwischen einer bewusst 'natürliche' Prozesstheologie zu einer traditionell in der Offenbarung gegründeten Trinitätslehre ist freilich noch tief. Breit ist auch der Graben zwischen einer eschatologisch erschlossenen Geschichtsauffassung und einer Gecshichtsauffassung, die vom Verständnis der Natur als Prozess herkommt."[91]

Trinitarian Time and Trinitarian Eternity

Moltmann's doctrine of the Trinity, in sum, locates the unity of the Trinity in the openness and self-surrender of the persons to each other and to the world. In that respect, the Trinity is not immanently closed, but eminently open. This means that that which is created *ex nihilo et continua* by the Trinity is also taken up with all history into the Trinity. The created order is neither extrinsic nor accidental to God, then, when God is construed trinitarianly. As with Barth, Jüngel, and others, Moltmann does not ground God's relatedness in time and history. It is God's trinitarian relatedness internally, and so externally, which is the ground for time and history. Furthermore, an eschatological trinitarian doctrine of God which posits the priority of the eternal future for God means that there is a proleptic direction in God which, I contend, can be understood only temporally. That is, temporality is in the eternity of God. O'Donnell, following Jüngel and Moltmann, captures the point this way:

> The Christian God is the God who suffers in time, who enters our history in the event of Jesus Christ. To think God in the light of this event is to think of a God whose being is in coming. God's coming to [humanity] proceeds from his sovereign freedom of overflowing love. In this sense God's coming is grounded in his transcendence. But since God's being itself is his coming, we cannot think of God without his creation or without [humankind or without temporality. Humanity and temporality are] not accidental or external to God but through the unfathomable mystery of his love are part of God's own self-definition.[92]

Moltmann understands that this doctrine of the Trinity implies much for the doctrine of Creation, and thus for the contemporary scientific world view. Because of this advance in his trinitarian thought, Moltmann was able to "turn to the world" with his Gifford Lectures of 1984 and 1985, published as *God In Creation, A New Theology of Creation and the Spirit of God.* In this book he seeks to "de-secularize" the world and "secularize" God. That is, he recognizes that the emphasis on God's transcendence in theology to this point (again we see his animus against abstract monotheism) has led to a crisis in humanity's understanding of itself and nature. Christian re-interpretation of the modern scientific world is therefore necessary, so that God's spirited involvement *in* the world can be recognized anew. Moltmann's doctrine of the Trinity enables him to do this and he consistently holds to his eschatology in the enterprise. It also means that Moltmann turns directly to a trinitarian re-explication of time and eternity vis-à-vis the modern scientific worldview.

Moltmann begins by summarizing and disposing of the notions of time as the Platonic, circular repetition of eternity and of time as the eternal present of Parmenides.[93] With Augustine, he agrees that time is created by God's resolve. Interestingly, Moltmann elaborates that God's resolve to create means a self-alteration of eternity so to make space for created time (recall the discussion we had above of the kabbalistic doctrine of zimsum). God makes "God's own time" so to create the creation by self-willing a kind of kenosis, by withdrawing his eternity into himself.[94]

Moltmann is both unclear and not comprehensive enough on this point. The question may arise as to why there first needs to be any transition. Why not simply say that time is created from within eternity? One might read Moltmann as if he were to say eternity is so contradictory to time that some kind of transitionary bridge needs to be established. But this is not his aim. Moltmann in fact desires to pose time and eternity in such a way that they are not defined over and against each other.[95] So Moltmann assumes the need for the transition. Still, he will not take up the option that eternity includes and transcends temporality. Why? Though Moltmann is unclear about this issue and is not thorough in thinking through the issue, he virtually identifies God with God's eternity, much as Gregory of Nyssa identified God with God's infinity. Therefore the distinction of God from creation by means of God's self-limitation is a safeguard for the position of *theism*. This is the way to avoid a panentheistic approach and to affirm God's trinitarian transcendence and immanence. Further, Moltmann would also identify God's transcendence with the transcendence of the eschatological future. This means, finally, that the distinction of God from the creation is a distinction of temporalities. And such are the distinctions that Moltmann proceeds to enumerate with his following of and elaboration upon Augustine's key notion of the subjective experience of time.[96]

Moltmann asserts that there is within the Trinity a particular sense of time he labels as eschatological. Eschatological time is God's time. It is the time which embraces all other times retroactively "from the future." Eschatological time is a means whereby Moltmann would now speak of God's trinitarian transcendence-in-immanence.[97] This sense of time, Moltmann asserts, is a *different* sense. It is not linear, but "future disjunctive" (my term). It relates to what transcendently lies ahead in the sense that creation relates transcendently to God's prior resolve. This is a very important point. In the eschatological time scheme of things the following applies. All things which are no longer ultimately determinative, such as sin, law, and death, belong to the past. All things which are already valid and efficacious, such as grace, reconciliation, and liberty, belong to the present. And all things which are now in the Christian life to be hoped for, though not yet experienced, including the resurrection of the dead, the redemption of the body, and eternal life, belong to the future.

> But this means that *the present time* of believers is no longer determined by the past. It takes its definition from the future. The believer's present is free from the past and open for the future of the Messiah. It is the present of the One who is to come. So it is by no means true that the Christian faith replaces the archaic, cyclical interpretation of time by a modern, linear one. What it puts at this point is its own messianic understanding of time, which distinguishes between the quality of past and future—which is the very opposite of setting them on a single line.[98]

Here Moltmann makes a provocative proposal. He recognizes that time accompanies events in a phenomenological fashion. There is no single past-present-future. There are different pasts, presents and futures of individual historical events. So, following the suggestion of some process studies and Augustine, Moltmann develops a scheme which gives to each mode of time its own past, present, and future.[99] Augustine had already spoken of the different modes of time at each moment of time in terms of *memoria* (the present past), *contuitus* (present present) and *expectatio* (present future).[100] Moltmann takes this further, arguing that the concept of linear time covers only simple series of events. This linear concept is inadequate, however, because these series actually are woven into a network of interrelations and multiple effects. If, over Augustine's historicization of time and the irreversible/reversible arrows of time, one were to add the constitutive presence of the future to every moment, the distinctions between the various time matrices would be as follows.

Linear time is still simply to be construed as the direction from Past (P) to Present (Pr) to Future (F) or, as Moltmann conceives it, P→Pr→F. Augustine's historicization of time (present past, present present and present future) would accordingly appear as PrP→PrPr→PrF, because the future is herein always mediated by the present. This Augustinian "temporal line," as it were, however can be understood only within the larger context of a "matrix" of times, such that we must pose two other "temporal lines" as follows: PP→PrP→FP and PF→PrF→FF. In the former, we see that the times are mediated by the past (P); in the latter by the future (F). Moltmann then adds these all together into a "network."

PrP→PrPr←PrF
  ↓   ↓
PrF→PrPr←PrF
  ↓   ↓
PrF→PrPr←PrF
  etc.←F[101]

Moltmann's point is to give us the image of an eschatologized network of times, in which all creaturely life is found. Beyond the PrF, the Future (F) is always the eschatological/ transcendent future. As Moltmann puts it:

The future as project always goes beyond the future as experience. The future that transcends all remembered, experienced and still-to-be-experienced present is what we call the eschatological future. We have to understand it not as future history, but as the future *of* history. As the future of history, it is the future of the past, as well as the future of the present and the future. In this sense, it is the source and the fountain of historical time. *The primary phenomenon of primordial and authentic temporality is the future.*[102]

Indeed, the eschatological future determines all modes of time. It also bears significance for our understanding of God's being insofar as God's transcendence and the transcendence of the eschatological future are mutually interpretive. Moltmann draws support from the futuristic text of Revelation 1:4 ("Peace to you from him who is and who was and who is to come."). This underscores, once again, discussion we have engaged above.

We would expect as a third term the words "...and who will be." But the future tense of the verb "to be" is replaced by the future of the verb "to come." This alters the third term in the concept of time quite decisively. God's being is in his coming, not in his *be*coming. So his being does not pass away when once it comes. If God and the future are linked together theologically in this way, God's being has to be thought of eschatologically; and then the future has to be understood theologically. But if "future" is thought of theologically, it acquires a continual transcendence compared with every present, and makes of every present a provisional transcendence. In this way the future becomes the paradigm of transcendence.[103]

So the "direction" of time is impelled by what is ahead. As eternity marks what transcendently lay beyond the past, the eschaton marks the future beyond the future. Moltmann argues that the future maintains an ontological priority over the other temporal modes and that the eschatological time of the all embracing future of God—eternity—is the ontological ground for all temporality. Indeed, though Moltmann earlier may seem to have desired distance between God's eternity and time, Moltmann's enumeration of different senses of time concludes with the positing of "eternal time," that "time of the new eternal creation in the kingdom of divine glory."[104] "Eternal time" is the transcendent manifold of God that includes temporal finitude. For those subject to temporal finitude, on the other hand, eternal time is the grand future where life will still carry on in the dynamism of the fulfilled immanent Trinity. Perceived proleptically from this present time, as Moltmann would have to argue it and as I argue, we may then conclude that temporality is indeed essential to the Trinity.

Critique

Moltmann's phenomenological recognition of time/events could have been significantly strengthened if he had paid more direct attention to the sciences. The acknowledgement that each event has its "own" time, for example, finds ready correlation with Special Relativity and with the "internal time" of event/objects in General Relativity, as Chris Isham pointed out. Furthermore, Moltmann's construction of a "network of times" may be somewhat comparable to Hawking's use of Feynmann's "sum over histories" and its parlay into "imaginary time," though it is arguable that anything can be gained from such a comparison. Finally, Moltmann's concepts of openness of the future, openness in the Trinity, and of creation as an "open system" would seem to find ready correlation in the fundamental indeterminacy of the quantum realm. Yet, Moltmann does not draw explicitly or with any depth from these or other possibilities. Though Moltmann is fond of referring to the natural order as a *laboratorium possibilis salutatis* (a laboratory of possible salvation) which can be changed and made adequate to its future in creation, Moltmann's self-conscious intent to remain theological barrs access to the laboratory, except for a few general references.

Questions which could be posed to Moltmann, then, may be these. First, are his general references to some physical science themes correct and rightly appropriated? Second, are there specific data and theories which could strengthen his program, and, if so how (such as those just mentioned)? Third, are there physical scientifc data and theories that we surveyed in chapters 4 and 5 that would challenge Moltmann's doctrine of the Trinity? These questions, of course, make the perhaps unusual assumption that natural science should inform theology and *vice versa*. But inasmuch as Moltmann has referred, at least, to the laboratory, it is appropriate now to take him up at his word and go there to ask these questions of his most operative term taken from the sciences.

The term which symbolizes much of Moltmann's theology, and seems to be the key component borrowed from the natural sciences, is "open system." Moltmann has mined this concept repeatedly in the elaboration of his eschatological theology.[105] So, we ask, is Moltmann's general reference to this physical science theme rightly understood and appropriated? It would seem that Moltmann's use of the sciences at this point is more metaphorical and less directly correlative with theological assertions than he would admit. While correlation is one's ultimate desire, it may well be that consonance—we recall Ernan McMullin's advice—is the more pragmatic and heuristically helpful goal, at least in the short term.[106]

One occasion in which Moltmann perhaps too quickly assumes correlation is indeed his general appropriation of the term "open system." He writes that this world, brought from slavery to freedom and created by God with a natural orderliness, is open to time, to the future, and to change. It is "an 'open system,' full of every potentiality."[107] Moltmann refers to the seminal work of Arthur Peacocke with this appeal to "open system."[108] But Moltmann does not sustain the strict scientific sense of the term, as does Peacocke. Moltmann rather likens open system to the process of communication in community and to orientation to the transcendent future.[109] The use of the phrase, at best, is only analogous to the scientific sense. It would better align with Pannenberg's use of the term "exocentricity" in his theological anthropology.[110] Indeed, Moltmann's argument in *God in Creation* is that God's creative activity in the world is intended to "open up systems which are closed up in themselves." God does this by suffering communication. The cross is paradigmatic, then, for God's relationship to natural physical systems. Furthermore, through this suffering mode of communication, God creates quite specific chances for "liberation from isolation," and quite specific chances for the evolution of the various open life systems. The eschatological future of creation, then, is the openness par excellence of all life systems.

This will be the identity of the new creation in the kingdom of glory, which will perdure in and through a new, infinite temporality.[111]

In the physical sciences, however, openness refers to the lack of external or internal constraints for growth and perdurance, and especially to the exchange of energy between systems and their environment. A "closed" system, in contrast, may perdure and grow, but is entirely energy self-sufficient. In the "open system," life continues as long as energy is given from "outside" the system. In a closed system, life will be exhausted in shorter order because the energy is limited. In either case, according to the given scientific scenario based on the limited amount of matter/energy in the universe, entropy will win out and cold death ensue. Furthermore, if "system" is applicable to the universe as a whole, one must acknowledge that various cosmological models pose the universe as expanding (open), steady state (open or closed) or retracting (closed).[112] It is not necessarily the scientific case that the universe is an open system. But it is scientifically so in any case that openness will result in a tired cold death and a closed system will result in an imploding hot one. Moltmann not only misconstrues the concept of "open system." He fails to understand that the universal system, open or closed, scientifically is slated for death. Indeed, Moltmann denies that entropy plays a role in an open universe; he glosses over its significance.[113] The general concept is misappropriated. The specific consequences challenge the very concept of an open future in Moltmann's theology.

But closer attention yet may show that this need not be so. If Moltmann were to acknowledge and carefully analyze the issue, he could propose at least two responses that are consonant with his own theological program. I shall only be suggestive, not comprehensive, on these points. First, Moltmann, in the Augustinian tradition, identifies God's love as the impetus for self-communication and creativity. This same love of God is also identified as the divine energies (*energeia*) that are shared in the Trinity. Moltmann assumes this from the "tri-versity" and discussion of the divine energies, rather than attributes, carried on by the Cappadocian Fathers.[114] The transcendence of love and its "energy" on God's part in Moltmann's program could give more descriptive content to what Moltmann means by affirming God as "the power of the future." Furthermore, assuming the premise that the economics of the trinitarian life say something about the trinitarian life *in se*, then we conversely may suppose that in some sense the energy of the trinitarian life *in se* is the resource for dynamic creations, like time, *ad extra*. This brings trinitarian reflection closer to giving an apt theological answer posed by the theodicy question nascent in the datum of entropy. Recognizing that the terminology may not exactly match, at least consonance is achieved in suggesting that the divine energies which make up the power of the future can transcendently overcome the lack of energy signed by entropy.

Second, and perhaps related to the first suggestion, Moltmann's appeal to the Theology of the Cross, inasmuch as it denotes God's suffering of the natural order, too, can also denote God's suffering of entropy or universal collapse. If the cross is paradigmatic for how God relates to the cosmos, then God will take into God's self the anomie of an ennervated universe or its heated and hysterical breakdown. And as God brought new order out of the chaos of Christ's death, symbolized in the shaking and shading of the universe around the cross of Christ on that fateful Friday, so also faith would hold that God will bring new order out of the chaos predicted by the sciences.[115] In this case, less is explicated for faith as in the former. But in both cases scientific theory is treated seriously and thus a more pertinent response is enabled from the side of theology. As for theology's answer, again, a direct correlative response may not have been entirely achieved. There is no possibility of identifying the divine energy exactly with physical energy, for example. But consonance here between science and theology, at the least, is achieved.

On the more positive side, Moltmann does recognize from quantum theory that there appears to be a *structural* openness to the future in the created order. This openness is enhanced in the evolutionary process which gives rise to new ever more inclusive structures. Thus Moltmann recognizes the role of wholism and the principle of emergence. He further argues that these phenomena would seem to characterize the universe as a "participatory" system and as an "anticipatory" system.[116] It appears that Moltmann's general intuitions are correct here, but he would benefit further from a more specific scientific reference. Appeal directly to the indeterminacy principle, for example, would support his argument. Appeal to Bell's Theorem and the principle of non-locality could bring positive support for the argument of the universe as participatory and wholistic; i.e., that it is to be characterized as a communicative community. In this respect, though quantum physics deals with discrete events, the emphasis on non-locality affirms still the relatedness of events, rather than reinforces the Cartesian dualism of the past, in which humankind's role was *maître et possesseur de la natur*. This is, of course, where Moltmann's doctrine of creation elides into ethics.[117]

With respect to temporality proper, however, there is much yet to be gathered from the sciences that might support Moltmann. Here is a case where Moltmann has not borrowed even any general themes from the sciences, other than that of indeterminacy. And that was discussed only in a different context and not applied directly to the problem of time.[118] As I noted above, some further support might be found for Moltmann with reference to relativity theory and further reflection on the concept of time posed by the quantum theory. An example of how these themes may be taken up into a doctrine of the Trinity will be shown in the following chapter. Conversely, what has not been articulated fully yet is how a program like Moltmann's may provide the context for answering problems posed by physics with respect to time and eternity. We gave but a hint with the critique of Moltmann's treatment of "open system."

In conclusion, it is clear that Moltmann's serious respect for the problem of history has been salutary in underscoring the significance of the doctrine of the Trinity as an articulation of how God and the world are related. I have found it helpful to characterize the Trinity along Moltmann's lines of a "social" model, borrowing as it does from the Cappadocian Fathers the notion of diversity-in-unity and the modern relational notion of person. I have not found this to be tri-theistic. Rather, such a model regains the soteriological significance of the doctrine of the Trinity, a significance that was lost in the speculative emphases on *de Deo Uno*, as Catherine Mowry LaCugna has observed.

Another advantage here is that the construction of the doctrine of the Trinity "from below" parallels the construction of scientific models and programs. Both start with concrete data and then search for explanation. In one case the data are, to be sure, historically revealed; in the other "naturally" revealed. With most contemporary theologians, Moltmann employs "Rahner's Rule," arguing that the "real" Trinity is revealed in its worldly economy. This means that a natural theology has its proper province in explicating "God" as long as it is understood that natural theology and empirical method are conclusive only when under the correction of revealed theology. Thus, Moltmann establishes God's transcendent "otherness," while yet avowing relation to the cosmos. Thus, also, the future stands as the pragmatic test and the eschatological source for the salvific completion of the natural-created order.

In all these implications, Moltmann's doctrine of the Trinity underpins, allows, and invites further discussion with the voices of the natural world, and does so in an internally consistent fashion. The remaining question is whether a doctrine of the Trinity such as this, informed and/or corroborated by other Trinitarian reflection, can lend to further development of theses, however begun by Moltmann, on time and eternity, and in similar mutual exchange with physical science. Suggestions of such theses will be posed in the following, concluding, chapter.

Notes

1. "Theology in the World of Modern Science," *Hope and Planning*, trans. by Margaret Clarkson (New York: Harper and Row, 1971) [English translation of *Perspektiven der Theologie*, 1968], hereafter noted as *HP*.

2. *HP*.

3. *Religion, Revolution and the Future*, translated by M. Douglas Meeks (New York: Charles Scribner's Sons, 1967), hereafter noted as *RRF*.

4. *Theology of Hope*, translated by James W. Leitch (New York: Harper and Row, 1967), 16; hereafter noted as *TH*.

5. See *The Future of Creation*, (Philadelphia: Fortress, 1979), trans. by Margaret Kohl, 14-17; hereafter noted as *FC*. Cf. also M. Douglas Meeks, *Origins of the Theology of Hope* (Philadelphia: Fortress, 1974), 87ff.

6. "A proper theology would therefore have to be constructed in the light of its future goal. Eschatology should not be its end, but its beginning." *TH*, 16.

7. "The Revelation of God and the Question of Truth," *HP*, 10.

8. *TH*, 258.

9. Cf. *TH*, 238-258, wherein Moltmann surveys hermeneutical methodology from F.C. Baur, through Dilthey to Heidegger.

10. "Planning must be aware of its origin in hope and of the projection of hope. If it puts itself in place of hope, it loses the transcendent impetus of hope and finally also loses itself." *TH*, 258.

11. *TH*, 76-77.

12. "Exegesis and the Eschatology of History," *HP*, 84.

13. It is important to note that the future about which Moltmann writes is not extrapolated from history, but comes *to* history from ahead. The difference to be noted is that between *adventus* and *futurum*. The advent of our God is that purposed by Moltmann. The future is coming and therefore impinges upon past and present. Therefore, if the future is the attribute of God's being, we may say that God's being is not in becoming, but is in God's coming.

14. *TH*, 33.

15. Of course, this position of eschatological theology is no longer unique. It is shared by many and has characterized whole theological careers. Among them, note Wolfhart Pannenberg's self-identification with the eschatological school with "The God of Hope" in *Basic Questions in Theology*, vol. II, trans. by George Kehm (Philadelphia: Fortress, 1971), 234-249; Carl Braaten, *The Future of God, The Revolutionary Dynamics of Hope* (New York: Harper and Row, 1969); Robert Jenson, *The Futurist Option* (New York: Newman Press, 1970). Ted Peters indicates his sharing of this perspective in *God, the World's Future* (Minneapolis: Fortress, 1992).

16. *FC*, "The Future As the Paradigm of Transcendence," 14-17. Cf. also *The Experiment Hope*, trans. by M. Douglas Meeks (Philadelphia: Fortress, 1975), ch. IV.

17. Cf. *TH*, 76-83.

18. *TH*, 201.

19. *The Trinity and the Kingdom*, trans. by Margaret Kohl (New York: Harper and Row, 1981); hereafter noted as *TK*, 212ff.

20. *TH*, 136.

21. *God in Creation*, trans. by Margaret Kohl (New York: Harper and Row, 1985), 213; hereafter noted as *GC*.

22. Moltmann no longer speaks so directly as to the doing of Christology from below. While he still affirms that the "economy" of God is the necessary place with and by which we begin theological and christological (even pneumatological) reflection, he agrees that thinking *only* in terms of a christology from below or from above is simplistic. Of course every beginning "from below" requires a dialectic of "from above"in response. There is always a context to be recalled in that reflection which begins from particulars, and there are always particulars to recall when we would begin reflection from a prior context or principle. See *The Way of Jesus Christ, Christology in Messianic Dimensions*, trans. by Margaret Kohl (San Francisco: Harper Collins, 1990).

23. *The Crucified God*, trans. by R. A. Wilson and John Bowden (New York: Harper and Row, 1974), 227; hereafter noted as *CG*.

24. *CG*, 214-215.

25. *CG*, 246.

26. *CG*, 254.

27. Moltmann takes up positively the imagery from Augustine and Richard of St. Victor here.

28. *CG*, 277.

29. *CG*, 278.

30. *CG*, 247.

31. See *TK*, 162ff. God's "fatherhood is defined by relationship to this Son, and by the relationship of this Son Jesus Christ to him. Consequently, in the Christian understanding of God the Father, what is meant is not 'Father of the Universe,' but simply and exclusively 'the Father of the Son' Jesus Christ. It is solely the Father of Jesus Christ whom we believe and acknowledge created the world...the name of Father is therefore a theological term—which is to say a trinitarian one; it is not a cosmological idea or a religious notion. If God is the Father of this Son Jesus Christ, and if he is only 'our Father' for his Son's sake, then we can also only call him 'Abba,' beloved Father, in the spirit of free sonship. It is freedom that distinguishes him from the universal patriarch of father religions." On this basis, Moltmann is able to affirm the feminist critique of patriarchy in God-language (aligned also with hierarchical "monotheism," as Moltmann sees it) without abandoning the Nicaean formulation of "Father, Son and Holy Spirit." It is a position amenable to the thought of less radical feminist theologians like Elizabeth Johnson, *She Who Is* (New York: Crossroad, 1993), and Catherine Mowry LaCugna, *God For Us*, 267ff.

32. *CG*, 267.

33. *CG*, 276.

34. This argument is not novel with Moltmann. The philosopher John Wisdom, with his famous "parable" of the gardener, indirectly denoted this state of contemporary consciousness. His parable, of course, was meant as a rejoinder to the excesses of logical positivism; it was a sympathetic defense of religious discourse. In the defense, however, he made it clear that one's perception of reality made all the constitutive difference in how a proof, even a logical proof, was to be constructed. Now the perception is commonplace that the universe is not as ordered as the one religious gardener thought. Rather, as we observed in chapter three, God's action is increasingly perceived in the indeterminacy and structural openness seemingly displayed at the quantum level.

35. *TK*, 8. I would argue, too, that the existential approach which seeks demythologizing and the deconstructive approach are the legitimate heirs to Kant's moral monotheism and thus deserving of similar criticism. They render faith into a pragmatism with no ontological claims.

36. *TK*, 3-9. Moltmann writes that the *via activa* requires a *vita contemplativa* to enrich and sustain it. The moral monotheism which Kant prescribes would starve life instead, because it particularly proscribes the resource of the Trinity. Moltmann quotes Kant, "From the doctrine of the Trinity, taken literally, nothing whatsoever can be gained for practical purposes, even if one believed that one comprehended it - and less still if one is conscious that it surpasses all our concepts." v. *TK*, 6.

37. This, of course, would obviate the need for systematic theology.

38. See Ernst Bloch, *Das Prinzip Hoffnung* (Frankfurt: Suhrkamp, 1959).

39. *TK*, 17.

40. *TK*, 18.

41. *TK*, 150.

42. *TK*, 19.

43. See *In der Geschichte des dreieinigen Gottes; Beiträge zur trinitärischen Theologie* (München: Chr. Kaiser Verlag, 1991). cf. especially ch. 6, "Die Gemeinschaft des Heligen Geistes;" hereafter noted as *GDG*.

44. Traditional trinitarian speculation, as we observed, ended in the affirmation either of *una substantia-tres personae* or *ein gottliches Subjekt - drei verschiedene Seinswesen*. "Mit dieser Formel wird die Einheit Gottes der Dreifältigkeit der gottlichen Personen vergeördnet...Wir gehen einen Schritt weiter, wenn wir sagen: die Einheit des dreieinigen Gottes besteht nicht nur in dem identischen, göttlichen Subjekt, sondern vor allem in der einzigartigen Gemeinschaft der drei Personen. Die trinitärischen Personen besitzen gemeinsam das göttliche Wesen und die göttliche Herrschaft. Darum geht ihre trinitärischen Einheit, ihre substantialle Einheit und ihre subjektive Einheit nach aussen voran. Der deutsche Ausdruck 'Drei-einigkeit' bedeutet eigentlich: *drei-Personen - eine Gemeinschaft*." *GDG*., 92-93.

45. For the same reasons of wanting to avoid speaking "monotheistically," Moltmann uses the German *Einigkeit* or *Vereinigung* rather than *Einheit* in speaking of the Trinity. The latter implies an ontological simple unity. The former terms imply more of a process of unification as well as the affirmation of distinction within the Godhead.

46. *TK*, 160.

47. *TK*, 161.

48. *TK*, 164-165.

49. *CG*, 215. He alludes, of course, to H. R. Niebuhr's *Radical Monotheism and Western Culture* (New York: Faber, 1961). If Moltmann read it, he did not understand Niebuhr's argument. Niebuhr does not argue against trinitarian thought. He writes, rather, in favor of what Moltmann should favor, though in a different language. Writing against the idolatrous objects of faith in culture, especially the dominant forms of henotheism and polytheism, Niebuhr defines radical monotheism as "reliance on the source of all being from the significance of the self and of all that exists." Radical monotheism "dethrones all absolutes short of the principle of being itself." Cf. 32 & 36. All Moltmann need do is substitute Trinity for "principle of being" for he and Niebuhr to be in agreement.

50. *TK*, 131.

51. *TK*, 133.

52. *TK*, 194.

53. *TK*, 142.

54. *TK*, 144. As Moltmann elaborates, if Barth had stopped at that point of securing God's sovereignty with this use of the doctrine of the Trinity, he would only be extending Schleiermacher's anthropology of humankind's feeling of absolute dependence. Ted Peters understands Moltmann to be making a somewhat stronger claim, that Barth focuses on that upon which we are dependent, and so implicitly accepts Schleiermacher's terms. I am not so sure. At any rate, Moltmann does allow that his criticisms seem to apply only to the "early Barth."

55. "Die Subjectivität Gottes und die Trinitätslehre: Ein Beitrag zur Beziehen zwischen Karl Barth und der Philosophie Hegels," *Grundfragen Systematischer Theologie, Gesammelte Aufsätze 2* (Göttingen, 1980), 96-111.

56. *TK*, 146.

57. *TK*, 148.

58. *TK*, 149-150.

59. Richard John Neuhaus, "Moltmann vs. Monotheism," *dialog*, XX:3 (Summer, 1981), 241. See also Ted Peters, *God As Trinity*, 129ff. and "Theology Update" in *dialog*, 31:4 (Fall, 1992), 272-279.

60. "Unitarian" might be one apt substitute for "monotheistic." Moltmann's translator even uses the term herself in a summary of the dangerous consequences of a substance onotology. "Finally, it is clear how much the substance of the Godhead, of which all three hypostases or Persons partake, threatens to obscure the trinitarian differences in a Sabellian, modalistic and ultimately unitarian sense." *TK*, 190.

61. Cf. *The Church in the Power of the Spirit*, trans. by Margaret Kohl (New York: Harper and Row, 1977) 289ff.; *Politische Theologie - Politische Ethik* (Mainz & München: Kaiser/Grünewald, 1984), 79-88, 166-191; *GC*, 276ff. Ted Peters, in *God As Trinity*, 235ff., objects to the social model of the Trinity as a paradigm for human relational ethics because of its second order status as a "model," arguing that the more primal "Kingdom of God" image is the biblical intent for conduct of human/worldly affairs. A student of Moltmann would respond that "proto-trinitarian" experience of God (e.g., in charismatic celebrations of the Spirit or prayerful/mystical encounters with Christ) is indeed "first order." It could be argued further that "Kingdom of God" and (a social model of) the Trinity are mutually interpretive on a first-level basis. See, e.g., Arthur H. Williams, Jr., "The Trinity and Time," *Scottish Journal of Theology*, 38:1 (1986), 65-81. I wonder if the symbols of the trinitarian experience, however, may have priority if they could be argued as "pre-narrative," while the Kingdom of God is a narrative image; i.e., the Trinity is the source of the story of salvation, while the Kingdom of God is the content.

62. This is clearly Moltmann's understanding expressed in *GC*, taken over from Luther's *theologia crucis*. For a fine study, see Walther von Löwenich, *Luther's Theology of the Cross*, tr. by Herbert A. Bouman (Minneapolis: Augsburg, 1976).

63. John Wright, S.J., seems to infer a tritheism in Moltmann's construction. He construes Moltmann to mean that "the divine missions of the Son and Spirit set up some kind of separation or division within God that is healed through our salvation." Cf. "The Holy Trinity: Mystery of Salvation," *CTSA Proceedings*, 35 (1980), 199. Claude Welch would argue that it is incorrect for Moltmann to argue that the New Testament bears primary reference to divine plurality. Indeed, Welch would contend (and still does) that

Moltmann can't get to divine unity from plurality. Cf. *In This Name*, 253, 264. I argue that Moltmann's reliance on the notion of "persons-in-communion" protects him from the charge of tritheism. Moltmann begins to fashion this anthropology as early as 1963. See "Die 'Weltoffenheit' des Menschen. Zur neueren philosophischen Anthropologie," *Verkündigung und Forschung* 8 (1963), 115-134.

64. "Moltmann, of course, does not himself hold to his own rule about speaking of God in trinitarian fahsion. He reverts time and time again to a simple concept of God, where God as such is the subject of the sentence without any trinitarian differentiation. It proves at last to be as unavoidable to him as it was to Barth." "A Trinitarian Theology of the Cross," *The Journal of Religion*, 65:1 (Winter, 1976), 117. The implication that Moltmann can't escape from Idealism is rather severe. To be fair, one can and should distinguish the use of "God" as popular convention (and expedience) from any intentional unitarian reference. I'd give Moltmann the benefit of the doubt here.

65. See Ted Peters, *God, the World's Future*, 123.

66. *GC*, 87ff.

67. *CG*, 250 and 281, n.36.

68. *CG*, 255-256.

69. E.g., John Cobb writes in summary of Whitehead's doctrine of God, "God always (and some temporal occasions sometimes) is the reason *that* each new occasion becomes. God, past occasions, and the new occasion are conjointly the reason for *what* it becomes. Whatever it becomes, it will always, necessarily, be a new embodiment of creativity." *A Christian Natural Theology* (Philadelphia: Westminster, 1965), 214.

70. Moltmann, "What is 'New' in Christianity: The Category Novum in Christian Theology," in *RRF*, 12-13.

71. Alfred North Whitehead, *Process and Reality* (New York: Free Press, 1978), 529.

72. One should note that Moltmann does not conceive of this completion as static. He argues in *God in Creation* that temporality, what we may call with the physicists "the arrow of time," continues infinitely within God's eternity as integral to the *new* creation. Moltmann calls this concept "eternal time." It is the consumation of four other sorts of "time." They are: kairotic, historical, messianic, and eschatological. See *GC*, 124.

73. "The Future As the New Paradigm of Transcendence," *RRF*, 196.

74. See John O' Donnell, *Trinity and Temporality* (Oxford: Oxford University Press, 1983), 179. He quotes Ogden: "Just as the reality of God the creator is not something belonging to the past of nature and history, but is their ever-present primordial ground, so the reality of God as a judge and redeemer is not a particular event of the future, but the ever-present final consequence of each passing moment in the stream of time."

75. *The Experiment Hope*, trans.by M. Douglas Meeks (Philadelphia: Fortress, 1975), 52. See also "Hope and History," in *RRF*, 210: "As far as I can tell, process theology, on the one hand, speaks of the 'becoming God' in the context of the dynamics of world process. Eschatological theology, on the other hand, speaks of the 'coming God' in the context of the dialectical dynamics, circumscribed by the symbols of *creatio ex nihilo, justificatio impii, and resurrectio mortuorum*."

76. I am much indebted here to O'Donnell's observations, 152ff.

77. Writing on Christology and the doctrine of the atonement, for example, Gerhard Forde writes, "The cosmic dimension [of Christ's rule] is *eschatological*. The crucified and risen one must reign until he has put all enemies under his feet. Then the kingdom is

handed over to God, who will be all in all (1 Cor. 15:28)." "The Work of Christ," *Christian Dogmatics*, Carl Braaten and Robert Jenson, eds., vol. 2, 93. See also the article by Hans Schwarz in the same volume entitled "Eschatology," 475-587.

78. John O'Donnell asks the same question; I follow much of his evaluation here.

79. O'Donnell, 152ff.

80. *GC*, 64. See also, "Creation As An Open System," in *The Future of Creation*.

81. *TH*, 180.

82. Peter Momose, *Kreuztheologie*, 158, noted in O'Donnell, 194.

83. O'Donnell, 194.

84. *The Experiment Hope*, 78.

85. John Cobb, *Christ in a Pluralistic Age* (Philadelphia: Westminster, 1975), 156.

86. Cobb, 155. Additionally, Cobb charges that the starting point of threeness "can hardly be distinguished from tritheism except for the insistence on perfect unity of purpose and character among the three persons."

87. John Cobb, "Reply to Jürgen Moltmann's 'The Unity of the Triune God'," *St. Vladimir's Theological Quarterly*, 28:3 (1984), 173-177.

88. Lewis Ford, "Process Trinitarianism," *Journal of the American Academy of Religion* 43,2 (June 1975), 297; quoted in O'Donnell, 195.

89. "Das Neue Testament als Zeugnis der trinitärischen Geschichte Gottes," unpublished Lecture Notes, Tübingen, Winter Semester, 1978. Quoted in O'Donnell, 196.

90. Joseph Bracken, S.J., interprets Moltmann to have combined a traditional, Barthian trinitarian theory with the perspectives of the process theologians. On that basis, Bracken then criticizes Moltmann for not showing how the reality of three distinct persons is possible within a process approach to God. This is a curious criticism. It assumes, first of all, a conscious intent on Moltmann's part to blend Barthian Idealism with process theology, while there is no evidence in any of Moltmann's work of a thorough reading of the process theological literature. Bracken imputes to Moltmann an intention that Moltmann did not have. Bracken also complains that Moltmann's positing of *pathos* in God leaves unexplained how this does or does not affect divine transcendence or human freedom. Again, this criticism is questionable precisely because Moltmann *does* engage in this defense amply, but not on the basis of metaphysics as Bracken seems to require. Moltmann is still in the Barthian camp here, and Bracken would make a philosopher out of him. In sum, Bracken criticizes Moltmann for not adopting Bracken's agenda. So, Bracken faults Moltmann for remaining "more at the level of pious metaphor than established hypothesis." *What Are They Saying About the Trinity?* (New York: Paulist, 1979), 33.

91. *GDG*, 20.

92. O'Donnell, 200.

93. *GC*, 104-112.

94. *GC*, 114.

95. *GC*, 114..

96. That experience is, of course, the intuition of time through memory, perception and anticipation. Thus Augustine renders the human side of time as the experience of present past, present present, and present future.

97. Again, Barth is influential here. Moltmann's argument is much like Barth's in *CD*, III/4, in which Barth refers to God as the "frontier" who arouses our attention. It is "what is to come" that gives the Christian character to time. So Barth writes, "What is at

issue is the manifestation of Jesus Christ as the One He is, as the Lord; and therefore the revelation of the beginning of time posited in Him, and also of its goal and end. It is with a view to this coming event that time still exists and men are still in it. Time is now the time in which those who have come from Him wait for Him and hasten to meet Him (2 Peter 3:12)...time as the time of this man is time ruled by the Lord who has already come but is still to be manifested." (*CD* III/4, 580-581).

98. *GC*, 123-124.

99. *GC*, 126-130.

100. Augustine, *Confessions*, XI, 20.

101. It is exceptionally important to note that I have taken the liberty to reverse this last arrow. Otherwise, as printed in the English translation of *GC* it does not fit with Moltmann's argument that the transcendent future is *coming*. Also, the Augustinian line of the English translation reads "PrP→PrPr→PF." This is clearly an error and I have changed it accordingly. Augustine spoke of the Present Future, not the past future (PF), when he spoke of the role of "expectatio." The German translation bears this out. In fact, one sees Moltmann's correct intent in a research article that was parlayed into this particular chapter of *GC*. Cf. "Verschränkte Zeiten der Geschichte, Notwendige Differenzierungen und Begrenzungen des Geschichtsbegriffs," *Evangelische Theologie* (Mai-June: 1984), 213-227. Therein GZ (the Present-Future, PrF) always points *back* toward the GG (Present-Present, PrPr) AND the final future, Z, is connected to the preceding "etc." only by a hyphen (!).

102. My emphasis. *GC*, 129-130.

103. *GC*, 133-134.

104. *GC*, 124. Moltmann says this after a survey of biblical traditions about time. In that survey, Moltmann finds: (a) "kairotic" time — that time which is determined by the event itself; (b) Historical time — determined by the mission of God's promise and acts of faithfulness; (c) messianic time — the time of dawn of the new creation inaugerated by the coming of the Messiah; (d) eschatological time — determined by the universal fulfillment of what was promised in historical time and what dawned in messianic time; and (e) eternal time.

105. Cf., e.g., 197-206; *FC*, ch. VIII.

106. Ernan McMullin, "Natural Science and Belief in a Creation," *PPT*, 49-79. Christians hastily have embraced — and coopted — scientifc theories when self-interest may be served (Of course, history is replete with hasty condemnation, too). Pope Pius X found proof in the initial theory of the Big Bang for the doctrine of *creatio ex nihilo*. But scientific theories of singularities and alternative cosmologies since have shown clearly that there is no proof that "$t=0$" equals "creation from nothing." The Principle of Complementarity, for another example, has been used to explicate the "two-natures" of Christ and has served as a synonym for theological paradox. When thus employed, the principle is robbed of its initially denoted content and serves only as a principle of metaphor. Metaphors are indispensable for theology, but the rendering of science into metaphor without acknowledgement that one has consciously changed "symbol systems" does disservice to an enterprise founded on relative exactitude and direct correlation. Rightly to apply the Principle of Complementarity to Christology would mean having to identify one of the "natures" with waves, the other with particles. The absurdity of that effort should be apparent. If taken naively, it could have the kind of devastating impact on theology that, for example, the shift of "hypostasis" from its original Greek milieu to the

Latin use incurred. In other words, clear acknowledgement about what can and cannot be assumed from science is required.

107. *TK*, 100-101. See especially the essay, "Creation As An Open System," in *FC*.

108. *Creation and the World of Science*, (Oxford: Clarendon, 1979).

109. See "Creation As An Open System."

110. Pannenberg, *Anthropology in Theological Perspective*, trans. by Matthew J. O'Connell (Philadelphia: Westminster, 1985).

111. *GC*, 213.

112. Recall my discussion of Robert John Russell's survey of the cosmological models in chapter 4.

113. *GC*, 204.

114. *TK*, 150, 178-185, 189, et.al.; Gregory of Nyssa, *Against Eunomius*, II/12; cf. also LaCugna, *God For Us*, 183-196.

115. Robert John Russell has written suggestively about this possibility of theologizing on the basis of Ilya Prigogine's theory that more refined orders may rise out of chaotic dynamical systems. See Russell, "Entropy and Evil," *Zygon* 19:4 (December, 1984), 449-467.

116. *GC*, 203-205.

117. In recognizing this relatedness, Moltmann finds the motivation for a repentant ethics of ecology. Koinonia can no longer brook a "master-slave" relationship to the natural world. The natural world cries out, too, under the cross as the groaning of creation for the revealing of glory through the voice of humankind. Humanity is to see its renewed role as *representative* of creation rather than a power over creation. Indeed, Moltmann, if he would, could again benefit from specific attention to the sciences here and draw helpfully from the Anthropic Principle. Humanity as the "representative" of creation is one way to image either a "soft" or "hard" reading of the Anthropic Principle. Cf. *GC*, pp.1-52, 69-71; FC, ch.I; *Creating A Just Future* (New York: Harper and Row, 1989), ch. III.

118. Indeterminacy was discussed in ch. 8 of *GC*, "The Evolution of Creation." It received no reference in the earlier chapter on "The Time of Creation,"ch. 5, nor in ch. 6, on "The Space of Creation."

VII

A Constructive Statement

Religion is the cultivation of some eternity, of whatever it is upon which a community relies to reconcile the discontinuities of time, to rescue our temporal tale from its threatening idiocy and give it plotted coherence, to make it indeed a tale. There are as many putative eternities as there are religions, or vice versa. To each putative eternity necessarily belongs a paired interpretation of time, and in the pairing of a particular eternity with its appropriate grasp of time, a particular apprehension of temporal continuity, of what eternity enables for time.

- Robert Jenson, *Unbaptized God*

With this concluding chapter we begin by recognizing that we already have covered much ground indeed and may be tempted to ask whether we have followed any particular map at all. To change the analogy, one might describe the exploration thus far as the proverbial walk into the forest. Having entered into the thick of it, we not only may have the nagging sense that we have lost sight of the forest for the trees, but that we have so closely looked at the trees that we have lost sight of them for their bark and the bugs in the bark.

After some scratching and looking about, this chapter of the map brings us out of the forest and, I hope, that we will do so with new appreciation of its shape and shades. We recall that with chapter 2 we surveyed the Christian concepts of time and eternity and found them wanting. The predominant Christian concept of time was deficient because it still presumed a Newtonian absoluteness despite the virtually institutional character of time's plurality as it is accepted in the scientific community. After all, nearly a hundred years later, graduate students in theology are still surprised to learn of the implications of Special Relativity, so far behind the Einsteinian and quantum revolutions is theology. In this discussion, we found the common Christian concept of eternity not only to be counter to temporality of any sort; it was recognized as the avenue by which an inappropriate Hellenistic idea of divinity as unchanging substantiality still compromises the authentic biblical view of deity. With chapter 3 we saw how contemporary theological reflection on the doctrine of the Trinity has begun to change this error and affirms that temporality itself derives from the dynamic interrelationship of the trinitarian persons.

Chapter 4 then occasioned a summary of current theories in physics and cosmology that could directly inform new theological thinking about time and eternity. With chapter 5 we also considered the diverse points of view of three active physicists in the effort to draw out some common themes from the excited and quickly changing state of physical science today. Those concepts and common themes led to my proposal of several theses regarding time and eternity at the conclusion of that chapter.

Finally, we engaged in a comprehensive discussion of the evocative work of Jürgen Moltmann and looked particularly to his treatment of matters related to the concepts of time, eternity and the doctrine of the Trinity. We discovered there that though there is much material with which he attends to the issue at hand, there is also opportunity for his position to be strengthened by drawing from the resources such as we outlined in chapters 4 and 5, and by some conversation with the theological trends we noted in chapter 3.

With this brief chapter I now hope to bring into synthesis what we have surveyed above. I hope to provide here a constructive statement that brings together the strengths I have identified above, so ultimately to give meaning to the assertion that the eternity of the Trinity is essentially temporal. By that core assertion I claim that eternity should be understood as the manifold for temporalities, rather than opposed to temporality of any sort. By that assertion I also mean to claim that the revised sense of temporality and eternity occasioned by contemporary physical theory can inform, support and be explicated by the doctrine of the Trinity. Of course, there are "doctrines within the doctrine." There are untold variations in explication of Trinitarian doctrine. I mean by the doctrine of the Trinity one which is close to Moltmann's and bears Barth's legacy that temporality itself derives from the inter-personal relations of the triune persons. In other words, the internal life of the Trinity, traditionally referred to as the "theological" or "immanent" Trinity, transcendent to human knowledge, is the heart of economic trinitarian temporalities. Relationality and dynamism are within God, which means, too, that time is in God and finds finitizations external to God "proper" in the economy of God.[1]

Finally, by the assertion that temporality is within and derives from the Trinity, I also mean to suggest that the dialogue of natural science and theology on this issue (at least) may provide the occasion methodologically to exhibit their mutuality. I noted how it may be that theology could be constructed along the lines of a Lakatosian scientific research program. The research program approach is widely thought to supercede the difficulties posed both by narrow positivism and by the ambiguities of Kuhnian paradigms. One fruit of this supercession is that theology may be seen methodologically to have more in common with the natural scientific enterprise, as first argued by Nancey Murphy. Therefore, a preliminary word about that is in order before we proceed to the posing of the theses themselves.

About Method

The positivist philosophical position that an assertion must be verifiable by appeal to a real and direct correlate of the assertion has been supplanted twice-over. It has been supplanted first by the neo-positivist position of such philosophers of science as Karl Popper and Carl Hempel. For Popper, scientific meaningfulness means hypothetical falsifiability. For Hempel, meaningfulness entails a hypothetical possibility that confirmation of a language reference could be achieved by direct deduction from theory to data.[2] The demise of Linguistic Positivism was assured, finally, by the historicist philosophers of science, premier examples of whom are Thomas Kuhn and Stephen Toulmin.[3] The latter have demonstrated that scientists operate by whole "paradigms" that control the choice and interpretation of data. If the necessary criteria for theory choice of consistency, applicability, confirmability, predictiveness and fruitfulness seem no longer to hold for a given theory, it may well be time for a paradigm-shift to occur; the theoretician may have to adopt a wholly different "way of seeing things."

This is not so easy to achieve. Paradigm shifts are influenced by culture and politics, as well as by lack of scientific progress.[4] A scientist within the paradigm may not know, and often cannot know, that that paradigm is changing. The historicist philosophers of science, therefore, have shown the need for a new positive methodology which will embrace the historicists' concerns as well as the positive content of previous schools of philosophy of science. Such a positive methodology is provided by Imre Lakatos.[5]

Lakatos contends that the history of science is characterized not as a history of successive paradigms, as Kuhn argues, but as a history of competing research programs.[6] A "research program" consists of a set of theories and data. That theory which is central to the research program is called the "hard core." Attached to it is a set of auxiliary hypotheses. This hard core and its auxiliaries, which make up the "protective belt" of the hard core, allow data to be related to the research program. If data arise which would contradict part of the auxiliary belt, the belt is adapted accordingly with the intent of safeguarding change or damage to the hard core. "A research program, then, is a series of complex theories whose core remains the same while auxiliary hypotheses are successively modified, replaced, or amplified in order to account for the problematic observations."[7]

A "progressive" research program, consequently, is one in which the core theory is unrefuted in each new version of the theory. It also predicts novel facts insofar as it has "excess empirical content over its predecessor" and corroborates some of those facts. On the other hand, a research program is degenerating when predictiveness pales and, above all, when damage is done to the hard core theory. Lakatos contends that the history of science is not a history of succeeding progressive paradigms, as Kuhn believes, but a history of competing research programs. Those programs which would be progressive are judged so specifically according to their ability to anticipate novel facts. The theory of General Relativity, for example was found to be a progressive research program because it anticipated that sometime a case would be found in which light is bent by mass. The predicted novel facts which confirmed this program are the perihelion effect of Mercury and the discovery of singularities (Black Holes). When the theory/research program was first proposed, scientists did not yet have the ability experimentally to confirm it; with the advent of higher quality radio-telescopes, the predicted novel facts were discovered. In short, the ability to predict novel facts is an objective criterion for selecting one research program over another.[8]

Murphy argues that the theological task ought not be so different. Construed as a research program, theology can be "scientific." Holmes Rolston is one scientist who would generally concur.

> ...in generic logical form science and religion, when done well, are more alike than is often supposed, especially at their cores...There are differing emphases in specific logical form in the rational modes of each. But both disciplines are rational, and both are susceptible to improvement over the centuries; both use governing theoretical paradigms as they confront experience.[9]

The hard core of such a scientific theological program would contain "the theologian's judgement about how to sum up the very minimum of the relevant community's faith."[10] Murphy even suggests that the trinitarian nature of God could be part of this hard core. As with many scientific programs, here a negative heuristic, that is, a rule which would protect the hard core from falsification, would also be added. For example, with respect to the Trinity, the *shema* of Deuteronomy 28 ("Hear O Israel, the Lord your God is one") may appear to be contradictory to the assertion that Christians are to be baptized "in the name of the Father, and of the Son, and of the Holy Spirit" (Matthew 28). The addition of an auxiliary hypothesis might mediate the semmingly conflicting claims as to the Godhead's identity. One such auxiliary hypothesis, for example, might be that "the intimacy of a relationship contributes to personal unity in that relationship" (as per the doctrine of perichoresis of St. John of Damascus, or the event of "concrescence" as described in Whiteheadian process theology). This hypothesis thus could explain that the "three identities" of Matthew 28 are indeed the one identity of Deuteronomy 28 when the three are understood "relationally." Thus the auxiliary theory, acting as a negative heuristic, would protect the hard core and perhaps even allow for prediction of novel facts.

Of course, a strong theological research program will have a positive heuristic, as well. A doctrine may be employed, for example, in the sense of its role as second-order discourse.[11] It places constraints upon the theologian not to stretch beyond prescribed orthodoxy. Yet it allows for new theoretical construction rather than mere repetition of old formulae. Further auxiliary hypotheses may be added in a full systematic theological research program to spell out the meaning of the hard core, as well as to provide the connections to the pertinent data.

> [The data] must be related to the core in such a way that the vision of God summed up in the core theory helps explain the doctrines, which in turn explains the data. In other words, the auxiliaries must be consequences of the hard core, and the data consequences of the auxiliaries. Explanation and confirmation being the two sides of a single coin, the core theory is confirmed by the data that it (indirectly) explains.[12]

It is in the context of theology as a research program that I would propose the theological issue of this thesis, and would further do so as a methodological experiment. Of course, a "full blown" research program likely would have as its hard core something more general than this particular aspect of the doctrine of the Trinity which I have considered. This thesis can only be but a partial example of a broader and deeper research program approach. Indeed, a full example would have to be a whole systematic theology constructed as a research program.

I would argue, though, that an affirmation of a trinitarian theology would need to be quite near the hard core, for only by its inclusion can so many otherwise seemingly contradictory lower-level theories be accomodated (e.g., that "Jesus is Lord," that the "Spirit" brooded over the waters at the Creation, that God did not die on the cross, yet shared the suffering and death of Jesus, etc.). Consider the thesis of this essay as a heuristic device then; that I would treat this thesis *as if* it were such a hard core theory. Thereby I hope to exemplify both the Lakatosian method and add credibility by this constructive proposal to the conversation between theology and the natural sciences.

Indeed, it may be helpful to suggest that this book itself may serve more appropriately as an exploration of auxiliary theses in a wider-ranging research program conducted under a more basic core thesis, e.g., that "God's Identity is Revealed as Trinity," or even "God Acts." The point here methodologically is not so much to conduct a full research program as partially to model one, while the fundamental concern is to explicate temporality in terms of God's trinitarian character.

With this chapter I propose, then, to format the discussion in a Lakatosian mode. I will do this first by asserting once again the core thesis. Following that I will pose a "protective belt" of auxiliary theses under thematic classifications. Finally, some predictions of novel facts will be offered, which could corroborate the viability of this research program. The following caveat needs to be emphasized, however. Because the following is, at most, a constructive *proposal* along the skeletal outlines of a partial research program, the speculations offered as the core thesis and auxiliary theses should be taken in that limited sense. They are offered in consideration of all the previous chapters of "data" we have entertained. But they are not offered as a definitive and comprehensively thought out research program. They can only be taken as starting points. To go further is beyond the scope of this argument. As with all proposed research programs, their realization in fruitfulness or stillbirth must come as the critic brings her own temporality to this enterprise. To put it another way, this chapter could perhaps serve equally as the first, with those chapters already written and read serving as the data and argument that might bring dissensus or credibility to this project. Either way, then, with these following suggestions, I am not required to be as thorough in the argument as I have sought to be in the prior exposition. Indeed, here I would prefer to be somewhat Wittgensteinian in the fashion of my proposals by keeping them brief and enumerated, with an occasional insertion of commentary.

Core Thesis
1.0.   The eternity of the Trinity is essentially temporal.

Auxiliary Theses
Definitions

1.1.   Throughout this essay I have been arguing that eternity is not the same as timelessness, as with the Hellenistic perspective. Even Augustine's impatience with those who asked about "time" before the creation of time[13] is not a presumption of eternity against time. Rather, I hold that temporality lies within eternity and is created from eternity, while yet eternity is more than temporality.

1.2.   Furthermore, though I have not explicitly put it this way so far, because I write out of Christian conviction I also mean to say that there is no eternity outside the Trinity. This is not to say that eternity is synonymous with the Trinity. In what may be construed as a paraphrase of Boethius's definition, I suggest that eternity is the fullness and the comprehensiveness of relatedness in the Trinity, from within which derives the temporality of the Trinity.

1.3.   This brings us to the understanding of "essentially" in the core thesis as I have intended it throughout. Clearly, if by "eternity" I mean something other than the Greek notion of immutable substance, then "essentially" could have no substantialistic connotation, either. It is the proposal that temporality is at the heart of eternity which I offer. Insofar as temporality necessarily issues from the dynamism of relationship that is characteristic of the trinitarian experience *ad intra*, so too temporality is at least logically central to trinitarian identity and thus to the eternity of the Trinity.

1.4.   Because eternity is not opposed to temporality, conversely, our own lived temporality does not mitigate the eternity of the Trinity so much as bring eternity into a focus. Any temporality is a finitization of eternity.

1.5.   "Temporal" is the predicate that applies to any of the temporalities of which eternity is the manifold.

Theses On Epistemology and Physical Concepts

2.0.   Temporality is a real property of reality understood wholistically.

2.1.   If eternity is the all-embracingness of time, then time is limitation from eternity. Time is disjunctive and passing, never comprehensive; or as already stated, time is a finitization of eternity.

2.2.   However, at the level of the quantum state, time is directionless; which is to say, per Hawking and Isham, it is not "real," but discrete and discontinuous.

2.3.   Quantum phenomena do imply, however, that a future pertinent to each phenomenon is at the "root of reality."

2.4.   The time of General Relativity is phenomenological; it is part of the four-dimensional space-time matrix itself. As phenomenological, time here is understood only within the horizon of particular masses and their particular spaces. In General Relativity, time is already to be understood "plurally" as time differs with each frame of masses and spaces.

2.5.   The theory of Special Relativity underscores the recognition that we must speak of a plurality of times even within a common frame of space. One inertial frame of reference may be discretely distinguished from another. There is no such thing as an absolute future in the Newtonian sense (though I would allow an absolute future in the transcendent eschatological sense), nor even of an absolute present, though we can speak of *some*thing given as a past.

2.6.   As a phenomenological construct, a person's (or a mass's) time can then be understood as derivative; it is a consequence of a variety of physical factors, though it is not reducible to any one of them. To put it another way, time is the result of the relationship of related matter in relative motion.

2.7.   Thus, time is emergent, though it is not able to be reified like the components of the related matter from which relationship time emerges.

2.8.   The future is open.

3.0.   An epistemology of critical realism is an appropriate response to the contested role of observership in the physical sciences today.

3.1.   This critical realist approach, combined with the recognition of the emergent character of time (2.7), requires wholistic explanation.

3.2.   Wholistic explanation employs complementary descriptions and includes top-down and bottom-up causal descriptions.

3.3. Wholistic explanation, together with the pluralities of past and present times, further implies the viability of a theory of a semi-block universe, in which past and present events are related and growing in their nexus as they are informed by new events of an expanding cosmos.

3.4.   A critically realistic and wholistic mode of explanation allows that a semi-block universe theory may be maintained regardless of whether one prefers the "finite eternity" conception of a closed universe or the "infinite eternity" of an ever inflationary universe.

3.5.   In either case, eternity is construable as an "envelope" of temporality rather than opposed to it.

4.0.   The concepts of transcendence and eschatology are integral in the critically realistic, wholistic description of eternity and temporality.

4.1.   Scientific abstraction from contingency to repeatability is ahistorical. An historical re-focus on contingency looks for continuity within the natural process.[14]

4.2.   The scientific, philosophical and theological endeavor to elucidate continuity in the natural process discovers breakdowns at each of the emerging levels of thermodynamics, biology and cosmology, such that there is always, as Pannenberg argues, insufficient explanation ultimately at that cosmological level, short of the presumption of a larger context.[15]

4.3.   The logical demand for an ever widening context, therefore, implies the ontological necessity of eschatological transcendence.[16]

4.4.   If eschatological transcendence is virtually synonymous with eternity, then the identification of God as the "power of the future" is appropriate.[17]

Theses About the Trinity (drawing from chapters 3 and 6).

5.0.   God is Trinity.

5.1.   The starting point for theological reflection on the Trinity is, so to speak, empirical,[18] insofar as the primary Christian experience of the presence of divinity is historically given in Christian scriptural revelation and worship. The *oikonomia* of salvation reveals God as the Trinity.

5.2.   The revelation of God in history is not only as a unity, but also as three identities.

5.3.   Recognition of the simultaneity of the three identities of God and the unity of God leads epistemologically to the positing of a necessary internal relatedness in God.

5.31. This internal relatedness itself is the ontological condition for the derivative epistemic realization of the external relatedness of the triune persons both to each other and to the creation.

5.32. This doctrine of the Trinity requires that we understand personhood in terms of *the* person-in-relationship.

Excursus

Even in the neoclassical position of process theology, which I criticized earlier in chapter six, Schubert Ogden argues in a fashion quite similar to mine, that God as a distinct identity exists only by "existing as the blessed Trinity of Father, Son, and Holy Spirit." God is a "distinct centre of activity and reactivity, and so a genuine individual in his own right." Simultaneously, God is *the* individual "whose own reality constitutes reality itself or as such." Thus God is transcendent to the world and immanent in the world as its source, "even as the world is immanent in him as its final end." But to call God an "individual" is allowable precisely because the "substantial unity" of God is the consequence of the intrinsic "personal plurality" — in my words: persons-in-relationship — of the three divine persons. Divine individuality is constituted by the personal plurality. This leads finally to an affirmation which even secular reason could conclude: that "there is one integral life from which and for which all other lives are lived."

By this assertion one may then bypass the problems inherent in the ancient doctrine of the *vestigium trinitatis*. I read Ogden's argument (though he does not explicitly say so himself) to mean finally, that this integral relatedness in God necessitates an "integral temporality" (my coinage), insofar as the relatedness in and of God can never be static; otherwise there would be no relationship.[19]

5.4. Triune relatedness is infinite, as asserted in the doctrine of perichoresis and Eastern Orthodox thought. Infinity is to be understood as unboundedness in the fashion after Gregory of Nyssa's and Robert Jenson's interpretation, as well as Pannenberg's.[20]

5.5. The movement of epistemological reflection to an ontological assertion leads next to the affirmation of Rahner's Rule, that "the economic Trinity is the immanent Trinity, and vice-versa."

5.6. The Trinitarian persons act in freedom and in mutuality.

5.7. Further, because the works *ad extra* of the Trinity are embedded in the relatedness-of-its-diversity, Rahner's Rule may now be construed as a cosmological statement.

5.71. This cosmological adaptation implies that a description of God's eternity (as the transcendent "omni-relatedness") as approached through the economy of God thus means it is approachable by way of temporality; so temporality is necessary to the economic and immanent Trinity.

5.72. Further, "reality" as created by the Trinity is also a field for the suffering love internal to the Trinity.[21]

5.8.   That there is yet freedom and transcendence in the divine persons means that the future enjoys priority. There is always an "open" future. There will be "always more." This is to say that the future is not fixed in phenomenal form and that, even when all is reconciled at the eschaton, an open future will still be offered. As Moltmann argues, even in the fulfilled time of eternity there will be temporality precisely because there shall always be the surplus of transcendence-freedom-future in the Trinity.

5.81. The perfect identity of the "economic" and "immanent" Trinity will not be fully realized until the eschaton. I follow several eschatological theologians on this point.[22] This is also to affirm that temporality and eternity will not be fully integrated and synonymous until the eschaton, when God is in all and all is in God.

5.9.   This transcendence is also a transcendence of the divine energies/love.

Synthetic Physical/Theological Theses

6.0.   The physical, epistemological and theological theses above may be fused into more complete reality statements.

6.1.   The requirement of wholistic explanation and the affirmation of a semi-block universe unite what is physically describable to a meta-physical theological explanation, and legitimately so. This is an extrapolation also of 4.2.

6.11. The assertions that future is at the root of reality (2.2), that the future is open (2.8), that God is the "power of the future" (4.4) and that there is the real possibility of asserting an absolute future in the transcendent eschatological sense (2.5) commends the further "physical" argument that future can be understood in terms of eternity's "all-embracingness" (3.4).

6.2.   Insofar as the theist maintains that God acts in the cosmos, thesis 6.1 (at least) implies that such action is, in part, describable by scientific theses in critically realistic fashion. And insofar as such theses illumine God's action, they further commend descriptives for a Doctrine of God, or, as in this case, a doctrine of the Trinity. Therefore theorems such as those of Special and General Relativity, and the Quantum Theory hold their own possibilities for describing God's action, but not God's self.

6.21.   Special Relativity may describe the kinesis in and of the Trinity. As acceleration leads toward infinite mass, so the kinesis of the Trinity may indicate the infinity, immediacy and omnipresence of God.

6.22.   As General Relativity describes how mass, energy and velocity are mutually influential, so too it may describe in part how a creator God is shaped and influenced (physically) by what is created, as well as how that which is created is composed by the mass, energy and "velocities" of the triune Persons.

6.23.   As the Quantum Theory posits freedom and open future at the root of reality, so also it may characterize and support the assertion of the freedom and future of God, i.e., of God's aseity and transcendence (6.1, 4.4, 2.8).

6.24.   The theory of Special Relativity commits to no fixed and absolute transcendent future. It can speak only to the shared causal future which one or more agents can affect. One agent's future outside the light cone may indeed be someone else's past. Thus, relativity theory requires a complex description of the Trinity's relatedness to time which avoids any talk of an absolute (or generic) future.

Excursus

Complex descriptions might be as follows.

Suppose persons A and B were placed on a horizontal axis and the light cone of each was extended directly upward from each person. Their "shared" future would be that common area in which the two cones intersect, one "level," as it were, away from the persons. If a third person is added, the future common to all three would be another "level" away yet. Based on this simplistic scenario, one might conjecture that God's temporality would be that complex future which is finally that shared area quite some distances away from the agents of the cones, multiplied by the billions of people who had populated and presently do populate this planet, if indeed we want only to speak of the human experience of temporality apart from the rest of cosmos. The extrapolation could be magnified infinitely further. Obviously this will not do as a description of a personal God who is intimate with God's people. It is also quite backward. The question, as Barth constructed it for us, is rather to conceive of God's complex temporality as causal for all aspects of our (and the rest of creation's) temporality. We must construct this description now, however, without contravening Special Relativity.

Somewhat like Moltmann's own attempt to depict a complex, causal future, one might pose three points (identities) of F, S and Sp. For simplicity's sake, we may place them on a horizontal axis. When one draws light cones from each point as we supposed above, the result would be similar to the first scenario. The shared temporal sphere would be one level away from the persons. But one shared axis is too limiting. As soon as one posits sheer mutuality *and* freedom of will and movement among the three identities (i.e., when we keep aseity together with the mutual reciprocity of the divine persons) as is appropriate to the triune persons, then cones may be drawn only in such a way that they include the other two persons and a common area of intense relationship—unity—at the "core" of the Trinity is established. These intersecting rays of the light cones, of course, would form a triangle at the "center" of the infinitely extending rays. The intensely shared "center," further, is the result of dynamic relationality of the triune agents and this center is analogous to the superposition of temporal trajectories in the quantum state. In other words, any temporality is possible and "specific" temporalities are, at this point, imaginary. Even outside this core there will be many shared areas of economy. With the creative work of the Father, the redeeming work of the Son and the ingathering work of the Spirit,—all performed in freedom and mutuality—this complex temporality extends to the created order, which in turn has its own temporalities. This follows the consonance we found earlier, e.g., with Philo, Augustine and Isham.

With the interior of this triangulation, we symbolically portray the priority of mutuality in the divine persons. However, as I suggested, the rays away from each point could be extended infinitely as the outlines of each agent's light cone, giving not only a triangular image to the "immanent" trinity, but also allowing that the cones unique to each divine agent have their own particular external consequences. This is to say, in other words, that the external works of the Trinity are distinguishable, while ultimately (eschatologically) co-inherent. This is an appropriate correction, I believe, of Augustine's maxim: *opera trinitatis ad extra indivisa sunt*. One should not stop there, however. Because divine relatedness requires dynamism or kinesis, this "triangle" is not at rest. The agents will "move" always with equal mutuality in respect to each other. The Son redeems what the Father has created and the Spirit will sanctify. Thus the horizons of influence which the divine persons effect are indeed both equally distinguishable and integrated.

Subject also to the laws of General Relativity,, and analogous to the reciprocity of mass and space, the *ad extra* work of the persons is influenced by that which is created. The Trinity, in a real sense, in reciprocal relationship with the created order, both influences and is influenced by the created order. Further, with the trinitarian effects of "bent" light cones extended infinitely "beyond" creation, all creation is seen as globally contingent upon trinitarian agency. This agency creates *ex nihilo* in the sense argued by Gilkey as of continuing ontological dependence. At the same time, the Trinity is further realized (shaped) by that which it creates.

The monotheism hereby affirmed is, as it were, a "singularity"[23] which, when applied beyond a two-dimensional plane, might seem interestingly like the unidentifiable point of causality that Stephen Hawking has argued in physical terms. However, we argue here, in accordance with assumptions of divine providence and trinitarian omnipresence, that the cones extended from the divine agents themselves describe fields of the Trinity's omnicausal agency. One may also construe this symbolically along the lines of a Big Bang cosmological model suggested by Chris Isham, in which the Real Time universe "emerges" from a primordial imaginary-time four dimensional sphere, such as in the Hartle-Hawking proposal.[24] In this respect, the global economy of the Trinity is indeed the theo-logical Trinity. This is an extension of Rahner's Rule.

Of course, the propositions made here reverberate in many other theological voices. These scenarios suggest that one may *approach* or *mimic*, though never conclusively realize, a physical description of triune temporality (however primitively constructed), given certain assumptions of divine agency, mutuality, freedom (analogous to omnipresence), and tri-unity. I am not suggesting that this possible description, however, is "merely" a metaphor. I argue that this physical type of divine description is consonant with physical description of cosmic processes. While this is not a collapse to or simple identification with the physical, divine action may be described as more like physical description than not. In fact, as divine transcendence should be understood as higher dimensionality which includes mathematical descriptions of "lower" dimensionalities, the divine *must* be consonant with the physical world and not disjunctive. Similar claims have been argued in process theological terms and kenotic christologies, as well as other theological genres with respect to divine effectiveness and passibility. In suggesting this, I have also extended upon Willem Drees's significant proposal that God's actions might be described by adding another dimension to physical description.[25] To be sure, the approach is limited by the confession that we are, after all, dealing with more than *physis* here when speaking of the Trinity. But we argue, nevertheless, that observable consequences, like time, have their origin in the penultimately unobservable Trinity.[26]

6.3.   The quantum theory evidences a structural openness to the future *and* the relatedness of events. This, too, is described by 6.24.

6.31. The structural openness to the future, as well as the assertions of 5.8 and 5.9, provide a better possibility by which to affirm Moltmann's suggestion that the creation is an open system.

6.4.   The causal agency of the Trinity, as discussed in 6.24 and also given an analogue in the discussion of the "divine energies" of the Trinity, is precisely that which is affirmed in the doctrine of *creatio continua*.

6.5.   The "model" of God suggested by this understanding of the Trinity and creation is more easily and economically rendered as theistic. That is, if the external works of the Trinity are not to be collapsed into *exactly* the same as those of the immanent Trinity, a caveat observed by Rahner's Rule, then it is difficult physically to describe this position in any terms of pantheism. At most, one might affirm a "pancumtheism" (or, *perhaps*, a nuanced panentheism, though this still tempts a collapse) wherein all is related to deity as a wheel by its spokes is related to the hub.[27]

6.51. This ongoing work of the Trinity may be construed as the infusion of energy into a system, which, when described at the quantum level, is then appropriately labelled as an open system, consonant with the scientific use of that term. Thus Moltmann's argument is appropriately corrected and provides an example of theology's right-headed use of original, even idiosyncratic, scientific terms.

6.6.   Time is emergent, because the Trinity is emergent, insofar as relationship among the divine persons is neither exhausted nor static, and shall not be fully realized until the eschaton (2.1, 5.81, and excursus of 6.24).

6.7.   The divine energies which constitute the power of the future can transcendently overcome the lack of energy signed by entropy. This is instantiated in God's suffering and overcoming of the cross.

6.8. Eternity itself will be temporal, though of a different sort than our common, narrow temporality. In other words, there will be the joyful experience of temporality without disjunction. The tensions asserted in 2.1 and 5.81 will be resolved.

Excursus

Each of these numbered auxiliary theses are based upon and implied by the correlative data of chapters 1 through 6. In a full-blown research program, that data would appear here conjoined with respective theses. I have chosen the more traditional expository style of traditional theological method in considering the data, employing that method as a bridge so to introduce this new possibility of method.

This enumeration could carry on quite further, too. One could suggest further auxiliary theses about the praxis of a life lived within this trinitarian universe-view. I would hold, for example, that the praxis of such a trinitarian outlook, concomitant with the argued understanding of time and eternity, frees the human person to shape the future in accord with the ever more realized trinitarian persons. I would suggest that there are consequences for prayer and worship life. I would underscore the "communitarian, perichoretic ecclesia," a personal church-in-communion, that issues from such a perspective. Such a church understands itself as continuous with all time and catholic tradition, in spite of the discontinuities of temporality, precisely because this church lives within and derives its purpose from the all-embracingness of eternity as that eternity exists from the Trinity.

One could go quite far with an ecclesiology within such a timely trinitarian horizon. Refreshing constructive proposals would be similar to those of Catherine Mowry LaCugna and John Zizioulas.[28] LaCugna emphasizes especially the worship and prayer life that would ensue from a properly Trinitarian understanding of faith. Zizioulas echoes, too, the sacramental shape a person's life would take within such a faith understanding. Most certainly these suggestions would resonate with Moltmann's continuing project to elicit and describe political theology's necessary relationship to and from doctrinal theology.

In these examples and more one sees predictions already that may be stated in the terms of this particular research program. It may be that some of these "novel facts" are laden with subjective values that would be peculiar in a strictly scientific research program. But "values" indeed are not alien to a progressive program. Karl Peters argues that all experience is value laden because "we are genetically informed and biologically constructed to experience in this way."[29] All the more, theological research programs too can be judged progressive only insofar as they yield a growth in value.[30] Increased depth in the community sense of the church, further perichoretic relationship within the wider social network; indeed, a concomitant peace and increase in joy and solicitude, however subjectively valued these qualities may seem to be: these are measurable marks of the progress of such a proposed theological research program.

I admit that these comments have something of a shape of Pascal's wager about them. One may not know the truth or falsity of them until it is quite too late for the cosmos. The tentativeness of any proposal, evenso, is necessarily qualified by the eschatological character of our subject, the Trinity, itself. Further predictions, which mark the advancing edge of a research program, always lead with the vulnerable limb. So, then, I will hazard some predictions of novel facts of a more objective type for theology and science which, methodologically at least, could show that some progress has been made in a research program like this one.

A Hazard of Predictions

7.0.   The doing of theology will become formally more like scientific research programs.

This is a general statement, perhaps even trivial, as only one more attempt other than mine at a Lakatosian style would prove the point. But this general statement is a necessary prolegomenon to the following assertions, which are meant, too, to specify its meaning.

7.1.   Theology will develop an instrument corresponding to or consonant with the descriptive four-dimensional geometry of space/time.

7.2.   This new instrument, a synthesis of previous scientific and theological constructions, will be a new, wholistically oriented set of emergent structures. The structures will be hierarchically ordered in multiple levels, though both "upwardly" and "downwardly" causal or implicative, and infinitely open to God the Power of the Future.

7.3.   This new instrument or system will profoundly clarify and simplify the task and body of Christian theology.

7.4.   Christian theology will thus be the stronger and its universality will be more rationally commended. Its veracity as a *scientific* theology will thus be the more philosophically and natural-scientifically recognizable.

7.5.   This will enable further ecumenical unity.

7.6.   In all these advances the unifying work of God as Trinity will be further substantiated, thereby further indicating that only an eternity with an essential temporality, the consequence of the relationality of the Trinity, is possible with and within this God.

Conclusion

Perhaps the reader recognizes that I have adapted predictions 7.1.-7.5. from the work of Thomas F. Torrance.[31] He argues that Barth himself had attempted to do for theology what scientists have been about in physics and cosmology: to develop a larger unifying theory, as it were, that incorporates both revealed and natural theology, both "corpuscular and undulatory theories of light."[32] With my proposals I would hazard that I may have gone a direction than Barth or Torrance at their times of writing might not have countenanced. Didacus Stella (1st century, A.D.) did comment, though, that dwarves on the shoulders of giants can see farther than the giants themselves. I would add that this is so if the eyes of the dwarves are open. I do suggest, whatever the mitigating circumstances, that the import of this proposal for a scientific theology is coherent with the claims of other significant theologians today.[33]

But ultimately, the demand as I see it and have described in chapter one that Christian theology must appropriate the insights of current physical theory, *starting with* the post-Einsteinian understanding of time, still remains. I have argued that Christian theology need not divorce itself from its basic doctrines to take this quantum leap. There is ample theological reflection in the tradition as to eternity's embrace of time, and ample classical and contemporary theological agreement as to an appropriate understanding of the Trinity so to give a Christian sensibility to current theory without being either fideistically non-scientific on the one hand, or materialistically atheological, on the other. The Eastern theological tradition since the Cappadocians and the blossoming work of so many thinkers about the Trinity since Barth are especially significant in this enterprise. They have not been without their areas of vulnerability, however, and exemplary of them, because he is exemplary in his healthy Barthian refocus on the Trinity, is Jürgen Moltmann. With the help of some insights of contemporary physics and cosmology, I attempted to point out some areas wherein Moltmann and the whole theological project might be strengthened. With that exposition concluded, I embarked on a short adventure in this chapter to show how projects like Moltmann's might be even further commended were they to take the shape of a progressive scientific research program along the thought of Imre Lakatos and commended to theology by Nancey Murphy. Though the adventure may have been perilous, the attempt was to suggest a new constructive statement based upon the data of the previous chapters.

Of course, time and the perchoresis of constructive criticism will evidence the degree or lack thereof of progress in this brief program. Its key assertion, the hard core theorem, has been that the eternity of the Trinity is essentially temporal. I have argued that the relationality of the Trinitarian persons with each other and, in turn, with the creation, is itself the origin of the complexity of times now elucidated by contemporary physical theory. With this reconstruction of the doctrine of the Trinity along social trinitarian lines I have sought to show that the previous inconsistencies within Christian theology's own concepts of time and eternity, as well as the external inconsistencies between science and theology, may be overcome.

Thus the reader has likely recognized by now another intention of this project: to show that the diastasis between science and theology may be overcome. Ironically, some of the diastasis in this era has been attributed to the neo-orthodox tradition consequent to Karl Barth, though it is Barth himself who in theological method and his doctrine of the Trinity set forth the new possibilities for convergence. Some theological reticence in appealing to the sciences for instruction and support is attributable to the argument that natural theology independent of revelation is to be shunned. While the arenas of science and theology have their respective areas of distinct responsibility, my argument about the need for theology to be in relationship with scientific advance, as exemplified in the case of physics and cosmology with respect to time, is ultimately one that is Barthian at its base.

If the theological hardcore belief is that God in God's self and as we know God in God's graceful revelation really is triune, then what can one make of the validity of any independent natural theology or analogous activity that concludes upon a god not of triune identity, but some god "in general"? This, for example, is the error Carl Sagan commits in his deistic eisegesis of Hawking's text. A trinitarian theology, in other words, must converse with partners of other thoughtful enterprises, for a trinitarian theology affirms that God enjoys a profound, hyper-complex relationship in God's self and to the universe. A trinitarian theology cannot separate God's being from God's acts, however such an act may elsewhere be described.

And this is indeed the Barthian claim. As Thomas Torrance puts it, "...if natural theology is included within the body of our knowledge of God as he really is, must it not be correspondingly trinitarian in its structure, and indeed precisely as trinitarian constitute the inner sub-structure of all sound theology?"[34]

In the end, it is not that we have been searching for some sort of trinitarian pattern for our physical worldview. Nor have we been attempting forcefully to lay a scientifc template over a dispirited theological corpus. We have, rather, been driven by the implicit trinitarian impulse that lies within both theological and scientific reflection so to recognize their consonance, if not their kinship. To what more may the need for wholistic explanation lead? And for what less could it possibly settle than time's embeddedness in the womb of eternity, and both science and theology's celebration of this new life?

These are perhaps broad concluding strokes. These suggestions are but a simple filtrate that has passed through a sieve of theological and physical observation. I trust, evenso, that they are suggestive for future research more than they make for any final conclusions. After all, subject as we are to the subject of time and eternity, "Only our concept Time makes it possible for us to speak of the Day of Judgement by that name; in reality it is a summary court in perpetual session" (Kafka). But faith and reason impel us ever more to seek fulfillment and ever more to enjoy God's future. However transient our hypotheses may prove to be, those very gifts of faith and reason will draw us into time's redemption.

Notes

1. Cf. Ted Peter's, "The Trinity In and Beyond Time," *Quantum Cosmology and the Laws of Nature*, 263-290.
2. Karl Popper, *Logik der Forschung* (Vienna, 1935), translated as *The Logic of Scientific Discovery*; Carl Hempel, *Aspects of Scientific Explanation* (New York: Free Press, 1966), and *Philosophy of Natural Science* (Englewood Cliffs, N.J.:Prentice-Hall, 1966).
3. Stephen Toulmin, *Foresight and Understanding* (New York: Harper, 1961); Thomas Kuhn, *The Structure of Scientific Revolutions*.
4. See Ian Barbour, *Myths, Models and Paradigms* (New York: Harper and Row, 1974), and *Issues in Science and Religion* (New York: Harper and Row, 1966), especially 138-174.
5. I am indebted to Nancey Murphy, *Theology in the Age of Scientific Reasoning*, for this argument and follow her summary of the Lakatos methodology.
6. Murphy, 59.
7. Murphy, 59.
8. Murphy, 61.
9. Holmes Ralston, III, *Science and Religion, A Critical Survey* (New York: Random House, 1987).
10. Murphy, 184.
11. Murphy takes George Lindbeck as an advocate of this understanding of doctrine. See Lindbeck, *The Nature of Doctrine* (Philadelphia: Westminster, 1984). Therein, Lindbeck argues that doctrine provides the "grammatical rules" by which to interpret the narrative sources for one's tradition. Specifically, Lindbeck argues that doctrine arises out of the regulative function of narrative. As "language games," according to Wittgenstein, place the conversation within a particlar world-view, with its own declension and horizon of meaning, so also is it the function of doctrine to provide a regulated discourse.
12. Murphy, 186.
13. See chapter 2.
14. This is the main argument of Pannenberg in his "Theological Questions to Scientists," which I discussed in chapter 6.
15. See chapter 2.
16. The similarity between this Pannenbergian argument and Anselm's ontological argument ought not be lost on the reader.
17. This, of course, echoes both Moltmann and Pannenberg.
18. The term "empirical" refers not directly to sense experience, but to the study of religious experiential belief. Nor does it refer to the specific intentions construed by the section on empiricism in the American Academy of Religion. This is another example of the language issue I discussed in the introduction to this dissertation; that we must be careful not to use terms in a new context that are robbed of their intended meaning in their original contexts. Yet often we must and do use words this way and, when we do so, we must be aware of their limits.
19. Cf. Schubert Ogden, "On the Trinity," *Theology* (March: 1980), 83: 97-102.
20. See chapter 2.
21. See the discussion of Moltmann, chapter 6.
22. See chapter 2.

23. Here I intend only metaphor.

24. See Isham, *QCLN*.

25. See chapter 5 and its note 71.

26. I say "penultimately" because Christian faith holds that the Trinity will be worshipped in fullness, which is to say "observed," only at the eschaton.

27. This, however, should count as a criticism of Moltmann's appeal to the Jewish mystical doctrine of zimsum. Moltmann gets the "geography" wrong by saying that the doctrine's imaging of God's withdrawing into God's self implies a panentheism. If anything, it implies that by God's withdrawal God creates a "belt" or external space for creation, subject still to God's agency because that space *ad extra* to God is nevertheless divine space.

28. The final chapter of LaCugna's *God For Us* is entitled "Living Trinitarian Faith" (see 377ff.). John Zizioulas's whole trajectory of discussion on the human as a relation-ecclesial being leads to a compelling vision of a renewed catholicity of the church which is non-hierarchical and deeply spirited. See *Being As Communion, Studies in Personhood and the Church* (Crestwood: St. Vladimir's Press, 1985). Ted Peters also devotes two final trinitarian theses to a discussion of practical life. However, he criticizes the communitarian vision of the Trinity as a model for human social life and prefers another vision (with which I have shown my disagreement elsewhere in this book) and with the final thesis turns to the experience of grace. Cf. *God As Trinity*, 184-187.

29. Karl E. Peters, "Empirical Theology in the Light of Science," *Zygon*, 27:3 (September, 1993), 308.

30. Karl Peters, 319.

31. Thomas F. Torrance, *Transformation and Convergence in the Frame of Knowledge, Explorations in the Interrelations of Scientific and Theological Enterprise* (Grand Rapids: William B. Eerdmans, 1984), 282-3.

32. Torrance, 280.

33. Cf. Wolfhart Pannenberg, *Theology and the Philosophy of Science*, trans. by Francis McDonagh (Philadelphia: Westminster, 1976) and Stephen T. Ostovich, *Reason In History, Theology and Science as Community Activities* (Atlanta: Scholar's Press, 1990).

34. Torrance, 297.

BIBLIOGRAPHY

Aquinas, *Summa Theologiae*, ed. Timothy McDermott (Westminster, Md.: Christian Classics, 1989).

Aristotle, *The Basic Works of Aristotle*, ed. S. McKeon (New York: Random House, 1941).

Augustine, *On the Trinity*, trans. Stephen McKenna, C.SS.R; vol. 45 of *The Fathers of the Church* (Washington D.C.: Catholic University of America Press, 1963).

___, *Confessions*, trans. R.S. Pine-Coffin (Middlesex: Penguin, 1961).

Balas, David L. "Eternity and Time in Gregory of Nyssa's *Contra Eunomium*, in *Gregor von Nyssa und die Philosophie: zweites internationales Kolloquium uber Gregor von Nyssa*, ed. H. Dorrie (Leiden: Brill, 1976),128-153.

Barbour, Ian, *Religion in an Age of Science, The Gifford Lectures,* vol. 1 of 2 (San Francisco: Harper Collins, 1990).

___, *Issues In Science and Religion* (New York: Harper and Row, 1966).

___, *Myths, Models, and Paradigms* (New York: Harper and Row, 1974).

Barr, James, *Biblical Words for Time* (London: SCM Press, 1962).

Barrow, John D., *The World Within the World* (New York: Oxford, 1990).

Barrow, John and Frank Tipler, *The Anthropic Cosmological Principle* (New York: Oxford, 1986)

Barth, Karl, *Church Dogmatics*, eds. G. W. Bromiley and T. F. Torrance (Edinburgh: T&T Clark, 1960), vols. I/2, II/1, III/2 and III/4.

___, *The Epistle to the Romans*, 6th edition, trans. Edwyn C. Hoskyns (London: Oxford University Press, 1933).

Baur, F.C., *Die christliche Lehre von der Dreieinigkeit und Menschwerdung Gottes in ihrer geschichtlichen Entwicklung*, I-III (Tübingen, 1843).

Bloch, Ernst, *Das Prinzip Hoffnung* (Frankfurt: Suhrkamp,1959).

Boethius, *The Consolation of Philosophy*, trans.V.E. Watts (Baltimore: Penguin, 1969).

Boslow, John, "The Enigma of Time," *National Geographic*, 177:3 (March, 1990), 109-132.

Braaten, Carl and Jenson, Robert, eds., *Christian Dogmatics*, 2 vols., (Philadelphia: Fortress, 1984).

Braaten, *The Future of God, The Revolutionary Dynamics of Hope* (New York: Harper and Row, 1969).

Bracken, Joseph, S.J., *Society and Spirit, A Trinitarian Cosmology* (Selinsgrove: Susquehanna University Press, 1991).

___, "The Holy Trinity as a Community of Divine Persons," *Heythrop Journal*,15 (1974),166-82, 257-70.

___, *The Triune Symbol: Persons, Process and Community*, College Theology Society Studies in Religion (Lanham: University Press in America, 1985).

___, "Philosophy and Trinitarian Theology," *Process Studies,* 8:4 (Winter, 1978), 217-230; 11:2 (Summer, 1981), 83-96.

___, "Subsistent Relation: Mediating Concept for a New Synthesis?" *Journal of Religion* (April, 1984), 188-204.

___, *What Are They Saying About the Trinity?* (New York: Paulist Press, 1979).

___, "The World: Body of God or Field of Cosmic Activity?", in *Charles Hartshorne's Concept of God*, ed. Santiago Sia (Dordrecht: Klower Academic Publishers, 1990).

Brown, Delwin, Ralph E. James Jr. and Gene Reeves, eds., *Process Philosophy and Christian Thought* (Indianapolis and New York: Bobbs Merrill, 1971).

Calder, Nigel, *Einstein's Universe* (New York: Viking, 1979).

Čapek, Milič, "Time in Relativity Theory: Arguments for a Philosophy of Becoming," J. T. Fraser, ed., *The Voices of Time*, 2nd. ed. (Amherst: University of Massachusetts Press, 1981), 434-455.

Capps, Walter, *Hope Against Hope: Moltmann to Merton in One Decade* (Philadelphia: Fortress, 1976).

___, ed., *The Future of Hope* (Philadelphia: Fortress,1970).

Clayton, Philip, *Explanation from Physics to Theology: An Essay in Rationality and Religion* (New Haven: Yale University Press, 1989).

Clayton, Philip D., "The God of History and the Presence of the Future," *The Journal of Religion*, 65, (Jan., 1985), 98-108.

Cobb John, and David R. Griffin, *Process Theology, An Introductory Exhibition* (Philadelphia: Westminster, 1976).

Cobb, John, "Reply to Moltmann's 'The Unity of the Triune God,'" *St. Vladimir's Theological Quarterly*, 28:3 (1984).

___, "Response to Ted Peters," *dialog*, 30:3 (Summer, 1991), 241-243.

___, *Christ in a Pluralistic Age* (Philadelphia: Westminster, 1975).

Cole-Turner, Ronald, "An Unavoidable Challenge: Our Church In An Age of Science and Technology," (Cleveland: The Division of Education and Publication, United Church Board For Homeland Ministries, 1992).

Congar, Yves, *I Believe In the Holy Spirit* (New York: Seabury, 1983).

Copleston, Frederick, *A History of Philosophy*, vol. 6 (Garden City: Image, 1960).

Cullmann, Oscar, *Christ and Time* (Philadelphia: Westminster, 1950).

Davies, Paul, *God and the New Physics* (New York: Simon and Schuster, 1983).

Drees, Willem, *Beyond the Big Bang, Quantum Cosmologies and God* (LaSalle: Open Court, 1990).

Dyson, Freeman, *Infinite In All Directions* (New York: Harper and Row, 1988).

___, "Time Without End: Physics and Biology In An Open Universe," *Review of Modern Physics*, 51 (1979), 447ff.

Eaves, Lindon, "Spirit, Method and Content in Science and Religion: The Theological Perspective of a Geneticist," *Zygon,* 24:2 (June, 1989), 185-215.

Einstein, Albert, *The Principle of Relativity* (New York: Dover, 1952).

___, *Relativity, The Special and General Theory* (New York: Crown, 1961).

Eliade, Mircea, *Cosmos and History: The Myth of the Eternal Return*, trans. Willard R. Trask (New York: Harper Torchbooks, 1959).

Eliade, *The Sacred and the Profane: The Nature of Religion*, trans. Willard Trask (New York: Harper and Row, 1965).

Fagg, Lawrence, *Two Faces of Time* (Madras: Theosophical Publications, 1985).

Feyerabend, Paul, *Realism, Rationalism and Scientific Method*, vol. 1 of *Philosophical Papers* (Cambridge: Cambridge University Press, 1981).

Ford, Lewis, *The Lure of God* (Philadelphia: Fortress, 1978).

Fraser, J.T., ed., *The Voices of Time*, 2nd ed. (Amherst: University of Massachusetts, 1981).

French, A.P., ed., *Einstein, A Centenary Volume* (Cambridge: Harvard University Press, 1979).

Gilberson, Karl, *Worlds Apart, The Unholy War Between Religion and Science* (Kansas City: Beacon Hill, 1993).

Gilkey, Langdon, *Maker of Heaven and Earth* (Garden City: Doubleday, 1959).

___, *Religion and the Scientific Future* (New York: Harper & Row, 1970).

Gregory of Nyssa, *Against Eunomius* in *The Nicene and Post-Nicene Fathers*, vol. V., trans. H. A. Wilson, Philip Schaff and Henry Wace, eds. (Edinburgh: T&T Clark, 1988).

Grib, Andrej, "Time and Eternity in Modern Relativistic Cosmology," unpublished paper presented at the Fourth European Conference on Science and Theology, Mondo Migliore, Italy, March, 1992.

___, "Quantum Cosmology, The Role of Observer, Quantum Logics," in Russell, et al., eds., *Quantum Cosmology and the Laws of Nature: Scientific Perspectives on Divine Action* (Rome and Notre Dame: Vatican Observatory and University of Notre Dame Press, 1993).

Griffin, David R., *Physics and the Ultimate Importance of Time* (Albany: SUNY, 1986).

___, *The Reenchantment of Science: Postmodern Proposals* (New York: SUNY, 1988).

Gunton, Colin, *Becoming and Being* (New York and London: Oxford University Press, 1978).

Haight, Roger, "The Point of Trinitarian Theology," *Toronto Journal of Theology*, 4:2 (Fall, 1988), 191-204.

Hawking, Stephen, *A Brief History of Time, From the Big Bang to Black Holes* (New York: Bantam, 1987).

Hilary of Poitiers, *De Trinitate*, Philip Schaff and Henry Wace, eds., *Nicene and Post-Nicene Fathers*, Second Series, vol. IX (New York: Charles Scribners Sons, 1899).

Hefner, Philip J., "The Creation," in Carl Braaten and Robert Jenson, eds., *Christian Dogmatics*, vol. 1 (Philadelphia: Fortress, 1984), 265-358.

Helm, Paul, *Eternal God* (Oxford: Clarendon, 1989).

Hempel,Carl, *Philosophy of Natural Science* (Englewood Cliffs: Prentice-Hall, 1966).

___, *Aspects of Scientific Explanation* (New York: Free Press, 1965).

Herbert, Nick, *Quantum Reality* (London: Rider, 1985).

Hodgson, Leonard, *The Doctrine of the Trinity* (New York: Charles Scribner's Sons, 1944).

Hodgson, Peter C., *God In History, Shapes of Freedom* (Nashville: Abingdon, 1989).

___, *Winds of the Spirit* (Nashville: Abingdon, 1994).

Hoffmann, Banesh, *The Strange Story of the Quantum* (New York: Dover, 1959).

Horvath, Tibor, "A New Notion of Time," *Science et Esprit* XL:1 (May, 1988), 35-55.

___, "Jesus Christ, The Eschatological Union of Time and Eternity," *Science et Esprit*, XL:1, (May, 1988), 17, 91-92.

Isham, C. J., "Creation As A Quantum Process," in Russell, et al., eds., *Physics, Philosophy and Theology, A Common Quest for Understanding* (Vatican: Vatican Observatory, 1988), 375-408.

___, "Quantum Theories of the Creation of the Universe," Russell, et al., eds., *Quantum Cosmology and the Laws of Nature, Scientific Perspectives on Divine Action* (Vatican City State: Vatican Observatory, 1993), 49-90.

Isham, C. J. and John Polkinghorne, "The Debate Over the Block Universe," Russell, et al., eds., *Quantum Cosmology and the Laws of Nature* (Vatican City State: Vatican Observatory, 1993), 135-144.

Jaki, Stanley, *The Purpose of It All* (Washington D.C.: Regnery Gateway, 1990).

Jenson, Robert, *Unbaptized God, The Basic Flaw in Ecumenical Theology* (Minneapolis: Augsburg Fortress, 1992).

___, "Jesus in the Trinity: Wolfhart Pannenberg's Christology and Doctrine of the Trinity," in *The Theology of Wolfhart Pannenberg*, ed. by Carl E. Braaten and Philip Clayton (Minneapolis: Augsburg, 1988).

___, "The Triune God," in Braaten/Jenson (eds.) *Christian Dogmatics*, vol. 1 (Philadelphia: Fortress, 1984).

___, *The Triune Identity: God According to the Gospel* (Philadelphia: Fortress, 1982).

Jüngel, Eberhard, *God As the Mystery of the World*, trans. Darrell L. Guder (Grand Rapids: Eerdman's, 1983).

___, *The Doctrine of the Trinity: God's Being Is In Becoming*, trans. Horton Harris (Grand Rapids: Eerdman's, 1976).

Kasper, Walter, *The God of Jesus Christ* (New York: Crossroad, 1976).

Kant, Immanuel, *Religion Within the Limits of Reason Alone*, trans Greene and Hudson (New York: Harper and Row, 1960).

Kelly, J.N.D., *The Athanasian Creed* (New York and London: Longmans, Green & Co., 1964)

Klaaren, Eugene, *Religious Origins of Modern Science* (Grand Rapids: Eerdmans, 1977).

Kuhn, Thomas, *The Structure of Scientific Revolutions*, 22nd ed.(Chicago: University of Chicago, 1970).

LaCugna, Catherine Mowry, "The Trinitarian Mystery of God," in *Systematic Theology: Roman Catholic Perspectives*, Francis Schussler Fiorenza and John P. Galvin, eds.,vol. 1, (Minneapolis: Fortress Press, 1991), 149-192.

___, "Current Trends in Trinitarian Theology," *Religious Studies Review*, 13:2 (April, 1987), 141-147.

194 Times of the Trinity

4

___, *God For Us, The Trinity and Christian Life* (San Francisco: Harper, 1991).

___, "Trinity,"" in *The Encyclopedia of Religion*, Mircea Eliade, ed., vol. 15 (New York: MacMillan, 1988), 53-57.

Lakatos, Imre, *The Methodology of Scientific Research Programmes: Philosophical Papers*, vol. 1, John Worrell and Gregory Currie, eds. (Cambridge: Cambridge University Press, 1978), 8-101.

___, "Falsification and the Methodology of Scientific Research Programs," *Criticism and the Growth of Knowledge,* Imre Lakatos and Alan Musgrave, eds. (Cambridge: Cambridge University Press, 1970), 91-196.

Larson, Duane H., "Review of Joseph Bracken, S.J., *Society and Spirit,*" *Center for Theology and the Natural Sciences Bulletin,*12:3 (Summer, 1992), 3-5.

___, "Theology Update: The Trinity and Time's Flow," *dialog*, 33:1 (Winter, 1994), 62-70.

___, "Pondering Pannenberg and the Trinity," *Lutheran Forum*, 28:2 (May, 1994), 32-35.

Leftow, Brian, "Boethius on Eternity," *History of Philosophy Quarterly*, 7 (1990), 123-42.

___, "Aquinas on Time and Eternity," *American Catholic Philosophical Quarterly*, 64 (1990), 387-99.

___, "Eternity and Simultaneity," *Faith and Philosophy*, 8:2 (April, 1991) 148-179.

___, *Time and Eternity* (Ithaca: Cornell University Press, 1991).

Lewis, Delmas, "Eternity, Time and Tenselessness," *Faith and Philosophy*, 5 (1988), 72-86.

Leyden, W. von, "Time, Number and Eternity in Plato and Aristotle," *Philosophical Quarterly*, 14 (1964), 35-52.

Limberg, David and Ronald Numbers, eds., *God and Nature, Historical Essays on the Encounter Between Christianity and Science* (Berkeley: University of California, 1986).

Lindbeck, George, *The Nature of Doctrine* (Philadelphia: Westminster, 1984).

Lucas, J. R., *The Future: An Essay on God, Temporality and Truth* (Oxford: Basil Blackwell, 1989).

Marion, Jean-Luc, *God Without Being, Hors-Texte*, trans. Thomas A. Carlson (Chicago: University of Chicago Press, 1991).

McFague, Sally, "Models of God For An Ecological, Evolutionary Era: God As Mother of the Universe," *Physics, Philosophy and Theology*, Russell, et al.,eds. (Vatican: Vatican Observatory, 1988), 249-271.

___, *Models of God: Theology for an Ecological, Nuclear Age* (Philadelphia: Fortress, 1987).

___, *Metaphorical Theology: Models of God in Religious Language* (Philadelphia: Fortress, 1982).

McMullin, Ernan, ed., *Evolution and Creation* (Notre Dame: University of Notre Dame, 1985).

Meeks, M. Douglas, *Origins of the Theology of Hope* (Philadelphia: Fortress, 1974).

Meijering, E. P., *Hilary of Poitiers On the Trinity, De Trinitate I, 1-19, II, III* (Leiden: E. J. Brill, 1982).

Moltmann, Jürgen, *Experiences of God*, trans. Margaret Kohl (Philadelphia: Fortress, 1980).

___, *The Future of Creation*, trans. Margaret Kohl (Philadelphia: Fortress, 1979).

___, "Christian Theology and Its Problems Today," *Theology Digest*, 19:4 (Winter, 1971), 308-317.

___, *The Church in the Power of the Spirit*, trans. Margaret Kohl (New York: Harper and Row, 1977).

___, *Hope and Planning*, trans. Margaret Clarkson, (New York: Harper and Row, 1971).

___, "Die Zukunft Christi. Kommt Jesus Wieder?," *Radius*, 1 (March, 1966), 6-13.

___, "Verschränkte Zeiten der Geschichte, Notwendige Differenzierungen und Begreuzungen des Geschichtsbegriffs," *Evangelische Theologie*, 44:3 (Mai-June: 1984), 213-227.

___, *God in Creation*, trans. Margaret Kohl (New York: Harper and Row, 1985).

___, *The Experiment Hope*, trans. M. Douglas Meeks (Philadelphia: Fortress, 1975).

___, *Politische Theologie — Politische Ethik*, (Mainz und München: Kaiser/Grunewald, 1984).

___, *Perspektiven der Theologie, Gesammelte Aufsätze* (Munich: Chr. Kaiser, 1968).

___, *In der Geschichte des dreieinigen Gottes, Beiträge zur trinitärischen Theologie* (München: Kaiser Verlag, 1991).

___, *The Way of Jesus Christ, Christology in Messianic Dimensions*, trans. Margaret Kohl (San Francisco: Harper, 1990).

___, et al, *The Future of Hope: Theology as Eschatology*, ed. Frederick Herzog, (New York: Herder and Herder, 1970).

___, "Die Kategorie Novum in der christliche Theologie," in *Ernst Bloch zu ehren*, ed. Siegfried Unself,(Frankfurt: Suhrkamp, 1965), 243-265.

___, *The Trinity and the Kingdom*, trans. Margaret Kohl (New York: Harper and Row, 1981).

___, "The Crucified God: A Trinitarian Theology of the Cross," *Interpretation*, 26:3 (July, 1972), 278-299.

___, *Theology of Hope: On the Ground and Implications of a Christian Eschatology,* trans. James W.Leitch (New York: Harper and Row, 1967).

___, *The Crucified God*, trans. by R.A.Wilson and John Bowden (New York: Harper and Row, 1974).

___, *Religion, Revolution and the Future*, trans. M.Douglas Meeks (New York: Charles Scribner's Sons, 1969).

___, "The Future As Threat and Opportunity," in *The Religious Situation, 1969*, ed. Donald Cutler (Boston: Beacon, 1969).

___, "Hope Beyond Time," *Duke Divinity School Review,* 33 (Spring, 1968), 109-119.

___, *Theology Today* (New York: Trinity, 1989).

___, "Eternity," *Listening*, 3 (1968), 89-95.

___, "Die Weltoffenheit des Menschen. Zur neueren philosophischen Anthropologie," *Verkundigung und Forschung,* 8 (1963), 115-134.

___, "Antwort auf die Kritik der Theologie der Hoffnung," in *Diskussion uber die Theologie der Hoffnung*, ed. W.D. Marsch, (München: Chr. Kaiser, 1967), 201-238.

___,ed., *Anfange der dialektischen Theologie,* 2 vols. (München: Chr. Kaiser, 1962, 1963).

___, *Umkehr zur Zukunft* (München: Siebenstern Taschenbuch Verlag, 1970).

Morse, Christopher, *The Logic of Promise in Moltmann's Theology* (Philadelphia: Fortress, 1979).

Murphy, Nancey, *Theology in the Age of Scientific Reasoning* (Ithaca: Cornell University Press, 1990).

___, "Scientific Realism and Postmodern Philosophy," *British Journal for the Philosophy of Science,* 41:3 (June, 1990), 291-303.

___, "Relating Theology and Science in a Postmodern Age," *The Center for Theology and the Natural Sciences Bulletin,* 7 (Fall, 1987), 1-10.

___, "From Critical Realism to a Methodological Approach: Response to Robbins, van Huyssteen and Hefner," *Zygon,* 23:3 (Sept., 1988), 287-290.

Neuhaus, Richard John, "Moltmann vs. Monotheism," 20:3 (Summer, 1981), 241.

Neville, Robert Cummings, *Eternity and Time's Flow* (Albany: SUNY, 1993).

Newton, Sir Isaac, *Sir Isaac Newton's Mathematical Principles of Natural Philosophy and His System of the World,* Cajori revision of 1729, trans. Andrew Motte (Berkeley: University of California Press, 1947).

Newton-Smith, W.H., *The Structure of Time* (London: Routledge & Kegan Paul, LTD., 1980).

Niebuhr, H. Richard, *Radical Monotheism and Western Culture* (New York: Faber, 1961).

Niebuhr, H. Richard, *The Meaning of Revelation* (New York: MacMillan, 1960).

O' Donnell, John, *Trinity and Temporality* (Oxford: Oxford University Press, 1983).

Ogden, Schubert, "On the Trinity," *Theology,* 83 (March, 1980), 97-102.

Ostovich, Stephen T., *Reason in History, Theology and Science As Community Activities* (Atlanta: Scholar's Press, 1990).

Pagels, Heinz, *The Cosmic Code: Quantum Physics as the Language of Nature* (New York: Simon and Schuster, 1982).

Pais, Abraham, *Subtle Is the Lord... The Science and Life of Albert Einstein* (Oxford: Oxford University Press, 1982).

Pannenberg, Wolfhart, *Jesus, God and Man*, trans. L.L. Wilkens and D. A. Priebe (Philadelphia: Westminster, 1968).

___, "Appearance As Arrival of the Future," *Journal of the American Academy of Religion*, 35 (1967), 107-118.

___, *Anthropology in Theological Perspective*, trans. by Matthew J. O' Connell (Philadelphia: Westminster, 1985).

___, et al., *Revelation as History*, trans. by David Granskou (New York: MacMillan, 1968).

___, "Theological Questions to Scientists," *Zygon*, 16:1 (March, 1981), 65-77.

___, "Die Subjektivität Gottes und die Trinitätslehre," *Grundfragen Systematischen Theologie*, II (Göttingen: Vanderhoeck und Ruprecht, 1963).

___, "Den Glauben an ihn selbs fassen und verstehen," *Zeitschrift fur Theologie und Kirche*, 86:3 (Juli, 1989), 365ff.

___, *What Is Man? Contemporary Anthropology in Theological Perspective*, trans. D.A. Priebe (Philadelphia: Fortress, 1970).

___, *Basic Questions in Theology*, trans. George H. Kehm, 2 vols. (Philadelphia: Fortress, 1970, 1972).

___, *Metaphysics and the Idea of God*, trans. Philip Clayton (Grand Rapids: Eerdmans, 1990).

___, "Problems of a Trinitarian Doctrine of God," *dialog*, 26:4 (Fall, 1987), 250-257.

___, *Systematische Theologie*, Band 1 (Göttingen: Vandenhoeck and Ruprecht, 1988).

___, *Theology and the Philosophy of Science*, trans. Francis McDonagh (Philadelphia: Westminster, 1976).

___, "The Doctrine of Creation and Modern Science," Zygon, 23:1 (March, 1988), 3-21.

___, "The God of Creation and Natural Science," CTNS Bulletin, 7:2 (Spring, 1987), 1-10.

Peacocke, Arthur, *Creation and the World of Science* (Oxford: Clarendon Press, 1979).

___, "The Theory of Relativity and Our World View," *Old and New Questions in Physics, Cosmology, Philosophy, and Theoretical Biology*, ed. Alwyn van der Merwe, (New York: Plenum, 1983), 733-752.

___, (ed.) *The Sciences and Theology in the Twentieth Century* (Notre Dame: University of Notre Dame, 1981).

___, *Science and the Christian Experiment* (London: Oxford University Press, 1971).

___, *Intimations of Reality, Critical Realism in Science and Religion* (Notre Dame: University of Notre Dame Press, 1984).

Pendergast, R.J., S.J., "A Thomistic Process Theory of the Trinity," *Science et Esprit*, XLIII/1 (1990), 35-59.

Peters, Ted, *God As Trinity, Relationality and Temporality in the Divine Life* (Nashville: Westminster/John Knox, 1993).

___, "Theology Update: Moltmann and the Way of the Trinity," *dialog,* 31:4 (Autumn, 1992), 272-279.

___, *God, The World's Future* (Minneapolis: Fortress, 1992).

___, "Trinity Talk," *dialog*, 26:1 (Winter, 1987), 44-48; 26:2 (Spring,1987), 133-38.

___, ed., *Cosmos As Creation, Theology and Science in Consonance* (Nashville: Abingdon, 1989).

___, "The Trinity in and Beyond Time," Robert John Russell, et al., eds., *Quantum Cosmology and the Laws of Nature* (Vatican City State: Vatican Observatory, 1993), 263-292.

Philo of Alexandria, *On the Account of the World's Creation Given by Moses*, trans. F. H. Colson and G. H. Whitaker (London: Heineman, Loeb Classical Library, 1981).

Plato, *Timaeus*, The Loeb Classical Library, vol.7, trans. R. G. Bury (Cambridge: Harvard University Press, 1942-67).

Plotinus, *The Enneads*, Book III, trans. S. MacKenna (London: Faber, 1969).

Polk, David P., *On the Way to God: An Exploration into the Theology of Wolfhart Pannenberg* (Boston: University Press of America, 1989).

Polkinghorne, John, *Science and Creation, The Search for Understanding* (Boston: Shambhala, 1989).

___, *Reason and Reality, The Relationship Between Science and Theology* (Philadelphia: Trinity, 1991).

___, *Science and Providence, God's Interaction with the World* (Boston: Shambhala, 1989).

___, "The Nature of Physical Reality," *Zygon*, 26:2 (June, 1991), 221-236.

___, *One World, The Interaction of Science and Theology* (Princeton: Princeton University Press, 1986).

___, *The Quantum World* (Prnceton: Princeton University Press, 1984).

Popper, Karl, *The Logic of Scientific Discovery* (New York: Harper, 1965).

Prigogine, Ilya and Isabelle Stengers, *Order Out of Chaos* (New York: Bantam, 1984).

Rahner, Karl, *The Trinity*, trans. J. Donceel (New York: Herder and Herder, 1970).

___, *Foundations of Christian Faith*, trans. William V. Dych (New York: Crossroad, 1984).

___, Karl, "Remarks on the Dogmatic Treatise *De Trinitate*," *Theological Investigations* IV, trans. Kevin Smyth, (London: Darton, Longman and Todd, 1966), 77-104.

Richardson, Cyril C., *The Doctrine of the Trinity* (Nashville: Abingdon, 1958).

Ricoeur, Paul, *Time and Narrative*, 3 vols. (Chicago: University of Chicago, 1984).

Rolston, Holmes, *Science and Religion, A Critical Survey* (New York: Random House, 1989).

Russell, J. L., S.J., "Time In Christian Thought," J. T. Fraser, ed., *The Voices of Time*, 2nd. ed. (Amherst: University of Massachusetts Press, 1981), 59-76.

Russell, Robert John; Nancey Murphy; C. J. Isham, eds., *Quantum Cosmology and the Laws of Nature: Scientific Perspectives on Divine Action* (Vatican City State: Vatican Observatory, 1993).

Russell, Robert John; William Stoeger, S.J., and George V. Coyne, S.J., eds., *Physics, Philosophy and Theology, A Common Quest for Understanding* (Vatican Observatory: Vatican City State, 1988).

Russell, Robert John, "Entropy and Evil," *Zygon*, 19:4 (December, 1984), 449-467.

Russell, Bertrand, *The ABC of Relativity* (New York: New American Library, 1962).

Rust, Eric C., "The Dynamic Nature of the Triune God," *Perspectives in Religious Studies*, 14:4 (Winter, 1987), 31-46.

Schilp, Paul, ed., *Albert Einstein: Philosopher-Scientist* (New York: Tudor, 1957).

Schlegel, Richard, "Time and Thermodynamics," J. T. Fraser, ed., *The Voices of Time*, 2nd. ed. (Amherst: University of Massachusetts, 1981), 500-523.

Schleiermacher, Friedrich, *The Christian Faith* (Philadelphia: Fortress, 1976).

Schmid, Heinrich, *Doctrinal Theology of the Evangelical Lutheran Church* (Minneapolis: Augsburg, 1875, 1961).

Schöpsdau, Walter, "Zeitlichkeit und Trinität: Theologische Anmerkungen zur Zeittheeorie Schellings," *Evangelische Theologie*, 38:1 (Jan-Feb, 1978), 37-61.

Searle, John, *Intentionality* (Cambridge: Cambridge University Press, 1983).

Searle, *Minds, Brains and Science* (London: BBC, 1984).

Sorabji, Richard, *Time, Creation, and the Continuum* (Ithaca: Cornell University Press, 1983).

Staniloae, Dumitru, "Der dreieinige Gott und die Einheit der Menschheit," *Evangelische Theologie*, 41 (Sept.-Oct.: 1981), 439-450.

Stead, Christopher, "Why Not Three Gods? The Logic of Gregory of Nyssa's Doctrine," *Gregor von Nyssa und die Philosophie, zweites internationales Kolloquium uber Gregor von Nyssa*, ed. H. Dorrie, Leiden: Brill, 1976).

Stout, Jeffrey, *Flight From Authority — Religion, Morality, and the Quest for Autonomy* (Notre Dame: University of Notre Dame Press, 1981).

Suchocki, Marjorie Hewitt, *God, Christ, Church* (New York: Crossroad, 1982).

Swinburne, Richard, "Conditions for Bitemporality," *Analysis*, 26 (1965), 47-50.

___, *Space and Time* (New York: MacMillan, 1968).

___, "Times," *Analysis*, 26 (1965),185-191.

Thompson, *Modern Trinitarian Perspectives* (Oxford: Oxford University Press, 1994).

Tillich, Paul, *Systematic Theology* (Chicago: University of Chicago, 1951) vols.1 and 3.

Torrance, Thomas, *Transformation and Convergence in the Frame of Knowledge* (Grand Rapids: Eerdmans, 1984).

___, *Space, Time and Incarnation* (Oxford: Oxford University Press, 1968).

___, *The Trinitarian Faith* (Edinburgh: T. &. T. Clark, 1993).

___, *Trinitarian Perspectives, Toward Doctrinal Agreement* (Edinburgh: T. & T. Clark, 1994).

Toulmin, Stephen, *Foresight and Understanding* (New York: Harper, 1961).

___, Return To Cosmology (Berkeley and Los Angeles: University of California Press, 1982).

Tracy, David and Nicholas Lash, eds., *Cosmology and Theology*, Concilium Series (New York: Seabury, 1983).

von Loewenich, Walther, *Luther's Theology of the Cross*, trans. Herbert J. A. Bouman (Minneapolis: Augsburg, 1976).

von Rad, Gerhard, *Old Testament Theology*, trans. D.M.G. Stalker, 2 vols. (New York: Harper and Row, 1962-65).

Weber, Renee, ed., *Dialogues With Scientists and Sages: the Search for Unity* (London and New York: Routledge and Kegan Paul, 1986).

Weinberg, Steven, *The First Three Minutes* (London: Deutsch, 1977).

Welch,Claude, *In This Name: The Doctrine of the Trinity in Contemporary Theology* (New York: Scribner, 1952).

Welker, Michael, *God As Spirit*, trans. John Hoffmeyer (Minneapolis: Fortress, 1994).

White, Andrew Dickson, *A History of the Warfare of Science with Theology in Christendom* (New York: D. E. Appleton and Co., 1896).

Whitehead, A.N., *Process and Reality* (New York: The Free Press, 1978).

___, *Science and the Modern World* (New York: Free Press, 1967).

Whitrow, G. J., "Time and the Universe, " J. T. Fraser, ed., *The Voices of Time*, 2nd. ed. (Amherst: University of Massachusetts Press, 1981), 564-581.

Wilber, Ken, *Quantum Questions, Mystical Writings of the World's Great Physicists* (Boston and London: New Science, 1984).

Wilken, Robert L., "The Resurrection of Jesus and the Doctrine of the Trinity," *Word and World*, II:1 (Winter, 1982), 17-28.

Williams, Arthur H. Jr., "The Trinity and Time," *Scottish Journal of Theology* 39:1 (1986), 65-81.

Zimmerman, E. J., "Time and Quantum Theory," J. T. Fraser, ed., *The Voices of Time*, 2nd. ed. (Amherst: University of Massachusetts Press, 1981), 479-499.

Zemach, E.M., "Many Times," *Analysis*, 28 (April, 1968), 145-61.

Zizioulas, John D., *Being As Communion, Studies in Personhood and the Church* (Crestwood: St. Vladimir's Press, 1985).

INDEX

research (cont.) 99, 110, 114-118, 167-
170, 180, 181, 183, 184
resurrection 28, 38, 51, 119, 124, 128,
129, 130, 132, 143-145, 150
revelation 4, 31, 39, 45, 50-54, 64,
126, 128-132, 136, 151, 173,
183
Richard of St. Victor 52, 158
Royce, Josiah 61
Russell, Robert John 12, 30, 34, 38, 39,
84, 87, 89, 118-123, 164
Russell, Bertrand 86, 93

sacramental 20, 180
Sagan, Carl 103, 183
Schelling, F. 61
Schleiermacher, F. 1, 5, 135, 160
Schoonenberg, Piet 66
Schweitzer, Albert 29
scientific method 7, 25
Searle, John 122
self-communication 49, 51, 65, 66, 153
sensation 25
simultaneity 39, 73, 112, 173
sin 129, 131, 150
singularity 84, 101-109, 120, 121, 178
social 26, 60, 61, 64, 68, 125, 137,
140, 147, 155, 160, 181, 183,
186
society 44, 58-61, 69, 70, 77, 88, 141
Soskice, Janet 105
space 6, 12, 17-19, 24, 25, 72-74, 82-
89, 93-95, 97, 100, 102-112,
120-122, 142, 149, 164, 172,
178, 186
special relativity,
theory of 72-73, 107, 112,
151, 165, 172, 176, 177
Spencer, Herbert 93
spirit 27ff., 34, 37, 41-48, 50, 52, 56,
58-60, 63-69, 98, 101, 111,
119, 131ff., 136, 140, 146,
149, 158, 160, 168, 169, 174,
177
Stead, Christopher 65
Stella, Didacus 182

Stengers, Isabelle 83, 89
Stern-Gerlach experiment 78
subjectivity 12, 27, 46, 49, 50, 58, 60,
83
subordinationism 43, 52, 64, 138
substance 18, 43, 44, 48, 63, 64, 66,
127, 133, 136, 137, 147, 160,
171
Suchocki, Marjorie Hewitt 60, 69
suffering 43, 125, 130-134, 153, 154,
155
sum-over-histories 101
superposition 76-78, 80, 101, 104, 177
supra-temporality 32

Templeton Foundation 92
Tertullian 45
temporalities 15, 166, 171, 177
temporality 6-9, 15-23, 28, 30-34, 40,
41, 46, 56-58, 61-69, 71, 91-
100, 104, 105, 110-116, 121,
145, 146, 148-155, 161, 165,
166, 170-172, 174-182; as
complex, 177; post-temporality
32
theocentricity 22
theodicy 125. 130, 131, 154
theologia crucis 124, 130, 160
theology 1, 3, 4, 8-13, 20-24, 27, 29-
33, 35-44, 47-51, 54-58, 61-
71, 91, 102, 104, 105, 118,
121, 124-136, 140-148, 152-
164, 165-169, 174, 179-186
thermodynamics 53, 72, 83, 119, 135,
173
Thompson, John 69
Tillich, Paul 15
time 4-9, 11, 12, 15-33, 34-56, 61-77,
82-88, 93-96, 125-133, 148-
151, 161-166, 170-172;
imaginary time 101, 102, 105,
108-111, 152
time dilation 73
timeless 15-17, 19, 36, 40, 44, 61, 104,
110, 113, 129
timelessness 16, 17, 19, 28-30, 38, 40,